TENTMAKING

TENTMAKING

A Misunderstood Missiological Method

KURT T. KRUGER

WIPF & STOCK · Eugene, Oregon

TENTMAKING
A Misunderstood Missiological Method

Copyright © 2020 Kurt T. Kruger. All rights reserved. Except for brief quotations in critical publications or reviews, no part of this book may be reproduced in any manner without prior written permission from the publisher. Write: Permissions, Wipf and Stock Publishers, 199 W. 8th Ave., Suite 3, Eugene, OR 97401.

Unless otherwise indicated, all Scripture quotations are from The Holy Bible, English Standard Version, copyright © 2001 by Crossway Bibles, a division of Good News Publishers. Used by permission. All rights reserved.

Scripture quotations marked ASV are taken from the American Standard Version (ASV): American Standard Version, public domain.

Scripture quotations marked KJV are taken from the King James Version (KJV): King James Version, public domain.

Scripture quotations marked (CEV) are taken from the Contemporary English Version Copyright © 1991, 1992, 1995 by American Bible Society. Used by permission.

Scripture taken from the NEW AMERICAN STANDARD BIBLE®, Copyright © 1960, 1962, 1963, 1968, 1971, 1972, 1973, 1975, 1977, 1995 by The Lockman Foundation. Used by permission.

Scriptures marked NIV are taken from The Holy Bible, New International Version®, NIV®, Copyright © 1973, 1978, 1984, 2011 by Biblica, Inc.TM Used by permission of Zondervan. All rights reserved worldwide. www.zondervan.com The "NIV" and "New International Version" are trademarks registered in the United States Patent and Trademark Office by Biblica, Inc.TM

Wipf & Stock
An Imprint of Wipf and Stock Publishers
199 W. 8th Ave., Suite 3
Eugene, OR 97401

www.wipfandstock.com

PAPERBACK ISBN: 978-1-7252-6515-8
HARDCOVER ISBN: 978-1-7252-6512-7
EBOOK ISBN: 978-1-7252-6513-4

Manufactured in the U.S.A.   09/22/20

To my Lord and Savior Jesus Christ.
He has never failed me, and he never will.

And because he was of the same trade he stayed with them and worked, for they were tentmakers by trade.

—Acts 18:3

Contents

List of Illustrations   ix
Preface   xi
Acknowledgments   xv
Abbreviations   xvii

1. Crucial Questions   1
2. A Purposeful Choice   8
3. Unpacking the Prevailing View   17
4. Paul's Self-Disclosed Reasons   28
5. Lack of Scholarly Consensus   40
6. Spiritual and Practical Considerations   53
7. Tentmaking in Church History   66
8. Roland Allen   83
9. Contemporary Church Planting Literature   103
10. Business as Mission   130
11. Paul's Tentmaking vs. Tentmaking in the Church   142
12. Defining Tentmaking   160
13. Bivocational Ministry and Contemporary Need for Tentmaking   168
14. Reviving Tentmaking   173
15. The Gift of Faith and the Spirit of God   182
16. Answering the Crucial Questions   187

Bibliography   191
Author Index   197
Scripture Index   201

List of Illustrations

Figure 1—Paul's understanding of tentmaking.   152
Figure 2—The contemporary church's understanding of tentmaking.   157

Preface

You are holding a book designed to bring clarity to an often misunderstood and neglected topic: tentmaking. The best way for the church to tackle any misunderstood subject is to go back to the Bible and determine, through careful reading and solid exegesis, what the Bible has to say about that particular subject. This is the task of determining what is normative, or what *ought to be*. Chapters 2, 4, and 6 lay out what is biblically normative regarding this topic, tentmaking.

We always go to God's word first and examine what God has said before we look at contemporary church practice. We do this in order to avoid the possibility of allowing the study and observation of ecclesiastical practice to influence our reading of Scripture. Even though we might *think* we already know what is right and what the Bible has to say on a particular topic, it would be better to study Scripture first and *then* to examine current practice within the church. If we instead start by looking at current practice, then there would be an increased temptation to find (or not find) what we wanted to within the pages of the Bible. I regularly preach the reminder to both myself and others: *We can justify just about anything.* This means that as believers who still wrestle with a sinful nature, we often seek loopholes in Scripture that will give us permission to continue to do what we want to do, instead of what Christ commands. It is the same thing with the church as a whole. Unless perennially called back to God's word, the church will often take up or continue whatever unbiblical practices are to her liking.

Moreover, things become problematic and unravel quickly anytime we use anything other than the Bible for determining what is normative. We must base our life and practice, both as individuals and as the church, on Scripture alone and not on what a particular social context may or may not demand. We must also not base our reading of Scripture on general revelation as interpreted and presented to us by the world, and certainly not on what the Christian community believes is normative. For example, there are some parts of the professing Christian community that do not believe repentance from sin is necessary for salvation. There are some parts of the Christian community that believe justification is something other than God graciously declaring us righteous based on the righteousness of Christ imputed to us. We cannot base our *ought to be* on something as shallow as whatever the Christian community views as normative or acceptable at a particular time in history. So it is with tentmaking. We cannot base our view and understanding of tentmaking on the church's past or current practice.

Once we have determined what *ought to be* from the Bible, then we can examine what the church is actually doing. In this case, how is the church practicing tentmaking? What does the church say, teach, and do when it comes to tentmaking? We simply want to *describe* what is currently going on. Chapters 3, 5, 7, and 9 set forth and describe how the church views and practices tentmaking.

After determining what is biblically normative *and* describing current church practice, we then need to compare the two and see if the current church practice accurately corresponds to what *ought to be*. Does the particular topic we are studying, in this case tentmaking, currently match what is normative as determined from Scripture? If so, praise God. No adjustments are required. If not, and this is the case with tentmaking, then the next and last step is to determine how to bring what *ought to be* into reality within the church. Chapters 11 through 16 compare the biblical norm with current practice and identify a pathway for tentmaking reform. It is both responsible and essential to complete this last step and identify a pathway, or a road map, that will take the church from where she is to where she *ought to be*.

This entire straightforward process can be summarized with these three questions:

1. What ought to be?
2. What is currently happening?
3. How do we bring what is currently happening into alignment with what ought to be?

The goal of this book is to bring clarity and reform to the often misunderstood missiological method of tentmaking.

As you may have already guessed, the answers to the above questions are not going to materialize on their own. In order to bring clarity to the subject of tentmaking, we are going to need to do some strenuous digging and heavy lifting. This means that we are going to be examining the work of some New Testament scholars and unpacking the writing of several contemporary church planting authors. At times, the reader will have to follow along with some fairly extended and sustained arguments. But don't let the prospect of this hard work cause you to holster your enthusiasm. You do not have to know biblical Greek or be familiar with the work of New Testament scholars to benefit from the information and conclusions I offer. I wrote this book so that it is self-contained and should stand alone without any outside reading. I also provide a couple of rest stops along the way in the form of quick reviews to make sure everyone is on the same page. And the main themes are repeated often enough to be helpful without being annoying. Although the book is designed to be read and understood by pastors, professors, missiologists, seminary students, church planters, and church leaders in general, it will be an enjoyable and illuminating read for anyone who is interested in tentmaking, missions, bivocational ministry, church planting, or church history. Anyone who has a passion for biblical truth should find this book gratifying.

The position I wish to defend in this book is that, based on the biblical evidence, tentmaking is a purposeful missiological method that should be intentionally selected based on the individual needs of the ministry context. The Bible shows us that Paul did not turn to tentmaking out of financial need or desperation, but instead made a purposeful choice to support himself as he established some (but not all) churches during his missionary journeys. If the church truly wishes to follow in the footsteps of Paul, then she must humble herself and commit to understanding and practicing tentmaking as the apostle Paul understood and practiced it. Tentmaking is the biblically grounded missiological method of complete self-support, which may be used purposefully and selectively by an internally (self) and externally (church) called and adequately trained Christian leader for evangelistic or didactic reasons when establishing churches.

Acknowledgments

I would like to begin by thanking Wipf and Stock Publishers for accepting my proposal for this book. They took a chance on a relatively unknown author, and without their partnership on this project the research, information, and conclusions presented here would have difficulty reaching my intended audience.

Steve Childers and Bob Orner were my faculty readers at Reformed Theological Seminary in Orlando, Florida. They encouraged me to publish my tentmaking work because they thought it would make a needed contribution to the greater church. Without their encouragement, this book would not have been written.

I am grateful to the ruling elders at Peace Community Church (PCA) in Frankfort, Illinois, for granting me a twelve-week sabbatical in order to complete this book.

Thank you to Mid-America Reformed Seminary in Dyer, Indiana, for responding quickly and positively to my request for sabbatical coverage. My deepest appreciation is extended to Dr. J. Mark Beach, Elijah De Jong, Dr. Alan D. Strange, Rev. Mark D. Vander Hart, and Aaron Vander Heiden, all of whom delivered strong Christ-centered preaching in my absence. They deserve to be recognized.

I have great respect for missiologist J.D. Payne at Samford University in Birmingham, Alabama. He read an early version of the manuscript and provided helpful feedback that revealed a few areas that needed clarification. I am sincerely grateful and honored that he took the time to do this.

The ongoing prayer support from my brothers and sisters has been deeply appreciated. Thank you, Peace Community Church, for lifting me up in prayer as I completed this work.

Thank you to my daughter-in-law, Anna, for assisting me with the creation of the flow charts that illustrate Paul's understanding and the contemporary church's understanding of tentmaking. For some reason, my word processing software would not convert what I had drawn up into PDF documents, so she had to recreate them in another program.

Finally, my most heartfelt thanks goes to my wife, Dawn, who has been proofreading my various writing projects for over thirty years. She graciously agreed to carefully pour through the manuscript multiple times, and each time revealed areas that needed correction or improvement.

Abbreviations

AD	*anno Domini*
ASV	American Standard Version
BAM	Business as Mission
BC	before Christ
BDAG	Walter Bauer, Frederick W. Danker, W.F. Arndt, and F.W. Gingrich. *A Greek-English Lexicon of the New Testament and Other Early Christian Literature.* 3rd ed. Chicago: University of Chicago Press, 2000.
CEV	Contemporary English Version
DMin	Doctor of Ministry
ERV	English Revised Version
GCC	Great Commission Companies
JBTM	Journal for Baptist Theology & Ministry
KJV	King James Version
m. Abot	Mishnah Abot
MDiv	Master of Divinity
MNA	Mission to North America
NASB	New American Standard Bible
NIV	New International Version
NRSV	New Revised Standard Version

NT	New Testament
OT	Old Testament
PCA	Presbyterian Church in America
RCA	Reformed Church in America
SPG	Society for the Propagation of the Gospel
TNIV	Todays New International Version

OLD TESTAMENT

Gen	1–2 Kgs	Song	Obad
Exod	1–2 Chr	Isa	Jonah
Lev	Ezra	Jer	Mic
Num	Neh	Lam	Nah
Deut	Esth	Ezek	Hab
Josh	Job	Dan	Zeph
Judg	Ps (pl. Pss)	Hos	Hag
Ruth	Prov	Joel	Zech
1–2 Sam	Eccl	Amos	Mal

NEW TESTAMENT

Matt	1–2 Cor	1–2 Tim	1–3 John
Mark	Gal	Titus	Jude
Luke	Eph	Phlm	Rev
John	Phil	Heb	
Acts	Col	Jas	
Rom	1–2 Thess	1–2 Pet	

1

Crucial Questions

When I was a boy, my mother read books to me. Lots of them. One of the books that I distinctly remember reading with her was called, *Take Another Look*.[1] It was a children's book full of optical illusions. For example, on one of the pages there was a simple drawing of a man's head wearing a tall top hat along with the question asking if the hat was taller than its base was wide. At first glance the top hat did appear to be taller than its base was wide because it was an example of what is called the *horizontal-vertical illusion* first observed by Wilhelm Wundt in 1858. But I did not know that. I just knew that when I first looked at the hat, it looked taller than it did wide. It was an optical illusion, and all the other illusions in the book were designed to function in the same way. The images and lines that appeared on each successive page looked uneven, crooked, or of different lengths at first, but after another closer and more careful look the truth could be discovered.

Some illusions, like the top hat, were more difficult than others. And the book actually encouraged readers to use a ruler if they had any doubts about what they were seeing. Which I did. Of course, once I read through the book and had checked all of the illusions with a second look and a ruler, I knew the truth. I never again had to read the book and wonder if the top hat was taller than its base was wide, because I knew it was not. The two

---

1. Carini, *Take Another Look*.

lengths were equal. I had used a ruler to measure and had confirmed that the two lengths were exactly the same.

There are some who have only taken a first look at tentmaking. Perhaps they remember reading somewhere in Acts that Paul made tents during his missionary journeys, but they cannot cite the biblical reference or remember where it was that he engaged in tentmaking. Or maybe they *can* cite Acts 18:3 and know that this was around the time Paul arrived in Corinth, but they have not given tentmaking any additional thought or reflection. It is an interesting detail, nothing more. The top hat looks taller than it is wide.

Then there are some who have taken another look at tentmaking. They may know their Bibles well and may have performed some in-depth study on Paul and his missionary methods. Some of these second-lookers possess advanced training and education in biblical studies and missiology. They have taken another look at tentmaking because they are interested in it professionally and want to understand why Paul made tents so they can learn from Paul's example and help explain it to the church.

But tentmaking is like the top hat optical illusion. It requires a second look *and* a ruler—the ruler of Scripture—in order to see it correctly. The whole ruler. Not just Acts 18:3, but every passage and verse that touches on Paul's tentmaking and his self-disclosed reasons for working in some of his ministry contexts but not others. You see, even among those who have taken another look at tentmaking and measured it with the ruler of Scripture, most still conclude that the top hat is taller than it is wide. They are not viewing tentmaking correctly. Maybe they are measuring the top hat diagonally, or attempting to find it's area, I do not know. But for whatever reason, after all the second looks and measuring, the vast majority of the church remains unable to see tentmaking for what it really is.[2]

The first time I took a second look at tentmaking was several years ago. I found myself responding to God's call and agreeing to be the lead pastor for a church plant that was enthusiastically supported by my denomination. I was given multiple evaluations and screening interviews, and was found

---

2. Rather than define tentmaking at this point in the book, I invite the reader to follow along as I build a biblical case for a correct understanding and definition of tentmaking. For those that want that information up front, you may jump ahead to chapter 12. However, I believe it will be much more satisfying to complete the journey from chapter 1 to chapter 11 before reading my definition. If you are completely unfamiliar with the concept of tentmaking, please understand that it does not refer to making literal tents. Typically, within the church, tentmaking is used to describe the practice of a minister or missionary who engages in some sort of secular employment in order to support themselves or augment their existing support while engaging in ministry. It is called tentmaking because, at times, Paul labored as a tentmaker (see Acts 18:3) during his missionary journeys.

to be an ideal candidate to lead a church plant. I was sent to our denominational church planting training, which lasted one week and took place in Grand Rapids, Michigan. In addition, I elected to take the Global Church Advancement church planting course in Orlando, Florida. A parent church was supplying the majority of the necessary financial support and our local denominational assembly was augmenting that support with several thousands of dollars. The Lord had provided and money was not an issue. I could move forward with the church plant unhindered by secular employment and give my full-time attention to God's work. Working another job to support myself while planting a church, or tentmaking, never occurred to me.

CONFLICTING MESSAGES

Before we had finalized our vision and mission statements and long before we held our first worship service I began to hear conflicting messages from various church planting authorities regarding secular employment and church planting. Denominational officials insisted that church planting was full-time work and it would be foolish to attempt to initiate a church plant without a combined salary and benefits package in place for the lead pastor. However, as I began taking another look, and as my reading and research on the topic of church planting deepened, I discovered that the literature was divided. Later in this book, we will examine several contemporary church planting authorities and their understanding of tentmaking in more detail. For now, it is enough to touch on a small sampling of the diverse opinions that I encountered.

One church planting author, Aubrey Malphurs, discouraged his readers from engaging in secular employment while planting a church. Malphurs writes that of all the possible funding sources for church planting, self-employment is "the least preferable because it limits the time the planter can give to the new ministry."[3] Malphurs' view was the opinion that most closely corresponded to the advice I was hearing from my own denominational network.

Others were open to the idea of a church planting pastor engaging in bivocational ministry or tentmaking, and based their receptivity on financial reasons. C. Peter Wagner states, "Frequently the founding pastor is bivocational or a tentmaker. This is one of the major ways of cutting the costs of new church development, and I highly recommend it."[4]

3. Malphurs, *Planting Growing Churches*, 52.
4. Wagner, *Church Planting*, 72.

Some recommended working outside the church and listed both financial *and* practical reasons. Stuart Murray writes that not only can church plants "be freed from the onerous financial commitment of supporting a full-time leader," but adds, "Bivocational leadership is not just a cheap option. There are advantages both for the churches who employ them and for the leaders themselves."[5] One of the advantages that Murray lists is that bivocational ministry makes it easier for churches to avoid the "lure of clericalism."[6] Murray explains, "A bivocational leader can give enough time to the church to prevent overcommitment from other members, but not so much that participants become passengers."[7]

Still others insist on some type of secular work for church planting pastors, but clearly communicate that the decision should not in any way be determined by the church's finances. Steve Sjogren and Rob Lewin write, "You desperately need to get into the community. You need to work no matter what your financial backing looks like. We encourage you to work outside the church until your plant reaches two hundred in weekend attendance."[8] Sjogren and Lewin's support for bivocational work is rooted in the belief that church planters must engage in bivocational ministry in order to generate the right perceptions and understandings among unbelievers in the community as well as among church plant attendees. For example, Sjogren and Lewin propose, "Taking an outside job creates an understanding in the church that you aren't there as their free therapist. It also creates an environment in which really emotionally sick people won't have you to lean on all the time, so they will find someone else."[9]

Yet another author believed that as long as there was a call to plant a church, support sources were relatively immaterial to the church planting endeavor. Ed Stetzer writes, "A secular job can also supply funding for the church planter . . . Finances are not the determining factor in God's will; God is the determining factor in God's will. If God expresses a call, the planter must help make a way where there is no other way—by working at bivocational employment."[10] If we were to adopt Stetzer's understanding, bivocational ministry becomes a type of battering ram utilized by church

---

5. Murray, *Church Planting*, 224.
6. Murray, *Church Planting*, 224.
7. Murray, *Church Planting*, 224–25.
8. Sjogren and Lewin, *Community of Kindness*, 172–73.
9. Sjogren and Lewin, *Community of Kindness*, 173.
10. Stetzer, *Planting Missional Churches*, 226. This is the exact same quote that appears in the 2016 edition of *Planting Missional Churches*. Stetzer and Im, *Planting Missional Churches*, 170–71.

planters who find it necessary to forcefully break through the gates of insufficient funds.

In retrospect, I can clearly see one commonality that all church planting voices shared regardless of their stance on whether or not pastors should work at a secular job while planting a church. No one considered the possibility that tentmaking is a church planting missiological method to be used purposefully and selectively based on the unique needs of each particular ministry context, as modeled for us in Scripture by Paul.

CLOUD OF CONFUSION

There seemed to be a dark gray cloud of confusion perpetually drifting over tentmaking that made it difficult, or rather impossible, for the church to see and agree on what tentmaking was and what to do with it. I began questioning why the church planting literature was so divided on this issue of secular employment and self-support for church planting pastors. I also found it peculiar that many of the church planting sources cited the Apostle Paul's missionary methods as a template to be followed for contemporary church planting, but failed to include any guided discussion of self-support under the banner of apostolic missionary methods. Instead, when tentmaking was mentioned, it was largely the author's opinion or experience that influenced what they wrote regarding how to properly utilize and apply tentmaking.

As we will see, and as outlandish as it may sound, many church planting authors completely ignore the topic of Paul's self-support. When it is included in the church planting literature, authors will often acknowledge that Paul made tents to support himself, but then they stop referencing Paul for the remainder of the discussion. They fail to follow up and develop contemporary theories and practices for self-support within church planting ministry contexts based on how *Paul* chose to implement self-support as revealed to us in Scripture. Why is that?

It turns out that there are an embarrassing amount of questions generated by the conflicting and often bewildering voices within the corpus of church planting and tentmaking literature. But that is not the only challenge created by the confusing haze. Tentmaking also has to deal with the openly negative stereotypes that have become associated with this apostolic practice.

Tentmaking has to overcome the image it conjures up in the secular world and, to an increasing extent, the church. The phrase *bivocational minister* usually brings to mind an image of a retired or relatively uneducated pastor serving a church that is rural, small, dying, or all three. Perhaps someone with limited formal training, licensed by a local church but not ordained by a denomination that requires an MDiv degree, is working at a full-time non-ministry job while simultaneously serving a church that is limping along and cannot afford a "real" pastor.

Dennis Bickers, who is a bivocational minister himself, writes, "The churches we lead are often smaller churches with few resources. Many of them have plateaued or are in decline. A large number of us serve with little or no formal theological training. Bivocational ministry is looked at by some as 'second-class' ministry performed by people who don't have the gifts to serve a larger church."[11] Bickers certainly has painted a bleak and unappealing picture. Many seminary graduates may not even consider bivocational ministry because of this stigma. Positions that require some form of tentmaking are often viewed as consolation prizes for candidates who have been passed over by more desirable churches.

How did we get here?[12] If the Apostle Paul utilized tentmaking and self-support in his ministry, why do so many in the church treat it like some sort of malady to be avoided?

Yet tentmaking is not avoided everywhere. For the most part, it appears that tentmaking has been relegated to missionary practice in places other than the United States. For example, some missiologists have taken tentmaking seriously when working oversees in cross-cultural contexts and especially in closed- or limited-access countries.[13] Consequently, tentmaking has been deemed acceptable, and in some cases preferred, within an overseas cross-cultural missionary placement but it is largely ignored in North American church planting contexts. Again, why is that? But even proponents of tentmaking as a missiological strategy to gain entrance into politically closed-off countries have their critics. Rundle and Steffen are two Christian mission-minded leaders, and they oppose using tentmaking as an entry tool into restricted nations. They state:

> One model that has little to commend it is the "missionary in disguise" approach. This is one that uses a business merely as a "cover" for people who quite frankly have little interest in business except for its usefulness as an entry strategy into countries that are off-limits to traditional missionaries.[14]

11. Bickers, *Bivocational Pastor*, 8.

12. A limited review of tentmaking in church history will be covered in chapter 7, and additional reasons for the church's departure from apostolic practice will be offered in chapter 11.

13. For example, Ruth E. Siemens views Paul's tentmaking, among other things, as, "a complete pioneering strategy for hostile environments." Siemens, "Vital Role," 129.

14. Rundle and Steffen, *Great Commission Companies*, 26.

Elsewhere they write, "Why would people feel that they need to fake their way into a country?" and, " . . . many Christians now recognize that this 'ends-justifying-the-means' approach to ministry is dishonest and a poor witness."[15]

Thankfully, there has been a growing interest in the writings of Roland Allen. Allen was an Anglican priest who lived around the turn of the twentieth century and a staunch advocate for the use of all of Paul's missionary methods, including tentmaking. Allen viewed Paul's tentmaking as a crucial component of his overall missiological strategy, as well as a timeless biblically prescriptive method for contemporary missiology with theological underpinnings. Allen writes these comments regarding Paul's tentmaking, "The finance of St. Paul's journeys is treated as an interesting detail of ancient history, not as though it had anything to do with his success as a preacher of the Gospel. St. Paul himself does not so treat it."[16] Because Allen stands out as a pioneering thinker who sought to view and understand tentmaking and self-support through a thoroughly biblical lens, we will spend some time unpacking his writings in later chapters.

In the end, when I began to take another look, I discovered that there were several crucial questions surrounding tentmaking and bivocational ministry that demanded answers. If the church wants to sweep away the swirling clouds of confusion and look down on tentmaking through clear sunny skies, then these questions must be answered: Was Paul's use of tentmaking during his missionary work intentional or pragmatic? Did he give any thought to it, or was it simply an expedient choice that he turned to when he needed money? Is tentmaking desirable for contemporary church plants, or is it a practice to be avoided when possible? Is it strategically and missiologically irrelevant? Should bivocational ministry be limited to contexts such as small rural dying churches or oversees missions? Is the relatively recent concept of Business as Mission really the same thing as biblical tentmaking? Are tentmaking and bivocational ministry synonymous? And perhaps the most important question of all, why is the church so resistive to following in the footsteps of arguably the greatest missionary of all time? Grab your ruler, because we are about to take another look at tentmaking.

---

15. Rundle and Steffen, *Great Commission Companies*, 26–27.
16. Allen, *Missionary Methods*, 49.

2

A Purposeful Choice

In order to answer the crucial questions surrounding tentmaking, we will have to start at the beginning. That means we will have to do our best to explore the origins of Paul's tentmaking. It also means that we will have to examine all of the commonly recognized methods of support available to first-century itinerant speakers. But most importantly, we will need to reach some conclusions about why Paul chose to support himself, or make tents, rather than accept payment in *some* ministry contexts, but not others.

TENTMAKING ORIGINS

Luke tells us that the Apostle Paul was a tentmaker, but he does not reveal when, where, or why Paul learned this trade.[1] One belief is that Paul learned tentmaking when he was a student of Gamaliel as part of a rabbinic code that combined Torah study with a trade. Those who fall into this camp cite the Mishnah which states, "Excellent is the study of the Law together with worldly occupation."[2] There are additional rabbinic sayings that strongly discourage receiving wages or income from teaching the Torah and so appear to complement the argument that Paul was following rabbinic practice.

---

1. Acts 18:3.
2. *m. Abot* 2:2.

For example, Hillel stated, "He that makes worldly use of the crown shall perish."[3] The suggestion that Paul made tents in order to avoid charging fees for preaching and teaching from the Bible because he wanted to honor Jewish customs is a popular one. But the idea of Paul allowing his life choices to be governed by rabbinical traditions and teachings seems unlikely. It is difficult to accept the idea of Paul honoring a Jewish custom when he so tenaciously argued against the spiritual usefulness of returning to Pharisaical traditions and works of the law. The book of Galatians comes to mind, as does Colossians 2:16–23. Furthermore, the NT records Paul uncompromisingly stating that teachers and preachers of the gospel *should* receive pay for their work.[4]

In contrast to the popular Torah and trade theory, Ronald Hock argues that "the ideal of combining Torah and a trade is difficult to establish much earlier than the middle of the second century AD, that is, long after Paul."[5] Hock buttresses his statement with research indicating that the ideal of combining Torah and trade did not surface until 140–170 AD in response to "the economic crises arising from the Jewish wars."[6] There is some attestation of rabbis who worked during the period between 70 and 125 AD, but their work appears, states Hock, "to have been more a consequence of their economic status than of their rabbinic self-understanding."[7] Hock concludes: "To sum up, the widespread view that Paul first learned and practiced his trade of tentmaking while a student of Gamaliel and so in conformity with a rabbinic ideal turns out, on examination, to be difficult to maintain."[8]

The most likely alternative to the anachronistic Torah and trade theory is that Paul learned tentmaking from his father. The practice of sons learning the trades of their fathers was widespread in both Jewish and Greco-Roman culture. Regarding first-century Jewish practice, Packer and Tenney state, "It was also the father's responsibility to teach his sons a trade or craft.

---

3. *m. Abot* 1:13. In the context of this quote, "crown" means extensive Torah knowledge that has resulted from a lifetime of dedicated and unwavering study.

4. 1 Cor 9:6–14; 1 Tim 5:17–18.

5. Hock, *Social Context*, 22.

6. Hock, *Social Context*, 23. Hock cites E.E. Urbach, "Class-Status and Leadership in the world of the Palestinian Sages," *Proceedings of the Israel Academy of Sciences and Humanities*, 2 vols. (Jerusalem: Central, 1968). A quote from this source indicates that combining Torah and trade did not arise until the Usha period which is dated from 140 to 170 AD. He also directs readers to J. Neusner, *The Rabbinic Traditions about the Pharisees before 70*, 3 vols. (Leiden: Brill, 1971).

7. Hock, *Social Context*, 23.

8. Hock, *Social Context*, 23.

For example, if the father was a potter, he taught that skill to his sons. One of the Jewish sages affirmed that 'he who does not teach his son a useful trade is bringing him up to be a thief.'[9]

F.F. Bruce flirts with the proposal that Paul's Roman citizenship was linked to his family trade of tentmaking. We know from Acts 22:28 that Paul was a Roman citizen by birth. This meant that his father and family were already Roman citizens. In order to explain how a Jewish family from Tarsus had been granted Roman citizenship, Bruce writes:

> Presumably Paul's father, grandfather or even great-grandfather had rendered some outstanding service to the Roman cause. It has been suggested, for example, that a firm of tent-makers could have been very useful to a fighting proconsul.[10]

PAUL'S SUPPORT CHOICE OPTIONS

The practice of self-support was rare, but it was not something that Paul invented. Paul was a missionary, but his itinerant ministry of proclaiming the gospel and planting churches resembled, at least in terms of public speaking, the philosophers that also traveled from city to city in the first century. Many of these public speakers charged fees or lived under the patronage of a wealthy host; however, there is evidence that at least some of them supported themselves by working. Hock writes, "Philosophers who worked to support themselves, even for short periods of time, were relatively few, with the Stoic Cleanthes, who worked as a gardener and a miller, the most frequently cited example."[11] The Cynic Dio Chrysostom labored "as a gardener and at other unskilled jobs."[12] Cleanthes lived from approximately 330 to 230 BC, suggesting that self-supporting public speakers had been around for several hundred years before Paul. Dio Chrysostom lived from approximately 40 to 120 AD and can be considered a contemporary of Paul. As a result, it can be concluded that, although not widespread, there were other public and professional speakers who practiced self-support by working.

Paul's contemporary philosophers usually chose other methods of obtaining wages and provisions before they turned to self-support. There were four primary means professional orators and philosophers used to secure

---

9. Packer and Tenney, *Illustrated Manners*, 456.
10. Bruce, *Paul*, 37.
11. Hock, *Social Context*, 56.
12. Hock, *Social Context*, 56.

funding and financial support.[13] The first means of support for itinerant philosophers was to charge fees:

> The practice of charging fees...was popularized by Sophists, with Protagoras of Abdera credited with taking the lead and with many other sophists—Gorgias, Hippias, Prodicus, Antiphon, Euthydemus, Evenus, and Isocrates—following suit. Fees were charged either by the lecture or for a course of study, and given the high fees charged by many Sophists—one-hundred minas for a course of study under Protagoras and Gorgias—we should not be surprised that many Sophists became wealthy, with Protagoras' and Gorgias' wealth becoming proverbial.[14]

Another method of support for itinerant philosophers and other public speakers was to live off of a wealthy patron. Hock writes:

> Entering a household . . . usually involved living in the patron's house, attending his banquets, and traveling with him. The responsibility of the philosopher, however, was to provide instruction for his patron's son(s), or simply to give counsel and so serve as the patron's resident intellectual. In either case, the philosopher, as part of a household, received a salary . . . or gifts from his patron.[15]

The third method of support that first-century philosophers, and ostensibly Paul, could have turned to was begging. Hock states, "Never as popular as charging fees or entering a household, begging was in fact closely identified with Cynic philosophers."[16]

The fourth and final option was working. Out of all of the abovementioned options, working was viewed as the least favorable choice. Hock comments: "Philosophers clearly preferred charging fees or entering a household. Begging appealed only to homeless and shameless Cynics. Working was the least popular option."[17]

Paul did accept support from some churches and fellow believers as we will see later, yet we know from the NT that Paul worked to support himself in at least Corinth, Thessalonica, and Ephesus. So the question

---

13. Ruth E. Siemens provides only three options for Paul as he planted churches and ministered: a) charging fees, b) receiving support from churches or from wealthy patrons, and c) earning his own living by working. For some reason she has omitted begging. Siemens, "Vital Role," 123.

14. Hock, *Social Context*, 52.

15. Hock, *Social Context*, 53.

16. Hock, *Social Context*, 55.

17. Hock, *Social Context*, 59.

becomes: Why did he choose to support himself in certain ministry contexts and not others?

PAUL MADE A PURPOSEFUL CHOICE

We know that Paul was not against receiving financial support from all churches. In 2 Cor 11:8, Paul wrote, "I robbed other churches by accepting support from them in order to serve you." The "other churches" in the above verse almost certainly included the church at Philippi. In 2 Cor 11:9, he continues, "And when I was with you and was in need, I did not burden anyone, for the brothers who came from Macedonia supplied my need. So I refrained and will refrain from burdening you in any way." Paul Barnett writes, "It is probable that the Macedonians were from the church at Philippi (Phil 4:14)."[18] I agree with Barnett.

Likewise, we know that Paul received financial support while he was ministering in Thessalonica, but not from the Thessalonians. Philippians 4:16 states that Paul received support from the church in Philippi while ministering in Thessalonica: "Even in Thessalonica you sent me help for my needs once and again."

In addition, in the midst of defending his apostolic status and authority, Paul wrote in 2 Cor 12:13 that he treated the church in Corinth the same as other churches, except that he did not accept support in Corinth: "For in what were you less favored than the rest of the churches, except that I myself did not burden you?" Murray J. Harris states this verse suggests that, "His [Paul's] refusal to accept the Corinthians' offer of maintenance while accepting it from other churches was the point of dissatisfaction."[19]

If Paul was not against receiving support from all churches, why did he refrain from accepting financial assistance from some churches? Was it an expedient, practical, or desperate choice borne out of necessity? This is the view that many people have adopted, as McCarty has observed, "The common thought has been that Paul had to make tents to support himself because the congregations could not support him."[20] However, others have challenged this conventional wisdom by pointing out that Paul did not accept support from one of the more wealthy churches, Corinth. If making tents was done out of necessity, we would expect to see Paul accepting support from the more prosperous churches but making tents when ministering to the poorer churches.

18. Barnett, *Second Epistle to the Corinthians*, 517.
19. Harris, *Second Epistle to the Corinthians*, 878.
20. McCarty, *Meeting the Challenge*, 24.

Let's take a closer look at Corinth and Philippi. April Nora Chiu Yamasaki argues that there is biblical evidence for viewing Corinth as one of the more affluent ministry contexts: "In an earlier letter, he [Paul] says that not many of the Corinthians were influential or of noble birth (1 Cor 1:26), which implies that some of the Corinthians were indeed from a more privileged class."[21] Yamasaki continues to highlight the fact that Paul often "addressed himself to a more educated and richer group within the church," such as those with intellectual gifts and believers who might appeal to a court of law when resolving disagreements.[22] Moreover, it should be noted that the primary reason there was division within the church over the Lord's Supper appears to be socioeconomic in origin. The rich were eating and the poor were being neglected and left out.

In a note explaining the Philippian support supplied to Paul in Corinth, Barnett contrasts the believers in Corinth with the believers in Philippi this way: "It is probable that the Corinthians from educated and affluent Corinth would have bristled at the very idea that the poor northerners of Macedonia would support someone who was ministering to them!"[23] Barnett's comment indicates that he views Corinth as a city of greater prosperity and wealth than Philippi. Paul describes the Macedonian churches in 2 Cor 8:2 with the phrase "extreme poverty," yet there is no indication in Philippians that Paul preached the gospel to them free of charge and engaged in a self-supportive tentmaking trade.

Anthony C. Thiselton concludes that the church at Corinth was diverse and contained both believers of high socioeconomic status as well as people who were of lowly account. While stating some fundamental points necessary to properly understand Corinth during Paul's missionary activity, Thiselton states, "*[T]he city community and the city culture felt themselves to be prosperous and self-sufficient*, even if there were many 'have nots' who were socially vulnerable or dependent on others."[24]

Scott J. Hafemann makes the following comments about Corinth: "Its location was strategic militarily and profitable commercially. Ever since the sixth century BC, a paved road existed across the isthmus, making Corinth a wealthy city because of its tariffs and commerce."[25] He continues by conceding that "most of the church was apparently from the middle, working classes of tradesmen, with only a few wealthy families," but concludes with

21. McCarty, *Meeting the Challenge*, 25.
22. McCarty, *Meeting the Challenge*, 25.
23. Barnett, *Second Epistle to the Corinthians*, 515.
24. Thiselton, *First Epistle to the Corinthians*, 4.
25. Hafemann, *2 Corinthians*, 22.

that "Corinth was a free-wheeling 'boom town' filled with the materialism, pride, and self-confidence that come with having made it in a new place and with a new social identity."[26]

In summary, a conservative assessment portrays Corinth as an extremely prosperous merchant city with both a wealthy and poor population. Within this picture, the biblical and historical evidence seems to favor a city with more than enough wealthy citizens to support Paul when compared to other churches that he planted. In fact, we would expect the church in Corinth to be more densely populated with wealthy believers because of the large quantity of merchants and the general commercial prosperity due to its strategic geographic location between the harbor of Cenchreae and the harbor Lechaeum. Barnett writes with finality, "The wealth of Corinth was guaranteed by the city's unique position."[27]

If Paul accepted support from some churches and not others based on expediency or necessity, we would expect to see him accepting support from the wealthy churches, but not from the poorer churches. But Corinth was one of the wealthier churches, and Paul refused to accept support from them. And Philippi was one of the poorer churches, and Paul accepted support from them.

The idea that Paul had to find some other means of support, at least in Corinth, rather than from the people he served because they were of lower social class and could not afford to support him appears untenable. Corinth does not emerge as less wealthy than some of the other churches Paul planted. It appears to be quite the opposite.

Moreover, the church in Philippi appears to be significantly less prosperous than Corinth, yet they were able to supply Paul's needs on a repeated basis. Paul received support from them when he was on site ministering to them, *and* he received support from them when he was ministering to other churches.[28] Paul chose to receive support in Philippi by agreeing to

---

26. Hafemann, *2 Corinthians*, 23–24.

27. Barnett, *Second Epistle to the Corinthians*, 2.

28. This observation that Paul accepted support from the church in Philippi both while he was ministering to them and when he was away ministering to other churches is going to be important as we move forward. Some say that Paul always supported himself and that he refused to accept support from churches because he was a tentmaker, which is not true. The NT tells us that he did accept support. Others attempt to draw sharp lines of distinction between support and gifts, which is something Paul did not do, so neither should we. Many others acknowledge that Paul accepted support at times, but postulate that he never accepted support from the people he was actively ministering to, which is also not true. The reason for these errors and others, I suspect, is because many people examining Paul's tentmaking attempt to force his support choices into a universal policy or a set of principles that governed the totality

enter the house of Lydia, which most closely represents the itinerant philosopher support method of entering the household of a wealthy patron. As we saw earlier in the chapter, this was widely recognized as a regular means of direct support or payment. Moreover, Acts 16:15 states, "And after she was baptized, and her household as well, she urged us, saying, 'If you have judged me to be faithful to the Lord, come to my house and stay.' And she prevailed upon us." In other words, Paul made no attempt to conceal the fact that he was receiving a large amount of support when he was ministering to one of the least affluent churches.

In addition, there is every reason to believe that Paul was receiving direct support from the entire Philippian congregation while he was on site ministering to them, and not just from Lydia. Paul mentions their collective financial support twice in his letter to them: once, in the beginning of the letter in Philippians 1:5 ("Because of your partnership in the gospel from the first day until now"), and once near the end of the letter in Philippians 4:15 ("And you Philippians yourselves know that in the beginning of the gospel, when I left Macedonia, no church entered into partnership with me in giving and receiving, except you only"). O'Brien acknowledges that while the word translated as *partnership* has "a wide range of applications," he concludes that in Philippians 4:15, "it denotes 'financial sharing.'"[29] In addition, O'Brien describes how to understand the phrase, "in the beginning of the gospel" in Philippians 4:15. He states, "It is better, therefore, to regard the expression from the standpoint of the Philippians, an interpretation supported by the NIV with its rendering 'in the early days of your acquaintance with the gospel', that is, from the time of their active participation in it. This view fits neatly with the reference in Phil 1:3–5, where God is thanked for the Philippians' *partnership in the gospel* 'from the first day until now.'"[30] I would agree with O'Brien that the Philippian church's financial partnership with Paul began when he began to minister to them with the gospel. Therefore, it was not just Lydia who supported Paul in Philippi. The whole church provided direct support for Paul and his needs while he was there. The word "you" in Philippians 1:5 and 4:15 is plural. It would be completely inconsistent and ungrounded for Paul to have been thanking the whole church for their support while he ministered to them if the whole church was not supporting him while he ministered to them.

---

of his missional behavior. The evidence against this type of thinking will be set forth in subsequent chapters.

29. O'Brien, *Epistle to the Philippians*, 534.
30. O'Brien, *Epistle to the Philippians*, 532.

Paul accepted traditional support from the church in Philippi while he ministered to them, both in the form of agreeing to stay in the household of a wealthy patron and in the form of direct monetary support from the members of the Philippian church. He also accepted support from the church in Philippi after he left them and was ministering in Thessalonica (Phil 4:16) and Corinth (2 Cor 11:9).

The conclusion then, is that Paul could have received adequate support from all the churches he founded, but instead he made a purposeful choice not to receive support in selected contexts. And just as significant, this purposeful choice does not appear to be linked to the prosperity of the ministry context. M.E. Thrall has come to the same conclusion. When responding to the idea that Paul made tents to supplement his income while ministering to poorer churches, Thrall writes that "this is an improbable explanation. As Holmberg points out, Mediterranean cities such as Corinth were in a flourishing condition, and Paul implies in 2 Cor 8.1–5 that the Macedonians were poorer than the Corinthians."[31] Thrall's observation aligns with everything else we have discussed in this chapter. Paul did not turn to tentmaking out of necessity when traditional support was unavailable. Why then did Paul choose to support himself in certain ministry contexts and not others?

---

31. Thrall, *2 Corinthians 8–13*, 706.

3

Unpacking the Prevailing View

It has been shown that Paul's purposeful choice to support himself in some ministry contexts but not others was *not* dependent upon the overall prosperity, or lack thereof, of the churches where he ministered. If Paul's tentmaking choices were not connected to the financial status of the congregations he ministered to, then what were they based on? Finding the answer to this question is essential because it is one of the keys to unlocking a proper understanding of biblical tentmaking. But for now, it will be helpful to examine what others are saying about Paul and his tentmaking. This chapter looks at the prevailing academic and popular view within the church. And by looking at the prevailing view, I mean unpack it. We need to explain it, interact with it, examine it with a critical eye, and test it against both itself and Scripture. So, we are going to unpack what we could call the current tentmaking understanding or the current tentmaking ideology that is circulating within the church. In addition, we will examine a particularly pivotal verse that, due to a translation choice, may be perpetuating a skewed and inaccurate understanding of Paul's self-support.

TENTMAKING VIEWED AS A FINANCIAL BACKUP PLAN

Let's start unpacking the current tentmaking ideology by looking at what F.F. Bruce has written. Bruce was an influential British biblical scholar who lived during the 1900s and wrote extensively on the NT. His writing is a fairly representative sample of the scholarship that has been published on the topic of tentmaking. We will interact with several other scholars and popular authors as we go on, but we have to start somewhere.

Bruce presents Paul's tentmaking as a financial backup plan, or a type of secondary option for support that he utilized only when necessary, not as a purposeful choice. Bruce writes:

> This may prompt one to ask how the missionaries normally supported themselves when hospitality such as Lydia's was not forthcoming. So far as Paul is concerned, the answer is not in doubt: he supported himself, and his companions where necessary, by his "tent-making."[1]

Later he states, "When, however, hospitality was spontaneously offered . . . he gladly accepted it."[2] Bruce has painted a picture of the Apostle Paul willing to accept more traditional support such as monetary gifts and hospitality when it was on hand and as ultimately provided by the Lord, but when such support was unavailable Paul turned to tentmaking out of practical need.

Bruce then gives a specific reason why Paul turned to tentmaking when circumstances necessitated self-support. He writes, "Many rabbis practiced a trade so as to be able to impart their teaching without charge. Paul scrupulously maintained this tradition as a Christian preacher."[3] But as we have shown in the previous chapter, Hock has presented compelling evidence witnessing to the fact that the ideal of combining Torah and trade did not surface until 140–170 AD in response to war-time economic factors. Assuming Hock is correct, it is difficult to see how Paul was scrupulously maintaining a tradition that had not yet developed.

Notice also that Bruce first states that Paul accepted support when it was offered, and that he resorted to tentmaking out of necessity when support was not forthcoming. But then he immediately turns around and declares that Paul made tents because he was scrupulously maintaining a rabbinic tradition of not accepting payment or support. Which is it? Did Paul scrupulously maintain a tradition of not accepting payment, or not?

1. Bruce, *Paul*, 220.
2. Bruce, *Paul*, 220.
3. Bruce, *Paul*, 220.

How could he be scrupulously maintaining a tradition of not accepting payment, and then accept payment whenever it was offered to him? Similarly, Bruce has acknowledged that Paul supported himself when hospitality and traditional support was not offered, but when describing Paul's arrival in Corinth he later states, "In accordance with his regular practice, Paul maintained himself in Corinth by his own manual labour."[4] What regular practice? Bruce has already stated that Paul sometimes accepted support and at other times supported himself. Bruce's statements seem to contradict each other. Bruce also states that Paul's regular practice was to support himself, but that is not true. He did not always support himself. It was not his regular practice.

Bruce supplies three reasons explaining why Paul chose to follow the alleged rabbinical practice of combining Torah and trade when traditional support or wealthy patrons were unavailable. One reason was "partly as a matter of principle," which this author believes is rather ambiguous.[5] What principle is that—a principle different from the Torah and trade tradition? Another reason was "partly by way of example to his converts," which immediately raises the question: An example of what?[6] An example of turning to trade work only when absolutely necessary, but live with a wealthy host when possible? And finally, the last reason Bruce offers was so that Paul could "avoid giving his critics any opportunity to say that his motives were mercenary."[7] But if Paul wanted to avoid the charge of being a charlatan or phony itinerant teacher, why not practice tentmaking in every ministry context and refuse all support?

Bruce's explanation of Paul's intermittent tentmaking is based on the presupposition that Paul was making an expedient and practical choice out of necessity, but the biblical evidence does not support this idea. Tentmaking was not a financial backup plan to be used when traditional support was unavailable. In addition, Bruce's secondary reasons for why Paul turned to tentmaking in observance of the alleged Torah and trade tradition become problematic as soon as they are lightly challenged or pushed to their logical conclusion. First, his suggestion that Paul was maintaining a tradition fails to align with the later development of the rabbinic ideal of Torah and trade on a historical timeline. Second, his remaining reasons present themselves as either vague and underdeveloped, or inconsistent.

---

4. Bruce, *Paul*, 250.
5. Bruce, *Paul*, 220.
6. Bruce, *Paul*, 220.
7. Bruce, *Paul*, 220.

A KEY PASSAGE

When high school students put on a play, they have to build a set from scratch. The students on the drama team in charge of building the set are collectively called the stage crew. The stage crew takes large sheets of plywood, saws, nails, screws, and paint and builds the set. The set includes walls, stairs, and door openings, but it also includes the background scenery. If a play takes place in the Midwest, for example, the background scenery might depict gently rolling hills and cornfields under a big blue sky with fluffy white clouds. Maybe a few trees are included in the foreground to give the two-dimensional set piece an illusion of depth. That is what the audience sees. What the audience does not see is the back of the set. In order for these heavy sheets of painted plywood to remain standing in place on the stage, there are support boards located strategically behind the set that diagonally connect a point midway up the back side of the set piece with another board extending out from behind the same set piece at the base. These support boards are vital to the integrity of the set piece. Without the support boards, the background scenery would be unable to remain upright.

One of the reasons modern scholars such as Bruce arrive at the conclusion that Paul used tentmaking as a financial backup plan is because the idea has been assumed for so long, it has become part of the biblical background scenery. The main attraction of Paul planting churches and fulfilling Jesus' command to go and make disciples is being performed on stage, while Paul's tentmaking is simply part of the set. During some scenes, such as Corinth, Ephesus, and Thessalonica, the plywood handpainted background scenery of Paul's tentmaking is rolled out on stage, but generally ignored while the live action and speaking parts are watched with great interest. Paul's background tentmaking set piece has fit nicely into the play for a long time, and there have not been any compelling reasons to inspect it.

The Scripture passage that has functioned as the main wooden support board for the tentmaking set piece is Acts 18:5: "When Silas and Timothy arrived from Macedonia, Paul was occupied with the word, testifying to the Jews that the Christ was Jesus." There is almost universal agreement that what this verse is saying is that because Silas and Timothy arrived from Macedonia with financial support, Paul could finally stop tentmaking and devote himself full-time to the task of proclaiming the word. In other words, *after* Silas and Timothy arrived from Macedonia with a financial gift, Paul could *then* become completely occupied with the word. Or so the thinking goes.

This interpretive assumption that Paul made tents because he had to may have even colored modern Bible translations. The King James Version translated Acts 18:5 as, "And when Silas and Timotheus were come from Macedonia, Paul was pressed in the spirit, and testified to the Jews that Jesus was Christ." But by the time the New International Version of the Bible was printed, the verse was translated as, "When Silas and Timothy came from Macedonia, Paul devoted himself exclusively to preaching, testifying to the Jews that Jesus was the Messiah."[8] The awkward "pressed in the spirit" phrase is absent, replaced with a different translation that supports the assumption that Silas and Timothy relieved Paul's financial burden so he could devote himself completely to preaching.

The old KJV translation and understanding of Acts 18:5 is communicating that Silas and Timothy found Paul pressed in the spirit (however one wants to understand what that phrase means), testifying and preaching Jesus. The NIV is communicating that because Silas and Timothy arrived, Paul could begin to devote himself exclusively to preaching Jesus. The more recent view captured by the NIV can be more easily seen in the New American Standard Bible version's translation: "But when Silas and Timothy came down from Macedonia, Paul began devoting himself completely to the word, solemnly testifying to the Jews that Jesus was the Christ" (Acts 18:5). Likewise, you can see this understanding in the Contemporary English Version: "But after Silas and Timothy came from Macedonia, he spent all his time preaching to the Jews about Jesus the Messiah" (Acts 18:5). There is a significant shift in translation *and* meaning from the old KJV to the newer NIV, NASB, and CEV.

This view is now so common it appears in reference books. For example, the widely popular *Evangelical Dictionary of World Missions* has this statement under the entry for "Tent-Making Mission":

> In Acts 18:1–5, we see Paul supporting himself by teaming up with Aquila and Priscilla as tent-makers. Later when Silas and Timothy arrived in Corinth from Macedonia, Paul devoted himself exclusively to preaching. Paul vehemently defended fully-funded spiritual ministry (1 Cor. 9:1–14). There are various ways of doing ministry. On his part, he opted not to receive church support, *not on principle but for a pragmatic reason*. For he has indeed successfully argued for the legitimacy of accepting church support for his ministry.[9]

---

8. This is actually the current 2011 edition of the New International Version. The 1984 New International Version is exactly the same except it uses *Christ* instead of *Messiah* at the end of the verse.

9. Moreau, *Evangelical Dictionary of World Missions*, 939. The italics in this quote and in all quotes throughout this book are found in their original sources.

Do you see how Yamamori goes out of his way to communicate the idea that Paul opted to support himself for pragmatic reasons? The understanding being presented by Yamamori is that Paul initially made tents for the pragmatic reason of needing money, presumably due to a lack of sufficient support, but after Silas and Timothy arrived, Paul devoted himself exclusively to preaching. And the whole explanation begins by quoting Acts 18:1–5: the main wooden support board.

This more modern interpretation of Acts 18:5 is widely popular among laymen and scholars alike. Some have accepted the traditional set piece without question and do not stop to inspect Acts 18:5 at all. For example, Bruce writes, "A gift of money from his friends in Philippi relieved him for the time being of the necessity to support himself by tentmaking; he was able therefore to concentrate on the preaching of the gospel."[10] In Bruce's commentary on Acts, he makes absolutely no other comment on this verse or on the Greek grammar. There is no presentation of any other alternative conclusions, other than Paul stopped making tents because he no longer had to.

Darrell Bock writes, "Silas and Timothy arrive from Macedonia as Paul begins to devote himself to preaching to the Jews that Jesus is the Christ. He may well have received support from Macedonia."[11] Bock continues by noting that the verb συνείχετο [syneicheto] can be translated differently. He writes, "The verb συνείχετο [syneicheto] is imperfect and has an ingressive force (became "absorbed in" or "devoted to"). The verb can have the meaning of being "constrained" or "compelled" to do something."[12] Bock does not expand on the alternate translations of συνείχετο [syneicheto], but at least he alerts readers to the range of semantic meaning.

David G. Peterson offers some of the same insight that Bock provides and struggles to make sense of the implications, but he unfortunately begins with the assumption that Paul was burdened by tentmaking work during the week and had an almost exclusive Sabbath synagogue ministry, and ends with the all too common conclusion that Paul changed his work pattern as a result of the financial assistance that was brought by Silas and Timothy. Peterson writes:

> Prior to their coming, Paul was engaged in a Sabbath ministry in the synagogue and was working with Aquila and Priscilla during the week. The Greek expression . . . if read as a passive, means "constrained by the word" (BDAG "wholly absorbed in preaching"). If read as a middle voice, it can be understood reflexively

---

10. Bruce, *Book of the Acts*, 349.
11. Bock, *Acts*, 578.
12. Bock, *Acts*, 578–79.

(TNIV "*devoted himself exclusively to preaching*"). The imperfect tense is often translated as a simple past continuous, suggesting that this is how Silas and Timothy found Paul when they arrived (NRSV "Paul was occupied with proclaiming the word"; ESV "Paul was occupied with the word"). However, this rendering gives no narrative significance to the arrival of Paul's coworkers at this stage. If the imperfect is taken inceptively, the meaning is that Paul began to be wholly occupied by preaching when they arrived. A possible reason for this changed pattern of work is that Silas and Timothy were able to support Paul financially or that they had brought money from Macedonia to supply his needs.[13]

Peterson dismisses the "constrained by the word" translation and states that the ESV translation "gives no narrative significance."[14] I would ask, which narrative? The biblical narrative, or the popular narrative that views Paul's tentmaking as a financial backup plan? Even though these men are objective scholars, the background scenery has been in place for so long that they either fail to raise their eyebrows at it (Bruce), or they attempt to shoehorn the text (Peterson) into the "tentmaking was a financial backup plan" presupposition. Is there another way? Could it be time to strike the set and allow fresh air to circulate backstage? I believe the answer is yes.

A TRANSLATION CHOICE

First, we need to set aside the widely held assumption that Paul was making tents because it was an expedient, practical, or desperate choice borne out of necessity. We covered that in chapter 2, and even though it continues to be a popular view, we know that tentmaking was not a fallback or secondary choice of support that Paul utilized for financially pragmatic reasons.

Second, we need to look at the immediate biblical context of Acts 18:5. Here is the NIV translation of Acts 18:3-6 that I believe presupposes the idea that the Macedonian gift allowed Paul to stop making tents and concentrate on full-time ministry:

> And because he was a tentmaker as they were, he stayed and worked with them. Every Sabbath he reasoned in the synagogue, trying to persuade Jews and Greeks. When Silas and Timothy came from Macedonia, Paul devoted himself exclusively to

---

13. Peterson, *Acts of the Apostles*, 510.

14. Peterson, *Acts of the Apostles*, 510. Peterson offers the translation, "devoted himself exclusively to."

> preaching, testifying to the Jews that Jesus was the Messiah. But when they opposed Paul and became abusive, he shook out his clothes in protest and said to them, "Your blood be on your own heads! I am innocent of it. From now on I will go to the Gentiles." (Acts 18:3–6, NIV)

The NIV has translated συνείχετο [*syneicheto*] as "devoted himself exclusively to." But as Bock and Peterson have observed, συνείχετο [*syneicheto*] in this context can also be translated as "constrained by." Even though both authors offer this translation, neither ends up using it in the passage because, I suspect, it does not fit the widely held assumption that the Macedonian gift relieved a financial barrier that was preventing Paul from turning his full attention to ministry. In what way would "constrained by" alter this passage, and would it make sense in the immediate and wider biblical context?

We know that Paul followed a pattern during his missionary activities. It is widely recognized that when Paul entered an unreached region, he proclaimed the gospel to the Jews first, then to the Gentiles. Kenneth Scott Latourette writes, "In going into a city for the first time Paul usually went to a synagogue and there declared Jesus to be the Christ. When, as generally happened, some heeded him but the majority, outraged, drove him out, he sought the Gentiles."[15] Likewise, missiologist John Mark Terry, within a work examining Paul's missionary methods, also acknowledges Paul's practice of Jews first, Gentiles second, and cites Scripture: "Paul believed the gospel was 'to the Jew first' (Rom 1:16)."[16] John Stott observes:

> As we watch Paul travel and proclaim the good news of Christ, we see a pattern that he follows when he enters each city. It is no different in Corinth and Ephesus. His first attempt is to persuade the Jews concerning Jesus. He begins in the synagogue where they meet, study Scripture, and pray. But when the Jews reject his message he turns to the Gentiles. In both cities Paul's bold step of going to the Gentiles was indicated by many people hearing and believing the gospel.[17]

I think most readers are aware of this pattern and will accept it as normative for Paul.

In the Acts 18:3–6 passage, we can see this pattern of Jews first, Gentiles second. In verse 4, Paul is ministering in the Jewish synagogue to Jews along with God-fearing Greeks who were also worshiping the God of the

---

15. Latourette, *History of Christianity*, 72.
16. Plummer and Terry, *Paul's Missionary Methods*, 163.
17. Stott, *Acts: Seeing the Spirit*, 81.

Jews. Then in verse 6, Paul stated that he would *from now on* go to the Gentiles. Paul gave the Jews in Corinth first priority because he understood the pattern that Jesus modeled of Jews first, Gentiles second.

There is another passage that clearly illustrates Paul's consistent pattern of going to the Jews first, then to the Gentiles. Acts 13:44–47 states:

> The next Sabbath almost the whole city gathered to hear the word of the Lord. But when the Jews saw the crowds, they were filled with jealousy and began to contradict what was spoken by Paul, reviling him. And Paul and Barnabas spoke out boldly, saying, "It was necessary that the word of God be spoken first to you. Since you thrust it aside and judge yourselves unworthy of eternal life, behold, we are turning to the Gentiles. For so the Lord has commanded us, saying, 'I have made you a light for the Gentiles, that you may bring salvation to the ends of the earth.'" (Acts 13:44–47)

There are many similarities between the accounts of Paul in Antioch and Paul in Corinth. Both passages present Paul proclaiming the gospel in a local synagogue. Both passages record Jews along with others present and listening to Paul's message.[18] Both passages indicate that the Jews' response to Paul's message was unfavorable and that they rejected him. Both passages state that Paul declared his intention to turn to a primary Gentile ministry in that city. The only significant difference between the two passages (if we hold to the presupposition translation of Acts 18:4–6) is that we have a statement about Paul being biblically grounded to minister to Jews first in Acts 13:46–47, whereas in Acts 18:4–6, we have a statement that says Paul "devoted himself exclusively to preaching." This is presumably because he was free to do so because of the Macedonian gift.

But what if we discard the presupposition that Paul was financially relieved, and therefore free to devote himself to full-time preaching? Would the "constrained by" translation make a better contextual fit? The answer is yes. Here is the ESV translation of Acts 18:4–6 with this author's changes underlined, specifically, with συνείχετο [*syneicheto*] translated as "constrained by" instead of "occupied with":

> And he reasoned in the synagogue every Sabbath, and tried to persuade Jews and Greeks. When Silas and Timothy arrived from Macedonia, Paul was <u>constrained by</u> the word, testifying to the Jews that the Christ was Jesus. And when they opposed and reviled him, he shook out his garments and said to them,

---

18. Acts 18:4: "And he reasoned in the synagogue every Sabbath, and tried to persuade Jews and Greeks."

"Your blood be on your own heads! I am innocent. From now on I will go to the Gentiles." (Acts 18:4–6)

Now, the account in Acts 13:46–47 and the account in Acts 18:4–6 are almost identical. In addition to all the similarities already stated, now both passages also share the common element of Paul being constrained by the word of God to preach first to the Jews, then to the Gentiles. Instead of Paul being "fully devoted to preaching the word" as a result of Silas and Timothy's arrival with burden-lifting money, Silas and Timothy arrive to find Paul being constrained by the word to preach to the Jews first, just as he was constrained by the word to preach first to the Jews in Antioch.

Moreover, in both Antioch and Corinth, Paul was in the synagogue on the Sabbath. Paul's weekly presence in the Jewish synagogue was also a pattern. We cannot assume that because Paul was ministering to the Jews in the local Corinthian synagogue on the Sabbath that it was because he was making tents during the week and *unable* to minister on any other day. The synagogue was the place where the Jews gathered for worship on the Sabbath. It was a suitable ministry context for proclaiming the gospel to the Jews and we would expect to find him there. It did not matter if Paul was making tents during the rest of the week or not. In fact, Paul was ministering in the synagogue on the Sabbath in Antioch, but there is no indication that the reason he was doing that was because he was engaged in tentmaking the rest of the week and the Sabbath was his only "day off." I believe that line of thinking originates in the presupposition of a necessity based view of tentmaking.

Finally, what should be obvious but is still worth mentioning, *nowhere* does it say in this passage or anywhere else in the NT that Paul actually stopped making tents after the arrival of Silas and Timothy. It is assumed, almost universally, because it is part of the presupposition background scenery that has been on stage for so long. In reality, the idea that Paul stopped making tents after his colleagues' arrival is an *argumentum ex silentio*, and an extremely weak one at that. Siemens writes, "It is generally assumed that they brought money from Macedonia and so he quit his manual labor to give full time to preaching . . . The larger context also show convincingly that he did not quit his manual labor."[19]

---

19. Siemens, "Vital Role," 122. Despite Siemens' agreement with me that the larger biblical context indicates that Paul did not stop making tents at Corinth upon the arrival of Silas and Timothy, she asserts that the text is saying that Paul was already engrossed in gospel proclamation. She writes, "The words in Greek suggest that they were surprised that he was already so deeply into his ministry." In other words, although Siemens believes that the Macedonian gift did not relieve Paul's burden of work so that he could devote himself to full-time ministry, she does not believe that Acts 18:5

Lest anyone think that I am attempting to produce my own novel translation, it should be noted that the American Standard Version (ASV) and the English Revised Version (ERV) have both translated Acts 18:5 exactly the same, "But when Silas and Timothy came down from Macedonia, Paul was constrained by the word, testifying to the Jews that Jesus was the Christ" (ASV).[20]

In summary, the "constrained by the word" translation provides a better immediate contextual fit because it is consistent with the NT biblical ministry pattern of Jews first, Gentiles second. It also makes more sense when comparing Paul's ministry in Corinth to his ministry in Antioch because it reveals evangelistic consistency and Paul's continued repeated obedience to his Lord's instructions. He was not willing to walk outside the boundaries that Jesus had put in place regarding the order of gospel proclamation.

Now that this support board of Acts 18:5 has been removed, the cumbersome set piece of Paul making tents out of necessity for pragmatic reasons has too little structural integrity to remain standing. Paul did not make tents because the churches were too poor to support him. Corinth was arguably one of the wealthier churches that Paul established and he did make tents in that city. Paul was not released to full-time ministry by the arrival of Silas and Timothy carrying moneybags. Paul was constrained by the word of God to proclaim the gospel in the Corinthian synagogue first to the Jews, then to the Gentiles.

Even though we have unpacked the prevailing popular view of tentmaking, we are still left with a compelling question: Why did Paul choose to support himself in certain ministry contexts and not others? In order to answer this question we will need to closely examine what Paul has already told us.

---

is stating that Paul was constrained by Scripture to proclaim the gospel to first to Jews and then to Gentiles, as I have argued.

20. The ASV was first printed in 1901 and was used extensively in seminaries.

4

Paul's Self-Disclosed Reasons

The NT reveals three primary reasons for Paul's purposeful choice to engage in tentmaking, and neither expediency nor desperate necessity are among them. Paul did not make tents as a financial backup plan when churches could not afford to pay him. The three reasons Paul chose to support himself in certain ministry contexts, and not others, were to correct a problem of idleness, to encourage benevolence, and to distinguish himself and his message from false teachers.

The first two reasons have the same didactic type of purpose and so we will group them together under a heading called *didactic*, which means: meant to teach or instruct. We could just as easily call the first two reasons pedagogical reasons. The third reason is evangelistic in nature. So we have two examples of tentmaking motivated by didactic goals and one example of Paul choosing to support himself for evangelistic reasons.

DIDACTIC: IDLENESS PROBLEM

There was a problem of idleness in the Thessalonian church. We know this because Paul addressed it in his two letters to the Thessalonians. In 1 Thess 4:11–12, Paul commands his readers to "live quietly, and to mind your own affairs, and to work with your hands, as we instructed you, so that you may

PAUL'S SELF-DISCLOSED REASONS

live properly before outsiders and be dependent on no one." Later in 1 Thess 5:14, Paul also writes, "And we urge you, brothers, admonish the idle." G.K. Beale makes this conclusion regarding the situation in Thessalonica:

> Most agree that the problem is Christians not working to support themselves because of a mistaken belief that Christ would return within the near future. The fact that the warning against slackness in working occurs both directly before and after (5:14) Paul's explicit teaching about Christ's final coming (4:13–5:11) supports this conclusion (Marshall 1983:117). Many guilty of such laxness would have become dependent on the charity of other church members as well as possibly on whatever welfare may have been available in the surrounding culture.[1]

Remember, we are not debating *why* there was a problem with idleness. The point of quoting Beale is to demonstrate his agreement that there *was* a problem of idleness among the believers in Thessalonica.

Some make the mistake here of concluding that Paul made tents so he himself could maintain a high reputation with outsiders by not being dependent on anyone. But Paul affirms elsewhere that ministers of the gospel may receive pay for their labor (1 Cor 9:3–14; 1 Tim 5:17–18; 2 Thess 3:9), as did Jesus (Luke 10:7). And, if you recall, Paul had entered the household of Lydia and received direct payment and support from the congregation at Philippi when he ministered to them. The reason Paul was teaching the church in Thessalonica to work was because *they* had a problem with idleness, not Paul. This passage does not support the notion that Paul was giving them a ministry model to follow that combined Torah and trade, or that *all* ministers of the gospel should engage in self-support. Paul did not turn to self-support in Thessalonica to ensure that outsiders did not mistakenly perceive him as a freeloader.

Due to the *Thessalonian* idleness problem, Paul sought to correct that problem by teaching them a strong work ethic. Although he could have received support from the Thessalonians (and did receive support from the Philippians while he was at Thessalonica), it would have appeared incongruent for Paul to exhort the believers there to work while he himself was receiving support from them, even though he was already laboring among them as a minister of the Lord. Paul was attempting to correct the problem of idleness by teaching them to work through oral instruction (1 Thess 4:11), written instruction (Thessalonian letters), and by way of example (supporting himself through non-ministry labor).

---

1. Beale, *1–2 Thessalonians*, 128–29.

Paul addressed the problem of idleness in 1 Thess 2:9 when he wrote, "For you remember, brothers, our labor and toil: we worked night and day, that we might not be a burden to any of you, while we proclaimed to you the gospel of God." Beale states, "Paul's earlier mention that he had worked 'night and day in order not to be a [financial] burden to anyone' is the positive example to follow."[2]

We might ask: A positive example of what, and for what purpose? We do not have to wonder for too long because Paul tells us in 1 Thess 4:11–12, "work with your hands, as we instructed you, so that you may live properly before outsiders and be dependent on no one." The purpose of Paul's example was to move the believers at Thessalonica to a point where they were no longer "living off the largesse of others who could easily afford it."[3] No society respects a person who *can* work but intentionally chooses joblessness and sloth. Paul exhibited a strong work ethic because he knew modeling is a powerful pedagogical tool. He wanted the believers in Thessalonica to live in a way that would "command the respect of unbelievers and not to be a burden on their fellow believers."[4]

We can see that the idleness problem had not abated by Paul's second letter to the Thessalonians. In Second Thessalonians, Paul approaches the topic of idleness with even more force. This passage warrants full quotation:

> Now we command you, brothers, in the name of our Lord Jesus Christ, that you keep away from any brother who is walking in idleness and not in accord with the tradition that you received from us. For you yourselves know how you ought to imitate us, because we were not idle when we were with you, nor did we eat anyone's bread without paying for it, but with toil and labor we worked night and day, that we might not be a burden to any of you. It was not because we do not have that right, but to give you in ourselves an example to imitate. For even when we were with you, we would give you this command: If anyone is not willing to work, let him not eat. For we hear that some among you walk in idleness, not busy at work, but busybodies. Now such persons we command and encourage in the Lord Jesus Christ to do their work quietly and to earn their own living. (2 Thess 3:6–12)

Interestingly, the reason Bruce supplies to explain why Paul accepted a living arrangement with a wealthy patron like Lydia is it "would have been

---

2. Beale, *1–2 Thessalonians*, 129.
3. Fee, *First and Second Letters*, 163.
4. Stott, *Message of 1 & 2 Thessalonians*, 90.

ungracious to refuse."[5] But in the above block quotation from Second Thessalonians, Paul writes that he did not even eat anyone's bread without paying for it. It seems farfetched to believe that Paul would agree to stay in Lydia's home and receive such generous support because he was motivated by a fear that he would appear socially ungracious, yet have no qualms about sending a strong unspoken social insult that would result from refusing the simple and comparatively inexpensive hospitality of a single meal or a loaf of bread from his Thessalonian brothers and sisters. In order to unearth Paul's motivation for self-support in some ministry contexts and not others, we have to dig deeper than social politeness.

In the above quote from Second Thessalonians, Paul reinforces the acceptability and legitimacy of his right to receive support from them. Paul did not have to make tents due to desperate financial circumstances. He could have received financial support from them, but he chose not to for didactic reasons. His words are explicit and remove any exegetical opacity: "It was not because we do not have that right, but to give you in ourselves an example to imitate" (2 Thess 3:9). It does not get much clearer than that. He is saying that he could have accepted traditional support and payment from them, but he chose not to because he wanted to give them an example to imitate. Paul gives us his reason for supporting himself at Thessalonica. Their particular circumstances required Paul to teach them not only with words, but also by example. In an effort to address the context-specific problem of *idleness*, he utilized every instructional tool at his disposal.

Before we move on, I want to clarify what Paul is saying when he uses the word *burden*, or the phrases *did not burden*, and *might not burden*, or other similar language. When you see those phrases, Paul is *not* saying that the reason he selectively turned to self-support was because he perceived it would have been difficult for the churches to pay him for his ministry. When Paul uses those *burden* phrases, he is using them to *describe* his free-of-charge ministry, not as *grounds* for his free-of-charge ministry.

This is true in his letters to the Thessalonians, and it is true in his letters to the Corinthians. Reading the expanded immediate context makes it clear he is not saying that he has decided not to bill them because he doesn't think they can afford to pay him, or that paying him would be too much of a financial hardship. He is using that language to *describe* his free-of-charge ministry.

Some people have looked at that language and concluded that one of the reasons Paul decided to support himself was so that he would not place a financial strain on the congregation he was ministering to at the time. But

---

5. Bruce, *Paul*, 220.

I do not believe there are any contextual grounds for rushing to that conclusion. Not only does it conflict with what we know to be true about Paul accepting payment from the poorer churches and supporting himself at the wealthier churches, but it also does not make any sense. Are we prepared to say that the reason Paul chose not to burden the church was because he did not want to burden the church? That is like saying, *The reason I did not go in to work today is because I did not want to go into work today.* At best, it is an arbitrary personal choice. It does not answer the *why* question: Why did Paul not burden the church in Thessalonica? Or, why did Paul provide a free-of-charge ministry at Thessalonica? Paul *tells* us in 2 Thess 3:9. It was to give them an example to imitate.

DIDACTIC: TEACHING BENEVOLENCE

The second reason why Paul made a purposeful choice to support himself in certain ministry contexts and not others was so that he could teach the Ephesians to obey Jesus' command to give to others in need. Luke has provided us with a detailed report of Paul's departing words to the Ephesian elders in Acts 20:18–35. The verses that pertain to Paul's tentmaking are his concluding remarks:

> I coveted no one's silver or gold or apparel. You yourselves know that these hands ministered to my necessities and to those who were with me. In all things I have shown you that by working hard in this way we must help the weak and remember the words of the Lord Jesus, how he himself said, "It is more blessed to give than to receive." (Acts 20:33–35)

Some believe that the above Scripture passage is a cautionary comment to the Ephesian elders, reminding them to serve Christ and his church for reasonable or zero pay. Bruce comments on this passage: "Paul reminds them finally that those who take care of the people of God must do so without thought of material reward."[6] But Paul is telling them that in all things, including his own self-support, he is showing them that believers should work hard in order to be in a position to help the weak and follow Jesus' command to give. Paul did not say that he made tents as a safeguard to protect himself from coveting material reward or to show others that ministry is never about the money.

Peterson reaches a similar but slightly different conclusion from Acts 20:33–35: "In addition to the danger of false teaching and persecution, Paul

---

6. Bruce, *Book of the Acts*, 395.

recognised the possibility that elders might misuse their position for personal gain."[7] If Paul wished to warn the Ephesian elders about leveraging their elder status to get rich, why did he say that he worked to show them how they must help the weak and follow the command of Jesus? Paul could have told them that he made tents in order not to minister for personal gain, but he did not. It makes more sense to accept the reason Paul actually states than to supply a reason Paul does not offer.

Peterson continues, "His aim here is to warn leaders of the dangers inherent in their position and to commend his own solution to the problem of greed."[8] Again, Paul does not say he made tents as a solution to combat greed. He said, "I have shown you that by working hard in this way we must help the weak and remember the words of the Lord Jesus." This error of removing the actual reason that Paul supplies and inserting a reason he does not provide invites us to go down a road that leads away from the text. Besides, helping the weak is not always an antidote to greed. Sometimes it is a psychological salve that aids in mentally justifying the accumulation and possession of extravagant or ill-gotten wealth.

Paul stated that the reason he worked hard to support himself in Ephesus was to teach the leaders by example that they must help the weak and put Jesus' teachings on giving into practice. Bock writes, "Using the term 'must' . . . Paul raises a moral obligation. It is a moral imperative to help the weak and be generous to them."[9]

Paul did state that he avoided coveting silver and gold. However, it is possible to still covet silver and gold while working and making tents. Paul's statement about not coveting could just as easily be linked with his previous statement about how the word of God is able, "to build you up and give you an inheritance among those who are sanctified" (Acts 20:32). The reason Paul did not covet silver or gold may have been because the apostle's mind was set on his spiritual inheritance rather than earthly wealth.

In fact, there are other places in the Bible where spiritual benefits are juxtaposed with silver and gold. Proverbs 16:16 declares, "How much better to get wisdom than gold! To get understanding is to be chosen rather than silver." And Acts 3:6 states, "But Peter said, 'I have no silver and gold, but what I do have I give to you. In the name of Jesus Christ of Nazareth, rise up and walk!'" In 1 Pet 1:18–19, Paul states how the blood of Jesus and its ability to make the spiritual ransom payment for our sin is much greater than silver or gold, "Knowing that you were ransomed from the futile ways inherited

---

7. Peterson, *Acts of the Apostles*, 572.
8. Peterson, *Acts of the Apostles*, 573.
9. Bock, *Acts*, 632.

from your forefathers, not with perishable things such as silver or gold, but with the precious blood of Christ, like that of a lamb without blemish or spot."

James 5:2–3 says this to the rich, "Your riches have rotted and your garments are moth-eaten. Your gold and silver have corroded, and their corrosion will be evidence against you and will eat your flesh like fire." Instead of pursuing gold, silver, and costly garments, they should have been helping the weak and giving to the poor. Finally, even though Jesus does not specifically mention silver and gold, his teaching in Matt 6:19–21 contrasts earthly treasures with spiritual treasures in heaven:

> Do not lay up for yourselves treasures on earth, where moth and rust destroy and where thieves break in and steal, but lay up for yourselves treasures in heaven, where neither moth nor rust destroys and where thieves do not break in and steal. For where your treasure is, there your heart will be also. (Matt 6:19–21)

If verses 32 and 33 are linked due to the contrasting relationship between spiritual inheritance and silver and gold, then verse 34 is when Paul began telling the elders about his practice of tentmaking and how it enabled him to live out the benevolent principle that Jesus taught. I see no reason why verse 33 must be linked to verse 34 over verse 32. The above-quoted verses may even favor a link between verses 32 and 33 as opposed to a verse 33 and 34 connection.

A third alternative could be that verse 33 serves as a bridge verse, originally linked to verse 32 and the concept of spiritual inheritance rather than silver or gold. Then, once Paul mentioned silver or gold or apparel, he may have been mentally and spiritually prompted to add his remarks about working for benevolent reasons.

Regardless of the exact relationship between verses 32 through 34, the idea that Paul includes these words about his self-support primarily as a warning against greed or misuse of power does not appear to be as solid as Bruce and Peterson respectively present. Primarily, because Paul does not provide those reasons.

There is one more powerful statement from Paul that lends support to the idea that he was addressing a ministry context-specific issue at Ephesus about giving to the poor. We find it in Ephesians. When discussing how believers should walk in the newness of Christ, he makes these comments in Eph 4:28: "Let the thief no longer steal, but rather let him labor, doing honest work with his own hands, so that he may have something to share with anyone in need." Paul tells us exactly why he commands the Ephesians to do honest work with their own hands, and it is not so they will avoid abusing the office of elder or succumb to greed. It is so that they will work and have enough to help the weak and follow Jesus' command to give to others.

It is worth pointing out that the command in Eph 4:28 is not being addressed *just* to the former thief. Paul is telling the former thief to discontinue stealing and join the rest of the Christian community in living rightly by working hard so that they have enough to follow Jesus' teaching and give to those in need. All followers of Jesus are to do honest work with their hands so they have enough to give to others, just as all followers of Jesus are not to have any corrupting talk come out of their mouths, as the next verse commands, "Let no corrupting talk come out of your mouths, but only such as is good for building up, as fits the occasion, that it may give grace to those who hear" (Eph 4:29). Paul is not saying in Eph 4:29 that only those who *used* to have corrupting talk come out of their mouths now need to refrain from that behavior, he is telling *everyone* to refrain from that behavior. Similarly, it is not just the former thief who needs to work hard with their own hands in order to be in a position to give to those in need, it is a command for all covenant people. One does not need to be a former thief in order to be under the command to engage in honest labor and give to those in need. Likewise, one does not have to be an Ephesian elder in order to be under the command to help the weak and remember the words of Jesus.

In summary, the second didactic reason that explains why Paul made a purposeful choice to support himself in some ministry contexts and not others was to teach the Ephesian elders (and by extension, all of God's image bearers) that they should be willing to work hard and go to great lengths in order to be in a position to give to the poor. There is no reason to doubt that Paul could have survived on the support of others at Ephesus, but he made the purposeful choice to support himself in order to teach the church by example that they must to do whatever it takes in order to be in a position to give to others.

EVANGELISTIC

The third reason that Paul chose to accept support in some ministry contexts, but to support himself through tentmaking in other ministry contexts, is evangelistic in nature and can be found in his two letters to the church in Corinth. The ministry context at Corinth, as revealed in the Bible, is convoluted. But we will continue building on the foundation we have previously established. Paul made a purposeful choice to accept support in certain ministry contexts and not others for reasons other than financial necessity or pragmatism.

There is one primary reason why Paul made a purposeful choice to support himself when he was in Corinth. Paul wanted as many people as possible to repent and believe in Jesus Christ. After presenting an airtight case arguing for his right to receive monetary support from the believers at Corinth in 1 Cor 9:1–12, Paul writes the following, "Nevertheless, we have not made use of this right, but we endure anything rather than put an obstacle in the way of the gospel of Christ" (1 Cor 9:12). Paul made a choice not to receive payment from them for evangelistic reasons.

Gene L. Green has recognized the different reasons Paul provides for self-support in the Corinthian and Thessalonian ministry contexts and writes, "In 1 Cor 9:1–18, Paul explains that he did not make himself a client of that congregation so as not to 'hinder the gospel of Christ' (9:12), but the motivation presented to the Thessalonians is different."[10]

The question now presented to us is, how would receiving support from them have put an obstacle in the way of the gospel? The answer is that if Paul received support from them, in Corinth at that time, it would have created the impression that the gospel was no different than the false teaching the "peddlers of God's word" were proclaiming to them (2 Cor 2:17). Paul's Jesus would have been placed on the shelf next to "another Jesus" that the false teachers were proclaiming (2 Cor 11:4). It would have been difficult to determine which Jesus and which gospel was genuine, because it would have been difficult to distinguish between speakers. If Paul accepted support, there would be a much greater possibility that he would appear to look like every other false teacher or philosopher vying for the Corinthian's attention. Paul did not want to blend in with his opponents because it would increase the likelihood that he would be rejected, for example, in favor of a more eloquent speaker. All things being equal, people may have been more likely to receive and follow a powerful, persuasive, articulate public speaker and reject Paul who by his own admission was not a skilled speaker. But to reject Paul was to reject Paul's gospel and Paul's Jesus; hence, the obstacle. Paul was willing to go to great lengths in order to eliminate that obstacle.

---

10. Green, *Letters to the Thessalonians*, 349. I extend congratulations to Green for not only distinguishing two different reasons for making tents in the two ministry contexts of Thessalonica and Corinth, but also for correctly identifying Paul's own self-disclosed reason for making tents in Corinth, that is, not to hinder or put an obstacle in the way of the gospel of Christ. It seems simple and straightforward, but as we will see later on, there are many who miss these important observations. Again, I believe it is because of the presupposition bias of reading what is expected into the text. There are many who cannot seem to break free from viewing Paul's tentmaking as a financial backup plan. Green also correctly identifies Paul's self-disclosed reason for self-support in Thessalonica. Green does not specifically address the Ephesian context.

We might ask, why did Paul go to Corinth and proclaim the gospel? The answer is to win people for Christ. In 1 Cor 9:22, which incidentally occurs immediately after Paul wrote that he did not make use of his right to support in order not to place an obstacle in the way of the gospel, Paul says, "I have become all things to all people, that by all means I might save some. I do it all for the sake of the gospel, that I may share with them in its blessings." In every ministry context that he encountered he became a chameleon to maximize the potential harvest. He was that way when he interacted with people, people groups, churches, cities, and regions. Paul went to Corinth to win people for Jesus and in order to maximize his potential effectiveness, and in that particular ministry context, it was necessary to select self-support.

In 2 Cor 11:12–13, Paul states, "And what I do I will continue to do, in order to undermine the claim of those who would like to claim that in their boasted mission they work on the same terms as we do. For such men are false apostles." When we remember that the gospel message and the authentic Jesus were inextricably joined to the man, Paul, we can see that Paul's goal to discredit his opponents is serving his overarching goal of reaching as many people for Christ as possible. If his opponents are perceived as valid apostles, then Paul's message is simply one of many valid messages competing for supremacy. Accepting support would have placed an obstacle in the way of the gospel. By refusing traditional support, Paul was distancing himself from the false apostles.

Paul again links his choice to support himself with his evangelistic goal in 2 Cor 12:14, where he states, "Here for the third time I am ready to come to you. And I will not be a burden, for I seek not what is yours but you." He chose to support himself because he wanted them to come to Christ.

Like we saw when we looked at Paul's letters to the Thessalonians, he continues to use the *burden* language in the same way in 2 Cor 11:9, "And when I was with you and was in need, I did not burden anyone, for the brothers who came from Macedonia supplied my need. So I refrained and will refrain from burdening you in any way." Paul follows the burdening language with 2 Cor 11:12, "And what I do [refraining from burdening them] I will continue to do, in order to undermine the claim of those who would like to claim that in their boasted mission they work on the same terms as we do." Do you see how he uses the *burden* language to *describe* his free-of-charge ministry and not as a *reason* that determines his self-support?

Roy E. Ciampa and Brian S. Rosner have identified gospel hindrance as Paul's reason for choosing self-support in Corinth. In their comment on 1 Cor 9:12 they state:

> So Paul is willing to go to the greatest lengths in order to avoid the very least of hindrances to the progress of *the gospel*. The *gospel* is mentioned for the first time here since 4:15, and it serves as the key to Paul's explanation of his decision to forgo the use of certain rights. The concept of the gospel is explicitly referred to in vv. 14 (x2), 16 (x2), 18 (x3), and 23, and it is the dominant concept in the remainder of the chapter. The primacy of the gospel trumps all other considerations when it comes to Paul's use of his rights.[11]

Although Ciampa and Rosner correctly recognize gospel hindrance as the reason for Paul's purposeful choice to forgo his apostolic right to support in Corinth, they claim that exactly how Paul's refusal to accept support in Corinth hinders the gospel remains unknown: "The question remains, why did Paul feel the gospel might be hindered by receiving support from the Corinthians? He does not tell us."[12]

Ciampa and Rosner continue with a discussion of recent scholarship centering on friendship and the patronage system in ancient Roman society and conclude that if Paul accepted support, then he would have no longer been free because he would be viewed as a client of a wealthy patron. Ciampa and Rosner write:

> Such a perception would have had potentially disastrous results for the ministry of the gospel. Paul would no longer be free (cf. vv.1, 19a) to be all things to all people (vv. 19b–22), but would be expected to be what his Corinthian patrons wished. He may also have not felt free to correct them as he saw fit. Others to whom he ministered (both within and outside the Corinthian church) could well think that he represented the interests of the

---

11. Ciampa and Rosner, *First Letter to the Corinthians*, 410.

12. Ciampa and Rosner, *First Letter to the Corinthians*, 410. When answering the question of how Paul receiving traditional support would have put an obstacle in the way of the gospel, Garland answers, "Potential converts may have shied away from converting to the gospel if they suspected that it came with strings attached: acceptance would cause them to incur financial obligations to support the one who brought them the gospel. Paul sought to avoid any impression that he was preaching only to acquire support. This policy of refusing assistance from converts caused him to endure privations." Garland, *1 Corinthians*, 413. Garland is unsure of why Paul maintained this so-called *policy*: "We can only surmise why Paul refused to accept subsidies from churches where he was preaching. His overriding concern in all that he did was whether it helped or hindered the gospel's advance (1 Cor. 9:12), and he refused to accept support at Corinth because he believed it would hinder the reception of the gospel." This is followed by a list of five possible reasons why Paul might have refused support, which Garland offers without committing to any one in particular. Garland, *1 Corinthians*, 419.

Corinthians who supported him rather than God's interest or their own.[13]

If these conclusions are correct, then why would Paul accept the patronage support of a wealthy host such as Lydia in Philippi? If Paul was concerned about his appearance to outsiders in regards to his freedom, why would he enter the household of anyone? In addition, I find the idea that Paul would have felt socially reserved and unable to correct someone's misunderstanding of the gospel because he was accepting support from them unconvincing. Is there any circumstance that would have prevented Paul from correcting someone about Jesus and the truth of the gospel?

It is noteworthy that Paul's opponents would have liked Paul to start accepting support in Corinth, because then they would have been on equal footing with him, and there would have been no distinction between Paul and the false teachers. However, Paul refused to accept support knowing that the false teachers would never stop taking money and begin supporting themselves. Paradoxically, the false teachers wanted to be regarded as equals with Paul who chose not accept support, but they also criticized him for not accepting support.

In summary, when we look at Paul's own self-disclosed reasons for choosing to support himself in certain ministry contexts, we find that Paul desired to correct a problem of idleness, to encourage benevolence, and to distinguish himself from false teachers. In order to achieve those goals, he intentionally chose to support himself.

---

13. Ciampa and Rosner, *First Letter to the Corinthians*, 411.

5

Lack of Scholarly Consensus

It has already been demonstrated that there is a prevailing view of tentmaking that understands Paul turning to self-support out of practical need when traditional support was unavailable. We have also seen how a skewed understanding or Acts 18:5 continues to perpetuate the widespread view that tentmaking was a financial backup plan. Tentmaking is generally considered something Paul utilized when he had to, but discontinued as soon as possible. However, the evidence has shown that Paul accepted support from one of the poorer churches, Philippi, and chose to support himself by tentmaking in Corinth, one of the wealthier churches. As a result, we can rightly conclude that tentmaking was not a a financial backup plan that he turned to when traditional support was unavailable. We have also seen how a clarifying translation of Acts 18:5 rejects the modern idea that Paul ceased tentmaking and began to devote himself exclusively to preaching after receiving money from Silas and Timothy. The prevailing view of tentmaking evaporates quickly when exposed to the heat of Paul's own self-disclosed didactic and evangelistic reasons for supporting himself.

    We have also examined some of the NT scholarship on Paul's tentmaking by Bruce, Peterson, Bock, Green, and Ciampa and Rosner. In this chapter, a few more authors and their tentmaking conclusions will be considered. I think it is important to show the lack of scholarly consensus on this topic. We need to see the cloud of confusion hanging over Paul's tentmaking. When multiple people are reaching such diverse conclusions when studying the same Bible and using similar exegetical methodology, it should be a red flag alerting the church to pay closer attention and investigate *why* there is such confusion and disagreement.

MURRAY J. HARRIS

Let us begin by looking at what Murray J. Harris has to say. Harris is a NT scholar who has written a single-volume commentary on Second Corinthians which is part of The New International Greek Testament Commentary series. In a comment on 2 Cor 11:7–12, Harris suggests some reasons why Paul chose self-support in Corinth:

> Paul does not restate his right to support (although this is implied in 11:9) but focuses on his reasons for financial independence of the Corinthians—to preach the gospel to them "free of charge" (11:7) and to avoid being a financial burden on them (11:9)—and his unwavering determination to remain independent (11:9–10, 12).[1]

Although the above statements are accurate observations, none of them provide a holistic answer to why Paul refused support in the Corinthian ministry context and not others.

For example, Paul did preach the gospel to them free of charge and was not a financial burden on them, but why? Harris explains that "By offering the 'price-less' good news totally free of charge, he was dramatizing in his own conduct the very appeal of the gospel as the good news of God's free grace."[2] Harris is saying that, by supporting himself, Paul was modeling the freeness of the gospel. This will be explored later in a discussion of the spiritual benefits of Paul's self-support, but again, if that was so important, why would Paul do that in some ministry contexts and not others? I agree, the gospel is free. Scripture teaches us that the free gift of God is eternal life in Christ Jesus our Lord. But why would Paul make such a personally difficult choice to support himself in one ministry context in order to model the freeness of the gospel, but then not do it in other contexts? All churches should be taught that the gospel is free. If in fact modeling the freeness of the gospel was so important in Corinth, why would it not be important everywhere? It doesn't make sense logically to offer up a reason for a selective choice by Paul that is not consistently true everywhere.

---

1. Harris, *Second Epistle to the Corinthians*, 753.
2. Harris, *Second Epistle to the Corinthians*, 765.

Paul did provide a free-of-charge ministry to them, to which Harris adds, "He probably saw this as an evidence of his love."[3] But why would Paul display an evidence of his love in Corinth and not in other places?

And, yes, Paul did demonstrate an unwavering determination to remain financially independent when ministering in Corinth. Harris states that this was to "maintain an advantage over any rivals who accepted payment for their services."[4] Okay, but what does that mean? How would Paul maintain an advantage? What was the advantage? Harris elaborates by stating, "No one could accuse Paul of preaching for profit."[5] Sharp readers will remember that this is essentially the same reason Bruce gave in chapter 3. Bruce gave three reasons Paul was allegedly following the Torah and trade tradition. Bruce wrote that refusing payment would mean that Paul could "avoid giving his critics any opportunity to say that his motives were mercenary."[6] While that might be an unintended byproduct, Paul did not make tents to deflect accusations of preaching for profit. What we see in Scripture is Paul creating distance between himself and his rivals because the true gospel message was fettered to the man, Paul. By maintaining a distinction between himself and his rivals, he maintained a difference between the true gospel and a false gospel. The problem with Harris' and Bruce's explanations are that while they are true, they fail to point to Paul's own self-disclosed reason why he supported himself in Corinth; namely, so that he would not place an obstacle in the way of the gospel of Christ (1 Cor 9:12).

What this means is that we cannot simply point to Paul ministering for free in Corinth and conclude that the reason Paul refused their support was because he did not want to place a *financial* burden on them. There are no grounds for that conclusion in the text. We have to keep going and see that refusing support from them was a means to an end, it was not the end itself. By laboring free of charge and not burdening them, he was removing an obstacle in the way of the gospel, and that obstacle was the blurring of distinguishable differences between Paul and his enemies who were proclaiming another Jesus and another gospel. By voluntarily refusing support from them, he was not attempting to help them out financially. He was making it easy for them to see the difference between himself and the other false apostles.

Harris concludes his point about Paul maintaining financial independence with the statement, "We may speculate on further reasons for

---

3. Harris, *Second Epistle to the Corinthians*, 765.
4. Harris, *Second Epistle to the Corinthians*, 765.
5. Harris, *Second Epistle to the Corinthians*, 765.
6. Bruce, *Paul*, 220.

his vigorous independence."⁷ Except we do not have to speculate, and we should not speculate. Paul has told us in 2 Cor 11:12–15.

Harris also comments directly on Paul's statement in 2 Cor 11:10: "As the truth of Christ is in me, this boasting of mine will not be silenced in the regions of Achaia." He notes that Paul's statement in this verse represents an oath before God. Harris writes, "If we define a biblical 'oath of confirmation' broadly as a direct or indirect appeal to the deity as the guarantor of the truth of a statement, especially one that the readers cannot verify for themselves, this verse constitutes an oath."⁸ Fair enough, but now that Harris has identified Paul making an oath before God, he has painted himself into a corner. He has no choice but to try and come up with a solution to Paul's inconsistent application of tentmaking and receiving support in varying ministry contexts. Otherwise, Paul is an oath-breaker.

Harris states, "How may we summarize Paul's policy regarding his financial relationship with his churches? Was it consistent? His conduct seems to have been governed by two principles."⁹ The two principles Harris suggests are: a) "Paul always refused financial aid for himself from those to whom he was currently ministering."¹⁰ And b) "Paul sometimes accepted gifts from distant fellow believers (2 Cor 11:8–9; Phil 4:16), or as he was leaving a region (2 Cor 1:16; Rom 15:24; 1 Cor 16:6), in each case to enable him to pursue new evangelistic of pastoral opportunities, not a payment for services already rendered."¹¹ The first principle that Harris states is simply not true. Paul did accept financial aid on site in certain ministry contexts. Acts 16:15 records Paul accepting direct support from Lydia in Philippi, and other verses that we highlighted in chapter 2 point to the entire congregation offering traditional support from the beginning of his ministry to them. The first part of Harris' second principle is true. Paul did accept financial support from believers outside his current ministry context. For example, Phil 4:14–16 states, "Yet it was kind of you to share my trouble. And you Philippians yourselves know that in the beginning of the gospel, when I left Macedonia, no church entered into partnership with me in giving and receiving, except you only. Even in Thessalonica you sent me help for my needs once and again."

But I am not so sure about the remaining part of Harris' second principle. Harris attempts to make the case that whenever Paul accepted outside

---

7. Harris, *Second Epistle to the Corinthians*, 765.
8. Harris, *Second Epistle to the Corinthians*, 763.
9. Harris, *Second Epistle to the Corinthians*, 765.
10. Harris, *Second Epistle to the Corinthians*, 765.
11. Harris, *Second Epistle to the Corinthians*, 765–66.

gifts, they were received and earmarked for the exclusive purpose of enabling Paul to move on from his current ministry setting and "pursue new evangelistic or pastoral opportunities, not as payment for services already rendered."[12] But even if we were to agree with what Harris is suggesting about Paul's outside gifts, it is not overly relevant to identifying why he refused direct support from the people he was ministering to in some ministry contexts and not others. Remember, Harris included this second principle primarily as a means to prevent Paul from being an oath breaker. Harris needs to insulate Paul from charges of accepting support while under oath not to accept support. Under Harris' view, Paul's second guiding principle of accepting outside support in the form of a *sending-you-on-your-way* gift is presented as an unusual exception to the general rule of never accepting support from the churches to which he was ministering, which Harris says is Paul's first guiding principle.

Like trying to close an over-packed suitcase, Harris is pushing down hard to make everything fit inside these two guiding principles that summarize Paul's support practices. However, we are still be left with the awkward Acts 16:5, Phil 1:5, and Phil 4:15 information about Paul receiving support from Lydia and the congregation in Philippi.[13] Pushing those aside for a moment though, if we could outright ignore the Act 16:5 verse and the Philippians verses cited above, then we might be able to force Paul's tentmaking practices into Harris' guiding principles. What other choice do we have? Paul made an oath before God.

But Paul did not make an oath before God to proclaim the gospel free of charge in all ministry contexts. He was not guided by a principle of always refusing financial aid "from those to whom he was currently ministering."[14] Paul did not make an oath before God to refrain from burdening all churches or maintaining a free ministry to all churches. If we look carefully at what Scripture actually says, we see something very different. Let's look at this verse again in the larger immediate context:

> Or did I commit a sin in humbling myself so that you might be exalted, because I preached God's gospel to you free of charge? I robbed other churches by accepting support from them in order to serve you. And when I was with you and was in need, I did

---

12. Harris, *Second Epistle to the Corinthians*, 766.

13. Harris side steps this fact by attempting to differentiate between accepting support and accepting hospitality, Harris, *Second Epistle to the Corinthians*, 766. But as we saw in chapter 2, staying with someone in their home was universally recognized as an acceptable form of receiving payment. Moreover, Paul was accepting support form the whole congregation at Philippi, not just Lydia.

14. Harris, *Second Epistle to the Corinthians*, 765.

not burden anyone, for the brothers who came from Macedonia supplied my need. So I refrained and will refrain from burdening you in any way. As the truth of Christ is in me, this boasting of mine will not be silenced in the regions of Achaia. And why? Because I do not love you? God knows I do! And what I do I will continue to do, in order to undermine the claim of those who would like to claim that in their boasted mission they work on the same terms as we do. (2 Cor 11:7–12)

Paul could have easily made his oath before God and ended it after the word *silenced*. In fact, that would seem to be the most natural way to make a forceful statement like an oath, especially if it was a universal policy or guiding principle. For example, if a missionary came to a church in Chicago and proclaimed, "As God is my witness, I will no longer accept support from churches," we could conclude that this was a blanket statement and that the missionary was no longer going to accept support from any church. But, if the missionary came to that same church and proclaimed, "As God is my witness, I will no longer accept support from churches in Illinois," we would naturally conclude that for whatever reason(s) the missionary was no longer going to accept support from any churches in Illinois, but we would also naturally conclude that they were going to continue to accept support from churches located outside of Illinois.

Instead of stopping after the word *silenced*, Paul qualifies his boast by limiting it to the regions of Achaia. Paul did not make an oath pledging to always provide a free-of-charge ministry in every single ministry context and church. He made an oath pledging to continue to provide a free-of-charge ministry to Corinth and the surrounding regions of Achaia. Why? He tells us in the very next verse. Despite pressure from his opponents, and most likely from those in the church, to conform to the generally accepted practice of accepting financial support in some way or form, Paul insists with an oath before God that he will continue his practice of delivering a free-of-charge gospel ministry so that he remains distanced from his opponents who are proclaiming another Jesus and another gospel.

Paul did not say that he preached God's gospel to everyone free of charge, he said he preached God's gospel to those in Achaia free of charge. This man, Paul, who went to extremes to become all things to all people, also purposefully tailored his missionary methods to the individual ministry contexts he encountered.

Attempting to find anyone else who takes note of Paul's qualifying phrase has been challenging. Thrall makes a slight reference to it, but it is buried in an excursus titled "Paul and Apostolic Maintenance" found in her *International Critical Commentary on Second Corinthians 8–13*. Thrall writes, "Perhaps we should take more notice of the limiting phrase (v. 10) 'in the regions of Achaia.' What does it limit?"[15] This comment is made within a larger discussion of how to reconcile Paul's seemingly inconsistent use of self-support. Thrall continues to ponder if the conditional phrase contained in Paul's oath completely limits his receiving any support from the church in Achaia for any reason, or if he is limiting the region (Achaia) where support from the Corinthians could be used. If the qualifier is to be understood in the second sense, Paul is anticipating that at some point in the future he might request the Corinthian church to provide support for him while he is ministering in another region, which is what the Macedonian churches had done for Paul while he ministered in Corinth.[16] I believe that Paul's use of the qualifying phrase "in the regions of Achaia" should be understood in the first sense. That is, Paul is declaring an oath not to ever receive support from the church in Corinth or in the region of Achaia while he ministered to them because that would make him indistinguishable from the false apostles in that region. If Paul received any support from them while he ministered to them, he would be leveling the ground between himself and his opponents who were proclaiming another Jesus. That would, according to Paul, place an obstacle in the way of the gospel of Christ.

PAUL BARNETT

We can now move on to Paul Barnett. Barnett is also a NT scholar and his commentary on Second Corinthians is published as part of The New International Commentary on the New Testament series. In a footnote from his commentary on 2 Cor 11:9, Barnett offers three reasons why Paul worked as a tentmaker: a) to distinguish himself from other itinerant speakers, b) to correct idleness, and c) to provide a sign of his "unique apostolicity."[17]

Barnett's first reason is valid, as we have just discussed. Paul did want to distinguish himself from other speakers in Corinth, but that was not the reason he turned to self-support in Thessalonica or Ephesus, so it does not work as an overarching explanation for why Paul turned to self-support. And this is where we see the breakdown in Barnett's approach to Paul's tentmaking. Keep in mind, Barnett is arguing that Paul worked to support himself in all ministry contexts so that he did not have to receive payment for his work. This first reason supplied by Barnett fits well with the Corinthian

---

15. Thrall, *Second Corinthians*, 707.

16. This is similar to what Harris was arguing when he was presenting his second guiding principle of sometimes accepting gifts from distant believers.

17. Barnett, *Second Epistle to the Corinthians*, 517–18.

ministry, but not everywhere. Furthermore, as Barnett continues it becomes clear that the end goal of distinguishing himself from other itinerant "lecturers or philosophers who were common in Greco-Roman culture" was so that Paul did not "suffer an evil reputation."[18]

Look carefully, because this is a significant observation that we do not want to miss. Barnett does identify one of Paul's self-disclosed reasons for his self-support, but he only *half* identifies it. Yes, Paul did want to distinguish himself from the other itinerant speakers, but only the ones who were claiming to have the same mission and work as Paul. Paul was concerned about the men he tells us about in 2 Cor 11:13: "For such men are false apostles, deceitful workmen, disguising themselves as apostles of Christ." He was not concerned about distinguishing himself from all general speakers and philosophers who were common in the Greco-Roman world. He was concerned about the men who were posing as apostles and ministers of the gospel, not all professional speakers. Yet, Barnett is saying that Paul was making tents in order to avoid garnering the widespread negative reputation that often accompanied professional speakers in general.

Paul tells us that he was seeking to avoid being confused with the men who were proclaiming, "another Jesus" (2 Cor 11:4). While it is true that these false apostles were greedy for financial gain, Paul was concerned about the gospel message being lost or confused, not that he might appear greedy. Paul writes that he will continue to refuse payment from them because he does not want to be confused with the gospel imposters who proclaim another Jesus. In 2 Cor 11:12, Paul states, "And what I do I will continue to do, in order to undermine the claim of those who would like to claim that in their boasted mission they work on the same terms as we do." So although Barnett lists Paul distinguishing himself from other speakers, he misses the fact that Paul was not aiming to distinguish himself from all speakers, but just the false gospel speakers. And just as important, Paul's motive was not to avoid being perceived as greedy, but to maintain a distinction between the true gospel and a false gospel, between the real Jesus and another Jesus. The only way to do that was to separate himself from the other false apostles by supporting himself.

Barnett's second point would also be correct, *if* he was limiting his discussion to Paul's didactic reason for tentmaking in Thessalonica. While I obviously agree that correcting idleness was one of Paul's reasons for self-support, I would strongly emphasize that it was the reason he chose self-support in Thessalonica, but his reasons for self-support in Corinth and Ephesus were different. Remember, Barnett is listing the three reasons Paul

---

18. Barnett, *Second Epistle to the Corinthians*, 517.

always supported himself. Unfortunately for Barnett, Paul was attempting to correct idleness in Thessalonica, but there is no evidence that he was trying to correct idleness in Corinth. Barnett states that idleness was "endemic in Greco-Roman society" but does not provide a reference."[19] Idleness did not seem to be an issue at Corinth, the "free-wheeling 'boom town' of merchants and trade."[20] Paul never mentions idleness in either letter to the Corinthians, and even more importantly, he never provides that as one of the reasons he was supporting himself in Corinth or Ephesus.

Barnett's third reason is based largely on 1 Cor 9:16–18, where Paul states, "Woe to me if I do not preach the gospel! For if I do this of my own will, I have a reward, but not of my own will, I am still entrusted with a stewardship. What then is my reward? That in my preaching, I may present the gospel free of charge, so as not to make full use of my right in the gospel" (1 Cor 9:16–18). Barnett writes:

> His obedience to God would have been diminished by receiving payment from others. His pay was to receive no pay. His work was between himself and God; he would not be paid for it. Gifts from the Macedonians were just that, *gifts*, not payment for work done . . . Paul the worker, who supported himself at such personal cost (see vv. 23–27), was a sign of his unique apostolicity; because God had called him, he could not be paid.[21]

There are two issues here. First, Barnett attempts to draw a line of distinction between gifts and payment or support for ministry work. However, Paul does not use the Greek word for gift δόμα [*doma*], in 2 Cor 11:8, he uses the Greek word for support ὀψώνιον [*opsonion*], "I robbed other churches by accepting support from them in order to serve you." Paul was not making tents and accepting outside gifts in Corinth, he was making tents and accepting outside support. It even comes across in the ESV translation. Even if Paul was using the word δόμα, and he does *not* in 2 Cor 11:8, I am not prepared to concede that Paul viewed financial gifts all that differently from financial support based on, for example, Phil 4:14–20.[22]

---

19. Barnett, *Second Epistle to the Corinthians*, 518.
20. Hafemann, *2 Corinthians*, 24.
21. Barnett, *Second Epistle to the Corinthians*, 518.
22. Incredibly, two page turns earlier in his book when commenting on 2 Cor 11:8, Barnett provides a footnote comparing Paul's support ὀψώνιον [*opsonion*], not gifts, to a soldier's rations. Barnett, *Second Epistle to the Corinthians*, 515. Barnett's unexplained decision to call the Macedonian support *gifts* in his footnote comment on 2 Cor 11:9, when in 2 Cor 11:8 Paul explicitly uses the word support ὀψώνιον [*opsonion*], reveals a strong desire to make Paul's choices fit neatly into a universal policy that does not exist.

Second, if Paul had a universal policy of receiving no pay, if Paul's "obedience to God would have been diminished by receiving payment from others," if "because God had called him, he could not be paid," if he "steadfastly declined" to be paid, then why did he receive support while ministering to other churches?[23] Paul was paid. We have biblical evidence that when Paul was ministering to the church in Philippi, he accepted the hospitality of a wealthy patron and general congregational support. Tentmaking was not a fallback solution to put bread on the table when traditional support was unavailable, it was not so that Paul could avoid being perceived as greedy by outsiders, and it was not because refusing payment was a sign of his unique apostolicity that, if abandoned, would have somehow diminished his obedience to God.

Later in his comments on 2 Cor 11:12, Barnett correctly narrows the focus of who Paul was attempting to distinguish himself from in Corinth. If you remember from earlier, near the beginning of this subheading on Barnett, we saw that he told us Paul was attempting to disassociate himself from Greco-Roman itinerant speakers in general, not from the false apostles at Corinth. Barnett stated that Paul, "was conscious that he may have been perceived as just one of many itinerant lecturers or philosophers who were common in Greco-Roman culture," and suggested that Paul "may have worked to support himself out of concern lest his ministry and the message of the gospel be associate with traveling philosophers."[24] But when we get to his comment on 2 Cor 11:12, Barnett identifies Paul's opponents not as general itinerant philosophers, but as "those (intruders) who seek to stand as equals with him in ministry."[25] However, just when it looks like Barnett might be following the right path and zeroing in on why Paul supported himself in Corinth, he doubles down on the idea that Paul refused payment in the churches where he ministered because it was his universal policy. Barnett writes, "Paul, however, has not received and will not receive payment from churches where he ministers the gospel."[26] Barnett continues to describe how God called Paul to be an apostle to the Gentiles and that proclaiming the gospel without payment was a badge of apostleship. If Paul was paid, says Barnett, then he would have been disobedient to God's calling as an apostle to the Gentiles. Barnett concludes, "His payment was to receive no payment. By not deviating from this policy Paul continued to wear the badge inscribed 'apostle to the Gentiles,' which his opponents—because

23. Barnett, *Second Epistle to the Corinthians*, 518.
24. Barnett, *Second Epistle to the Corinthians*, 517.
25. Barnett, *Second Epistle to the Corinthians*, 521.
26. Barnett, *Second Epistle to the Corinthians*, 521.

they received payment—could not wear."²⁷ But again, Paul was paid. Do we conclude that Paul took his badge of apostleship off in places where he accepted support like Philippi? Paul's self-support was not a sign of his obedience to God or a badge of apostleship, it was a purposefully and selectively chosen missiological method.

ATTEMPTS TO PROVE PAUL'S CONSISTENCY

We know that Paul made tents in Thessalonica for didactic reasons to teach a strong work ethic and to combat the problem of idleness. Paul made tents in Ephesus for didactic reasons to teach the church there that they should go to great lengths in order to have enough to give to others and be obedient to the benevolent principles that Jesus taught. And, we have seen that Paul made tents in Corinth for evangelistic reasons. He was interested, as he always was, in winning as many people for Christ as possible. In Corinth, that meant he had to make a clear and visible distinction between himself and the other false teachers who were proclaiming another Jesus. In the Corinthian ministry context, itinerant speakers were expected to charge fees for their services or live at the expense of a wealthy host. Paul did neither in Corinth. His strategic use of self-support, combined with some outside support, allowed him to minister in Corinth free of charge.

The problem with Barnett, Harris, and others is that they attempt to provide an explanation of Paul's tentmaking that is universal. They are looking for some kind of umbrella policy that adequately answers why he made tents no matter where he was ministering. But as we have seen, there is no policy or principle that will function in that manner. There is no *one-size-fits-all* reason why Paul engaged in tentmaking. And, as we have seen, the principles that have been suggested do not work because they are simply not true all the time. I would suggest that the comments made by Barnett and Harris are their best attempts to make ordered sense out of the biblical witness that testifies to Paul's missionary practices, but these and other existing theories have holes in them and are subsequently both incorrect and inadequate.

I have to recognize Thrall. By far, she has taken the most time and ink to examine and explore all the possible motives and influences behind Paul's self-support choices. Yet, she too is impeded by the impulse to prove Paul's consistent behavior among the churches. In fact, her concluding subheading that brings her discussion of Paul's apostolic maintenance to a close is,

---

27. Barnett, *Second Epistle to the Corinthians*, 522.

"*Was Paul inconsistent?*"[28] She asks many of the right questions, but gazes at all the answers with an attempt to fit them into a uniform policy. She writes, "There have been various suggestions, aimed at restoring some measure of consistency to his policy as regards maintenance."[29] She concludes by suggesting that during Paul's later unrecorded visit to Corinth (assumed to occur after Second Corinthians was written), he may have started accepting support from the Corinthians. She offers this possibility as a way of resolving the "inconsistent" tension. Thrall writes:

> It is possible that Paul was not quite so inconsistent as he appears ... When he eventually arrived in Corinth for the long-promised third visit, did he maintain his practice of refusing maintenance? ... If his letter in 2 Cor 10–13 had achieved its effect and destroyed the influence of the rival missionaries, and if his close relationship with the Corinthian church was about to be loosened, continuing consistency might have come to seem less important, and a desire to make up differences may have prevailed. In any case, one might still argue for a basic consistency in principle.[30]

It appears that most scholars, including Thrall, feel an obligation to prove that Paul's use of tentmaking and self-support in general were consistent. There seems to be a fear that if it could be proved that Paul inconsistently accepted payment in some ministry contexts, but not others, then he would somehow be dishonoring his calling as an apostle. As a result, some, like Barnett and Harris, end up walking to the end of a narrow plank by insisting that Paul's consistent non-use of support was universal. Others, namely Thrall, ask all the right questions and answer individual pieces of the puzzle correctly, but fail to see beyond the *we-have-to-make-sure-Paul-was-not-being-inconsistent* screen. Most everyone feels compelled to bring order to what at first glance appears to be muddled and messy. The thinking is that if the whole Pauline corpus is examined closely enough, a consistent practice will emerge, and if it does not, then the closest theory will have to suffice, even though there are awkward discrepancies and exceptions. Or, alternatively, speculative suggestions are made that go beyond Scripture.

There is at least one serious writer who is willing to tip his hat and acknowledge that Paul did not have a universal policy that governed his tentmaking and self-support. In the context of discussing Paul's weaknesses and forfeiting his rights, David J. Bosch writes, "His [Paul's] decision to

---

28. Thrall, *Second Corinthians*, 706.
29. Thrall, *Second Corinthians*, 706.
30. Thrall, *Second Corinthians*, 707–8.

support himself through the work of his own hands and not to accept any financial support from the churches he has founded (except, interestingly enough, the church in Philippi; cf Phil 4:15) has to be understood in the same spirit."[31] While not providing a solution to the visible exception, at least Bosch humbly acknowledges it.

In conclusion, we have seen that theories with holes, inconsistencies, and exceptions are not the answer; nor are speculative guesses. When we allow Scripture to stand alone and clear away our pre-existing biases, a consistent policy does not float to the surface. What we *can* see are the different reasons for tentmaking and self-support that Paul actually provides in his letters as he ministered in varying ministry contexts that all had unique missiological needs. Paul did not make tents out of desperation or as a pragmatic fallback strategy when traditional support was unavailable. It was not a financial backup plan. He was not honoring some long-held rabbinic code. He was not driven by a fear that he would be disobedient to God if he accepted traditional support. Paul *did* make tents as a carefully chosen missiological method for didactic and evangelistic reasons.

---

31. Bosch, *Transforming Mission*, 133.

6

Spiritual and Practical Considerations

I want to make sure we are all on the same page up to this point. So far we have examined the biblical and theological foundations for understanding the nature of the Apostle Paul's missiological method of tentmaking and self-support. Paul made a purposeful choice to support himself in some ministry contexts and not others. While some have stated that Paul worked because he was honoring a rabbinical code that yoked the teaching of the Torah with a trade, this custom did not develop until after Paul had died. Hock states conclusively,

> We have seen how difficult it is to sustain the assumption that Paul's role as artisan-missionary simply reflects a rabbinic ideal of combining Torah and trade; such a position has problems not only because of doubts about Paul's rabbinic training but also because of the likelihood that the rabbinic ideal itself arose only after the time of Paul.[1]

The suggestion that Paul made tents because the churches he served were poor and unable to provide for his needs is unsubstantiated and untenable. Moreover, while the idea that tentmaking was a fallback secondary option that Paul utilized when traditional forms of support were unavailable is

---

1. Hock, *Social Context*, 66.

broadly popular among scholars and reference books, it cannot be supported from the biblical witness.

Some might be tempted to conclude that Paul made tents because Ephesus, Thessalonica, and Corinth were all port cities and that Paul could generate sustenance-level income through tentmaking in those locations, but not elsewhere, but this sort of speculative explanation fails for a couple of reasons. First, it would have to be shown that first-century tentmakers only worked and sold tents lucratively out of port cities. Second, Paul tells us why he made tents, and it was not because he was living near the sea. Who would remove Paul's own self-disclosed reasons found in Scripture and insert reasons not found in the text?

I have also demonstrated that the traditional portrayal of Paul as the pragmatic tentmaker has been on the biblical stage for so long, it is rarely challenged or closely examined. It is a set piece that has become part of the background scenery. One of the primary sources of biblical support for the prevailing tentmaking view has been Acts 18:5, but when the word συνείχετο [syneicheto] is translated as "constrained by" (as it already has been by the ASV and ERV), it makes more contextual sense and fits the overall Pauline missionary practice of Jews first, Gentiles second. The idea that Paul stopped working upon the arrival of Silas and Timothy because they brought money and relieved Paul of his need to work is not found in Scripture. The Bible does not say Paul stopped working in Corinth after the arrival of Silas and Timothy.

For some reason, almost everyone who looks upon Paul and his tentmaking sees something that is either insignificant and not worthy of serious study or comment beyond a few dismissive remarks, or they see something that unless it can be shown that there is some consistent principle at work, threatens Paul's apostolic integrity in some way. As a result, several writers have attempted to make (sometimes forceful and rigid) blanket statements that supply consistency to Paul's use of self-support. Unfortunately, these theories and universal statements contain blatantly spurious claims, or they inexplicably ignore obvious inconsistencies.

Why did Paul choose to support himself in certain ministry contexts and not others? The answer is because Paul made a purposeful choice based on didactic and evangelistic reasons. Paul was a man who became all things to all people, so that by all means he might save some. Paul did not have a universal policy or apostolic principle that guided his acceptance of support in all ministry contexts. Instead, he carefully selected his missiological methods based on the individual needs of the specific ministry context of each region. For some ministry contexts, it was not strategically necessary to support himself. For other contexts, it was necessary.

Within the ministry contexts where self-support was required, it was required for unique reasons. In Thessalonica, it was for didactic reasons to teach a strong work ethic and correct the problem of idleness. In Ephesus, it was for didactic reasons to teach the church to go to great lengths so they would be able to give to the poor and follow the benevolent teachings of Jesus. In Corinth, it was for evangelistic reasons so that he could differentiate himself from the competing false apostles who were proclaiming a different gospel and a different Jesus. Paul made tents and supported himself so that he would stand in stark contrast to the false apostles. This in turn meant that his Jesus and his gospel stood out and could be distinguished from the counterfeit gospel and the false Jesus his opponents were proclaiming. In this way, he removed a substantially large obstacle that would have prevented many from repenting and believing in the true Jesus who saves people from their sins. Now, if you have been following along, then this is all review, but I want to make sure there are no outstanding questions before proceeding.

I want to take some time at this point to present some of the spiritual and practical aspects of Paul's tentmaking. These arise from and are connected to his purposeful choice to support himself, but they are not the same as the three self-disclosed reasons we identified in chapter 4. It might be helpful to think of Paul's self-disclosed didactic and evangelistic reasons for self-support in certain ministry contexts as operating on a *horizontal* plane in a strategic sense, while the spiritual aspects of his tentmaking can be understood as operating on a *vertical* plane in a personal sense between Paul and his Lord. Lastly, the practical aspects of tentmaking are simply the unavoidable realities of Paul's self-supporting tentmaking labor.

SPIRITUAL

Freeness of the Gospel

The first spiritual aspect of Paul's tentmaking can be found in 1 Cor 9:15–18. This is the passage where Paul explains that he is not making use of his right to receive support in Corinth because he would rather die than have his *free-of-charge* boast be taken away at Corinth. Paul continues by expressing the burden he feels to proclaim the gospel, and the outcome of not proclaiming it. In 1 Cor 9:16, Paul states, "Woe to me if I do not preach the gospel!" The passage continues, "For if I do this of my own will, I have a reward, but not of my own will, I am still entrusted with a stewardship. What then is my reward? That in my preaching I may present the gospel free of charge, so as not to make full use of my right in the gospel" (1 Cor 9:17–18).

Some make the mistake of placing these verses on the horizontal strategic plane as one of Paul's reasons for always supporting himself. But as we have shown earlier, and as others have observed, Paul did not always support himself. Therefore, these verses correctly belong in the vertical-relational plane and highlight Paul's obligation to his Lord and Savior, Jesus Christ. They are *also* part of his defense against his opponents who might have been criticizing Paul's refusal to receive traditional support as a sign of illegitimate apostolic status (1 Cor 9:1–2). Paul is not saying that he will never make use of his right to receive payment. These verses present the spiritual benefits of his context-specific choice to present the gospel free of charge in Corinth. Paul is expressing his private thoughts and motivations related to his deeply serious commitment to his Master as one who has been entrusted with a stewardship (1 Cor 9:17). Bosch writes:

> Paul's sense of concern for the Gentiles of the Roman Empire evinces itself in a deep awareness that it is his *obligation* to proclaim the gospel to them... Obligation to him who dies produces obligation to those for whom he died. Faith in Christ creates a mutuality of indebtedness; it recognizes that the believer is as deeply indebted to unbelievers as to Christ. Yet in no sense does it depend upon the tangible contributions of the creditors to the debtors, only and wholly upon the gift of God in Christ. Precisely for this reason the idea of "reward" does not enter into the picture; that would presuppose that Paul is of his own choice engaged in mission in order to gain something from it.[2]

I would agree with Bosch that Paul is as deeply indebted—in an evangelistic sense, of course—to unbelievers as to Christ and that indebtedness is in no way dependent on tangible contributions. Paul is duty-bound to proclaim the gospel to those for whom Christ died, and he does so with and without pay depending on the needs of the specific ministry context.

It should be noted that in remaining faithful to the stewardship he had been entrusted with, he also serves the horizontal strategic goal of not placing an obstacle in the way of the Corinthian believers. If, for example, Paul was not faithful with the stewardship he received, then that would obviously have a negative impact on his mission, no matter what form the unfaithfulness took.[3] We need to recognize that Paul is explaining that the vertical

---

2. Bosch, *Transforming Mission*, 135.

3. We must resist the urge to simplify Paul's reasons for a free-of-charge gospel proclamation or reduce and limit the declaration in 1 Cor 9:15–18 to a single horizontal

reason he chose to not make use of his right to receive support from them is because of his passion and sense of duty and loyalty to Jesus. That is what 1 Cor 9:15–18 is all about. If in completing his mission *for* Jesus, Paul offers a free-of-charge ministry to the Corinthians, then so be it. It honors Christ. It serves the overall big picture mission of remaining faithful to Jesus. Fee writes, "Thus his 'reward,' as his 'boast,' is to be found in the 'weakness' of working with his own hands so as not to hinder the forward progress of the gospel."[4] Paul's reward was to preach the gospel and complete the mission at Corinth exactly how Jesus had charged him to complete it (1 Cor 9:18).

Paul's proclamation of the gospel free of charge in selected ministry contexts also mirrors the freeness of the gospel presented throughout the NT.[5] This vertical plane spiritual benefit of tentmaking corresponds to God's gracious offer of forgiveness in Christ. Rom 5:15–16 states:

> But the free gift is not like the trespass. For if many died through one man's trespass, much more have the grace of God and the free gift by the grace of that one man Jesus Christ abounded for man. And the free gift is not like the result of that one man's sin. For the judgment following one trespass brought condemnation, but the free gift following many trespasses brought justification.

Likewise, 1 Cor 2:12 says, "Now we have received not the spirit of the world, but the Spirit who is from God, that we might understand the things freely given us by God." Eph 2:8–9 similarly states, "For by grace you have been saved through faith. And this is not your own doing; it is the gift of God, not a result of works, so that no one may boast." And Rev 22:17 gives this invitation, "And let the one who is thirsty come; let the one who desires take the water of life without price." All of these verses present and highlight the freeness of the gospel.

---

or vertical plane. In other words, we cannot say that Paul's declaration in this passage is relegated to the vertical spiritual plane with *no* impact on the horizontal strategic missional goal, even though it can be categorized as a spiritual vertical plane aspect of tentmaking.

4. Fee, *First Epistle to the Corinthians*, 421.

5. This is what Harris was talking about when he stated, "By offering the 'price-less' good news totally free of charge, he was dramatizing in his own conduct the very appeal of the gospel as the good news of God's free grace." Harris, *Second Epistle to the Corinthians*, 765.

Lowly Status that Identified with Christ

Paul preached Christ crucified which was a "stumbling block to Jews and folly to Gentiles" (1 Cor 1:23). Fee writes, "One may have a Messiah, or one may have a crucifixion; but one may not have both—at least not from the perspective of merely human understanding. *Messiah* meant power, splendor, triumph; *crucifixion* meant weakness, humiliation, defeat."[6] Jesus as a crucified Messiah assumed a lowly status. Not only did he become incarnate and descend to earth, but he descended to a low social status. He gave the appearance of a common criminal executed by the worldly powers of Rome and the hard-hearted Jerusalem leaders. Phil 2:6–8 states:

> Who, though he was in the form of God, did not count equality with God a thing to be grasped, but made himself nothing, taking the form of a servant, being born in the likeness of men. And being found in human form, he humbled himself by becoming obedient to the point of death, even death on a cross.

Paul lowered himself and followed in the footsteps of his Master when he chose to engage in self-support and tentmaking. Paul writes in 1 Cor 4:10, "We are fools for Christ's sake, but you are wise in Christ. We are weak, but you are strong. You are held in honor, but we in disrepute." Part of the reason Paul was considered weak and was held in disrepute was because he worked with his hands in Corinth. We know this because in the Corinthian ministry context, itinerant speakers were expected to charge fees for their services or live at the expense of a wealthy host. Paul did neither in Corinth. This accomplished the task of setting himself apart from the other false teachers, but it also carried a large amount of social stigma. Barnett states that "those who worked with their hands were generally held in low esteem."[7] Hock comments on artisans, "Stigmatized as slavish, uneducated, and often useless, artisans, to judge from scattered references, were frequently reviled or abused, often victimized, seldom if ever invited to dinner, never accorded status."[8] Hock also states that, "a free man who took up a trade was viewed as having done something humiliating."[9] 1 Cor 4:11–12 states, "To the present hour we hunger and thirst, we are poorly dressed and buffeted and homeless, and we labor, working with our own hands."

Paul had told the church in Corinth that he shared abundantly in Christ's sufferings (2 Cor 1:5). Jesus told his disciples that he must suffer

---

6. Fee, *First Epistle to the Corinthians*, 75.
7. Barnett, *Second Epistle to the Corinthians*, 513.
8. Hock, *Social Context*, 36.
9. Hock, *Social Context*, 36.

and be rejected in Luke 9:22, "The Son of Man must suffer many things and be rejected by the elders and chief priests and scribes, and be killed, and on the third day be raised." Paul was identifying with Christ as he suffered and experienced rejection as a manual laborer.

Just as Jesus lowered himself from a high status, indeed the highest status possible, and remained cognizant of his true identity and origin during his incarnate ministry, Paul also must have shared similar feelings, albeit on a much smaller scale. It is one thing to experience hardship, suffering, and rejection; it is another thing to experience that same affliction with the continual lingering knowledge that you could bring it to an end at any time and return to a more comfortable status. Jesus experienced this, as did Paul. Hock writes:

> Artisans generally and Paul in particular could not avoid experiencing the hostility and contempt directed toward them by representatives of the dominant ethos. Indeed, these experiences must have been doubly difficult for Paul, who, though he shared the life of artisans, was by birth a member of the socially elite, the very circles that maintained this social world.[10]

Emptying Himself Physically

Making tents was hard work. In 1 Thess 2:9, Paul states, "For you remember, brothers, our labor and toil: we worked night and day, that we might not be a burden to any of you, while we proclaimed to you the gospel of God." Hock has provided the most vivid picture of Paul the tentmaker:

> Leatherworking involved two essential tasks: *cutting* the leather, which required round-edge and straight-edge knives; and *sewing* the leather, which required various awls. These tasks would have been done at a workbench, with the leatherworker sitting on a stool and bent over forward to work.
>
> With respect to tentmaking, an apprentice like Paul would have learned how to cut the leather pieces so that their placement would take advantage of the natural strengths of the leather and thus best withstand strains and pulling. An apprentice like Paul would have also learned how to sew these leather pieces together, using either a basting stitch, a seam stitch, or a

---

10. Hock, *Social Context*, 35.

felling stitch, the latter two being used where seams needed to be waterproof.[11]

When Paul chose to support himself, he chose to engage in labor-intensive work. We can imagine Paul at his workbench, bent over with aching fingers, hands, and forearms. He would have put in long hours with little pay. When Paul states that he suffered "in toil and hardship, through many a sleepless night, in hunger and thirst, often without food, in cold and exposure" (2 Cor 11:27), some of those specific sufferings may have been directly or indirectly a result of his choice to support himself through tentmaking.

Jesus, of course, completely emptied himself physically on the cross and surrendered his life. Paul modeled Christ-likeness by emptying himself physically through tentmaking labor and the lifestyle that accompanied that choice. As a result of his labor, he was often weak and exhausted, and we know that Paul associated and identified his weaknesses with his obedience to Christ. Paul, at least in part because of his tentmaking, proclaimed these words, "For the sake of Christ, then, I am content with weaknesses, insults, hardships, persecutions and calamities. For when I am weak, then I am strong." (2 Cor 12:10)

In summary, there are spiritual aspects that emerge from Paul's purposeful choice to engage in tentmaking in certain ministry contexts that operate on a vertical plane between Paul and Jesus. Some of them mirrored the ministry of Jesus, others displayed Paul's willingness to follow in the suffering footsteps of his Master. We should remember that these spiritual aspects of tentmaking on the vertical plane are not in opposition to the horizontal strategic plane. The spiritual and strategic complement one another. It is not a choice between either/or, but rather an embracing of both/and.

PRACTICAL

In addition to the spiritual aspects associated with tentmaking, there were some practical realities, both positive and negative, of choosing this missionary method of self-supportive tentmaking. We should approach these practical realities with a circumspect attitude and make a point to recognize and acknowledge them, while at the same time keep them separate from the actual didactic and evangelistic reasons Paul gives for his tentmaking work.

---

11. Hock, *Social Context*, 24–25.

Reliable and Portable Means of Support

If someone were to run their eye over a NT historical map of Paul's missionary activity, they would observe that the three cities that Paul indicates as places where he made a purposeful choice to support himself are all port cities.[12] Corinth, Thessalonica, and Ephesus form somewhat of a neat triangle around the Aegean Sea. Corinth is on the western side of the Aegean and occupies one of the base corners; Ephesus is practically on the same latitude as Corinth, but on the opposite shore of the Aegean Sea, occupying the other base corner of the triangle; and Thessalonica is located on the northern coast and serves as the slightly off-center tip. These cities would have been ideal places to set up a tentmaking business because of the high-volume traffic of soldiers and travelers. Both groups used tents. Hock states:

> Tents were used, of course, by soldiers, but Paul's customers were more likely to have been civilians—persons whose occupations entailed much travel, such as the oarsmen who pitched tents for several days while their ship was in port; or persons who could travel in style, such as Clitophon and this party, who set up tents on a ship bound for Alexandria, and the rich who used tents, often deluxe tents, when attending one of the great festivals.[13]

The location of these cities and the people who traveled to these cities would have ensured that Paul had a reliable means of support while he was working in those places. Therefore, Paul's trade of tentmaking was portable. Hock notes, "At the conclusion of his apprenticeship Paul might have been given his own set of tools. The requisite knives and awls, incidentally, would have made tent-making an easily portable trade."[14] If Paul had his own set of tools, the only other requirement for him to ply his trade would be a workshop, which according to Hock, "could be located almost anywhere."[15]

Workshops could be part of a house, either the front or the back. They could be located in the city or outside the city; however, Hock writes that "most workshops would be located in or near the *agora*, or marketplace . . . workers having the same trade tended to locate their shops in close proximity to one another, so that areas of a city might be known by the

---

12. It is true that Corinth was not situated on the actual Aegean Sea coastline and does not technically qualify as a port city. However, because of its strategic location of lying in close proximity between two ports and the overland passage that ran by Corinth, it is well known to have exhibited robust characteristics of a port city especially in terms of commercial trade and volume of travelers, sans any actual harbor.

13. Hock, *Social Context*, 33–34.

14. Hock, *Social Context*, 25.

15. Hock, *Social Context*, 32.

trades clustered there, such as a 'cabinetmakers' street' in Athens."[16] The combination of a continuous supply of customers who traveled and used tents regularly and the ease of securing a workshop in any of the port cities were some of the practical aspects of tentmaking that allowed Paul to have a reliable and portable means of self-support.

Making Local Connections

Acts 19:11–12 states, "And God was doing extraordinary miracles by the hands of Paul, so that even handkerchiefs or aprons that had touched his skin were carried away to the sick, and their diseases left them and the evil spirits came out of them." The text does not require us to understand that people were coming to Paul at his tentmaking workshop and interacting with him throughout his ministry, but it certainly opens up the possibility. Paul's workshops could have served the dual purposes of work and ministry.

Hock once again sheds some light on the suggestion that Paul's workshop was a meeting place for gospel discussions and ministry. Hock cites Socrates as an example of a philosopher who lectured in alternative social settings, "Socrates, for example, could also be found talking in the stoas and other public buildings, in the gymnasia, and in the houses of friends . . . In other words, intellectual activity—conversing, lecturing, teaching, reading—was carried on in a variety of social settings, with the workshop being only one of them."[17] After an additional brief survey of Stoic and Cynic philosophers combining lecturing with work, Hock concludes, "We can affirm that the workshop, including that of the shoemaker or leatherworker, was recognized as a conventional social setting for intellectual discourse, a setting, though, that was used primarily by Cynic philosophers. On occasion the philosopher was also the artisan, whose shop became known as a place to engage in philosophical discussions."[18] Additionally, a tentmaking workshop would have been relatively quiet and suitable for oral instruction, as opposed to a blacksmith shop or a cabinet maker.

Just as we have pointed out earlier that Paul would not have limited his proclamation of Jesus to Sabbaths only, he would also not have limited his proclamation to outside of work hours only. Since the workday was commonly regarded as lasting from sunrise to sunset, Paul would have been restricted to a nocturnal ministry if he only talked about Jesus outside of his work hours. From what the Bible tells us about Paul, that seems highly

16. Hock, *Social Context*, 32.
17. Hock, *Social Context*, 38.
18. Hock, *Social Context*, 41.

unlikely. What is more natural to assume is that since workshops were used by others to engage in philosophical discussions, Paul also capitalized on the opportunity to engage people while making tents.

Tentmaking in the Aegean Sea port cites of Corinth, Thessalonica, and Ephesus was ideally suited for making local connections with a variety of citizens within those cities, including the wealthy Aegean and Mediterranean travelers, Roman soldiers, and general marketplace patrons. Paul would have been able to plant innumerable gospel seeds as he labored. Making tents in the same workshop day after day would also yield a predictable location for people to find him if they were interested in speaking with him or learning more about Jesus and the kingdom of God.

Financial Flexibility and Freedom

We have shown above that Paul's intentional choice to support himself in selected ministry contexts was not due to financial reasons; however, when Paul did choose to support himself, it did produce a practical benefit of increased financial flexibility and freedom. While some have labeled financial independence as a motivating factor influencing Paul's tentmaking practice, it should instead be placed here under the rubric of practical aspects. Financial independence was a result or outcome of tentmaking, not the basis for choosing to make tents.

Please note that Paul's hours in the tentmaking workshop did not allow him to live extravagantly, and often not even comfortably. Hock's research indicates that artisans were often barely able to buy food or clothing.[19] Paul's work did not provide him with a luxurious lifestyle.

Disadvantages

Not all of the practical aspects of tentmaking had a positive or complementary relationship with the horizontal plane strategic missional purposes. There were two chief disadvantages that accompanied Paul's purposeful choice to support himself in select ministry contexts. The dominant disadvantage was that Paul's apostolic status was challenged. The second and relatively minor disadvantage (compared to the first), was that his time spent in the workshop was time that he could not selectively use to minister outside of the workshop.

---

19. Hock, *Social Context*, 34.

Paul opened both letters to the Corinthian church by identifying himself as an apostle of Jesus Christ by the will of God. In addition, Paul made it clear in 2 Cor 3:1–3 that he did not need to furnish them with a letter of recommendation or to further establish his credentials as a true apostle because they themselves were the visible proof of his apostolic ministry and status. Before he came to Corinth, there was no church. But now, as a result of his apostolic ministry, the presence of a Christ-following Spirit-filled group of believers served as evidence of his apostolic status.

This was, ostensibly, not enough for the church because there were some who began to doubt whether or not Paul was the real deal. Paul wrote in 2 Cor 2:1 that he did not want to make another painful visit to them. Part of the pain he experienced the last time he visited was rooted in the fact that they were not listening to his instructions and commands, and that they were allowing false apostles to make inroads into the church.

We know that some of the people in the Corinthian church were challenging Paul's apostolic status, either directly or indirectly. This may have been due to Paul's choice to be self-supportive. Thrall writes that Paul's choice to refuse their support would have garnered a hostile attitude, "Whilst 'sin' may still be somewhat too strong a term, in Greco-Roman society the refusal of a proffered benefaction would nevertheless be seen as an insult to the benefactor(s) and as likely to engender hostility."[20] Moreover, receiving support and payment for ministry served as a validation of such ministry. Since true apostles did have the right to receive payment, it seemed unnatural for a true apostle not to receive payment.[21] The connection that some appeared to be making in their mind was that if Paul was not accepting payment, then maybe he was not a true apostle.

In 1 Cor 9:11–12a Paul wrote, "If we have sown spiritual things among you, is it too much if we reap material things from you? If others share this rightful claim on you, do not we even more?" Fee believes the "others" in verse 12 refers to Apollos and Peter. Fee writes:

> "Others" have been receiving the kind of patronage that Paul is arguing for as his own "right." At this distance we cannot be sure who is intended by these "others." Although it may refer to the "numberless guardians" of 4:15 or the "others" of 9:2, most likely it refers to Apollos and Peter. It seems likely that their accepting material benefits from the Corinthians is what has put Paul on

---

20. Thrall, *Second Corinthians*, 683.

21. 1 Cor 9:14 states, "In the same way, the Lord commanded that those who proclaim the gospel should get their living by the gospel." See also Barnett, *Second Epistle to the Corinthians*, 513.

the defensive. On this matter his own failure to accept patronage has made it appear as if he did not have the right to such.[22]

Other apostles *were* accustomed to receiving support. This is, parenthetically, evidence against any suggested and so-called universal "apostolic policy" of refusing support for ministry that supposedly governed Paul and all other apostolic ministers. But note also that by refusing his own legitimate support and patronage from them, he made himself appear less than a legitimate apostle.

Paul continues throughout the rest of the chapter to defend his right to support as well as his right and reasons for refusing their support. However, even though Paul provides his reasons and explanations to the Corinthian church, he is still left with the negative consequences of his choice to refuse their support. Specifically, the social insult and hostility it had elicited and the implied apostolic illegitimacy.

Finally, although Paul's time in his tentmaking workshop was used as much as possible for evangelistic conversation and theological discussion as covered above under practical benefits and making local connections, there must have been occasions when work simply demanded his exclusive and full attention. We can be sure that there were at least some times when Paul would have preferred to have gone out to meet someone or to speak to a group but, in order to maintain his personal reputation and integrity with outsiders as an artisan and laborer who honored deadlines and agreements with his customers, he was forced to postpone ministry outside the workshop.

---

22. Fee, *First Epistle to the Corinthians*, 409–10.

7

Tentmaking in Church History

At the outset of this chapter it should be mentioned that there are *relatively* few examples of tentmaking throughout church history.[1] What are some of the reasons for the relative historical silence on tentmaking?

For one thing, if tentmaking is understood as something the church does only when traditional support has evaporated or is non-existent, then there has been no compelling reason to turn to tentmaking since the time of Constantine. It has been said that a friend of the thirteenth-century scholastic Thomas Aquinas pointed to a chest full of gold and, referencing Acts 3:6, exclaimed, "Look Thomas! No longer can the church say I have no silver and gold." To which Thomas supposedly replied, "Neither can she say rise up and walk." The point is that one of the reasons for the historical silence may be because the church has been sufficiently financed for most of history. It may be that there are not many historical examples of tentmaking because the church has viewed tentmaking as something reserved for times of desperation and financial necessity.

Another reason may be that just as the majority of modern scholarship has viewed tentmaking as part of the background scenery of Acts, the

---

1. I want to emphasize the fact that there are relatively few examples of tentmaking in church history, but not an *absence* of examples. Moreover, I will be limiting my brief and selective historical review of tentmaking, except for a few examples, from the mid-eighteenth century to the present day.

historical church may have also viewed tentmaking as primarily a descriptive part of the biblical narrative instead of an integral part of Paul's missionary strategy. If Christians believe that tentmaking is one of those things *described* but not *prescribed* in the Bible, then there is no compelling reason to use it.

Lastly, people do not naturally choose to do something that is more difficult and time-consuming when there is an easier way made available. It should not surprise us that in the absence of a correct understanding of Paul's self-support, the church has avoided tentmaking when possible.

TAKING A TOUR

J.D. Payne has recognized J.C. Wilson's reputation as "the father of the contemporary tentmaking movement."[2] Therefore, I thought Wilson would be best suited to serve in the role of tentmaking historian and tourguide. In just a moment, we will allow him to guide us through a limited tour of church history in order to identify some of the more prominent examples of tentmakers who have followed in the footsteps of the Apostle Paul. But first we should allow Wilson to paint us a picture of what he believes tentmaking looks like.

Wilson crafted his definition of tentmaking by first defining a missionary: "Thus, the technical meaning of 'missionary' is a person who has been sent to witness to those of another culture."[3] Wilson then divides missionaries into two types and concludes that tentmakers are missionaries who support themselves:

> But the Scriptures say that there are two types of cross-cultural witnesses. The first are those who receive full support from churches. This is the way the Apostle Peter was supported. On the other hand, the Apostle Paul earned his own salary by making tents. Even today, cross-cultural witnesses or "missionaries" fall into these two categories. Some are funded by the contributions of fellow Christians, while others support themselves through various professions.[4]

Wilson provides several definitions of tentmaking from other sources, but he is ultimately content with the above-quoted division between paid and

2. Payne, "Tentmaking," 2.

3. Wilson, *Today's Tentmakers*, 14. An extended discussion or debate over the definition of *missionary* is beyond the scope of this book. I am merely providing Wilson's definition without further interaction so that I am able to show how he arrived at his definition of tentmaking.

4. Wilson, *Today's Tentmakers*, 15.

unpaid missionaries and the concept that tentmakers are missionaries who support themselves, like Paul.

If you have been following along in the book so far, you will immediately spot a problem with what Wilson is saying. When he presents Peter and Paul as apostolic examples of missionaries and states that Peter was supported while Paul earned his own salary, he is giving us an oversimplification of what is actually written in the Bible. Wilson is essentially saying that there are two and only two types of missionaries: those who are supported by others and those who support themselves. Well, that's not exactly correct, is it? Paul did not always support himself when ministering to others. Sometimes he did. Sometimes he did not. And sometimes he refused support from the people he was ministering to while accepting outside support from other churches. Paul was not an example of an apostolic missionary who always supported himself. Wilson's presentation of Peter and Paul as the only two biblical models for us to choose from lacks sustained reflection on Paul's actual practice as recorded for us in Scripture. Unfortunately, it is clear that Wilson continues to build his case for defining who qualifies as a tentmaker on this inaccurate oversimplification. Now, let us keep moving as Wilson guides us through church history and shows us his examples of tentmakers.

While information about tentmaking from the time of Paul to the fifth century is scarce, Wilson concludes that many of the Christians who fled or were exiled during the persecution by the Zoroastrians in Persia between 339 and 448 AD practiced self-support while spreading the gospel. Therefore, they should be called tentmakers.[5] To support his case for calling the above group of Christian refugees tentmakers, Wilson helpfully states, "They supported themselves and yet their main vocation was that of being ambassadors for Christ."[6] If by *ambassadors*, Wilson means people who brought the gospel to a new area and planted churches, even small house churches, then we might be able to tentatively call these people tentmakers who were following in the footsteps of Paul.[7]

Wilson's research into this group of people indicates that these early tentmakers did in fact establish not only churches, but also Christian

---

5. Wilson, *Today's Tentmakers*, 26.

6. Wilson, *Today's Tentmakers*, 26.

7. Ultimately, everyone who claims to be a follower of Jesus Christ, who makes any sort of evangelistic effort, and who works could claim to be a tentmaker. The disadvantages of such a broad definition of tentmaking will be discussed later, but it should be noted here that each of the historical examples provided by Wilson (with the exception of this first group and the Moravians) can only be called tentmakers if we are prepared to use such a broad definition.

communities and monasteries in Central Asia, India, China, Korea, Japan, and Southeast Asia.[8] It is difficult to speculate on whether these early Christians were attempting to follow biblical missionary methods by purposefully choosing to support themselves, or if it was their only option. It is also unknown if these early Christians began accepting support once local churches were established.

Wilson provides several other examples of tentmakers throughout church history, but his examples seem like he is straining the definition of tentmaking. Some of his examples do not even conform to his own definition. For example, Wilson points to Marco Polo as an example of a tentmaker, but supplies only one sentence to back up his assertion, "When Marco Polo (1254–1323) went to China in the latter part of the thirteenth century, the extension of Christianity was one of the motives for his travels."[9] True, Marco Polo did travel to Asia, and he was Roman Catholic, but he is remembered as a merchant and an explorer with more contributions to the field of cartography than Christianity.

Just because someone traveled and was also a Christian does not mean they utilized tentmaking. Polo is said to have visited previously established churches, but he did not plant churches. Polo was not trained or sought to prepare himself for ministry, and as far as we know, he did not set out with the intention of planting churches. There is no record of ministry calling or any reason to believe that he viewed himself as a church planter or a self-supporting missionary. Polo was an explorer and storyteller and, yes, he held Christian beliefs as did many people from Venice in the thirteenth century, but I do not believe we could identify him as someone who utilized tentmaking unless we use a definition of tentmaking that is so broad it no longer has any distinctive meaning. In addition, I think there are too many unknowns surrounding Marco Polo to be showcasing him as a tentmaking missionary.

Wilson continues by holding up Christopher Columbus as a historical example of a tentmaker. While referencing August J. Kling, Wilson argues that Columbus' vision for global Christianity and his voyages across the Atlantic qualify him as a tentmaker.[10] However, it is common knowledge that Columbus did not support himself with a trade as Paul did, nor did Columbus pay for his exploratory or, if Wilson prefers, missionary journeys. Columbus would not have made his voyages without financing from the Spanish Catholic Monarchs Queen Isabella I and King Ferdinand II. In his discussion of Columbus, Wilson quotes Kling, "Christopher Columbus was

---

8. Wilson, *Today's Tentmakers*, 27.
9. Wilson, *Today's Tentmakers*, 27.
10. Wilson, *Today's Tentmakers*, 27–28.

one of the most remarkable Christian laymen of all time."[11] Columbus may qualify as a Christian layman, but are all Christian laymen tentmakers?

Wilson also points to the chaplains of the East India Company as examples of tentmakers, but these chaplains were paid clergy. Wilson describes the origins of these chaplains:

> When the East India Company began, Sir Thomas Rowe was its first ambassador to the Mogul Court from 1607–1612. Since he was a dedicated Christian, he was accompanied by his chaplain. The East India Company then continued to secure clergy to minister to its employees.[12]

I fail to see how men who are paid clergy, that is, receiving direct payment and support for their ministry services from those they minister, can qualify as tentmakers.[13]

Despite all of the above questionable historical tentmakers, Wilson eventually strikes the exemplar anvil with a strong reference to the Moravians. William J. Danker provides us with a description of the Moravians and how they arrived on Count Nicholas Ludwig von Zinzendorf's estate in Germany:

> These Moravians were one remaining strand of reform efforts arising in the wake of the burning of John Hus in 1415. About 1458, a group of lay people who had been seeking to live as Christian brethren decided to take the Bible as the rule for doctrinal questions and as the pattern for the renewal of the apostolic church. Originally they had called themselves the *fratres legis Christi*, later *Unitas Fratrum*. They also had certain roots in the Eastern Church. They were persecuted frequently, but most severely through the Thirty Years' War and the Counter-Reformation. It was a small group of German-speaking Moravians who fled to Saxony and found refuge on Zinzendorf's estate,

---

11. Wilson, *Today's Tentmakers*, 28.

12. Wilson, *Today's Tentmakers*, 28.

13. Again, I believe this shows that Wilson's definition of tentmaker is too broad. Here he is stating that paid clergy who are employed by a trading company are tentmakers. A minister traveling abroad does not qualify as a tentmaker. The East India Company clergy example does not even meet Wilson's own definition of a tentmaker that he provided earlier in his book. Just a few pages earlier, he described tentmakers as missionaries who support themselves. The East India chaplains were not missionaries; they were chaplains to the East India employees. And the East India chaplains did not support themselves through secular work; they were paid to minister to the East India employees.

where they formed a spiritually and economically integrated community.[14]

These refugees were Protestants with a desire to spread the gospel, and Count Zinzendorf was not only sympathetic towards them, but he had listened to missionary stories as a child and had "covenanted with his friend, Count Frederick de Watteville" to reach the unreached of the world.[15] God had sovereignly brought together the persecuted Moravians and a Count with a heart for missions. Wilson writes:

> While he [Zinzendorf] was attending the coronation of the Danish King Christian VI, his cousin by marriage, he met a black slave from the West Indies who told him of the spiritual and physical misery of his people on the island of St. Thomas. He shared this need with the Moravians, and two artisans immediately volunteered to go there as self-supporting missionaries. They were Leonhard Dober, a potter, and David Nitschmaun, a carpenter. They arrived in the West Indies in 1732 and supported themselves by their trades.[16]

Corey Wilson states, "Contrary to most missionaries that are sent out today from North America, the Moravian missionaries were required to earn their own living."[17] Zinzendorf required this because he believed finances were not neutral and impacted not only the level of humility in the missionary, but also the impression that the missionary projected on the target people group. C. Wilson writes:

> Zinzendorf put much emphasis on the inner condition of his missionaries. He stressed that humility must be a key characteristic in their life and that his humility should lead to a distinct type of lifestyle. In turn, this distinct lifestyle would be a key element in winning the heathen to Christ ... Zinzendorf's application of this emphasis in the financial realm resulted in his belief that each missionary had a duty to earn their own living.[18]

The first two missionaries, Dober and Nitschmaun, were given "one gold coin each by Zinzendorf on the morning of their departure."[19] After this initial support they, and the other Moravian missionaries who followed

---

14. Danker, *Profit for the Lord*, 17.
15. C. Wilson, "Evaluation of the Missiology," 3.
16. Wilson, *Today's Tentmakers*, 30.
17. C. Wilson, "Evaluation of the Missiology," 5.
18. C. Wilson, "Evaluation of the Missiology," 4–5.
19. C. Wilson, "Evaluation of the Missiology," 5.

them, were expected to support themselves. By this method, the Moravian missionaries went to "the Eskimos in Greenland, the Indians in North America, and various indigenous peoples in Sweden, Russia, South America, and Africa—none of whom had previously enjoyed a Gospel witness among them."[20] C. Wilson does identify both a practical and a theological rationale for this tentmaking strategy: "The practical aspect was the church would save money and could send out more missionaries . . . The theological reason for maintaining this policy was to show the heathen the biblical example of the responsibility to work diligently to support one's family."[21]

The historical example and the self-supporting pattern of the Moravian missionaries aligns with Paul's tentmaking more than any other group we have considered thus far. They set out to reach new people groups with the gospel and establish local churches, and they purposefully chose to support themselves. While one of those purposes was related to financial necessity or expediency, the other purpose was based on the needs of the ministry context and most closely resembles Paul's didactic reason for correcting the idleness problem at Thessalonica. While the Moravian motivations may not completely mirror Paul's purposes, they do seem close enough to warrant positive comparison.

William Carey (1761–1834) has been called the father of modern missions because of his book, *An Enquiry into the Obligations of Christians to Use Means for the Conversion of the Heathens*, and his role in awakening a renewed world-wide interest in missions. But we must ask the question, was Carey a tentmaker? John Cox portrays Carey as making a purposeful choice to support himself and engage in missionary activity. Cox writes that Carey left "the shores of his home land, to take his last and set up as a shoemaker in India with the primary purpose of sharing his faith with the people of the sub-continent."[22]

On the other hand, Wilson records Carey securing traditional support before leaving England, "Before he left England, he had told the Christians who had agreed to support him that his leaving them was like one going with ropes down into a mine. He pleaded with them to continue holding the ropes. However, when he got to Calcutta, the people back home forgot him financially . . . He therefore took his family into the interior of the country and worked as manager of an indigo plantation."[23] Carey did not set out to make shoes in India so he could support himself while he shared his faith

---

20. C. Wilson, "Evaluation of the Missiology," 3.
21. C. Wilson, "Evaluation of the Missiology," 5.
22. Cox, "Tentmaking Movement," 113.
23. Wilson, *Today's Tentmakers*, 31.

with the people there, he set out as a traditional missionary and pleaded with people to continue providing him with traditional support.

No one denies that Carey worked as a cobbler before traveling to India, but it is also beyond denial that Carey purposefully set out on his missionary work expecting support from the benevolent giving of others. He did not turn to self-support until after his traditional funding was withheld. Again, obviously Carey did work to support himself on the mission field, but it was a fallback strategy that he utilized after conventional support was no longer available. In other words, Carey's tentmaking was born out of desperation and expediency. He used tentmaking as a financial backup plan. Carey's tentmaking was not a carefully selected missiological method based on the model of Paul in the NT.

In fact, we can turn to Carey's own writings to understand what type of support he was envisioning as he proposed a renewed pursuit of the Great Commission. Almost at the very end of *Enquiry*, he writes this concerning how missionaries were going to supported:

> In respect to *contributions* for defraying the expenses, money will doubtless be wanting; and suppose the rich were to embark a portion of that wealth over which God has made them stewards, in this important undertaking, perhaps there are few ways that would turn to a better account at last . . .
>
> If congregations were to open subscriptions of *one penny*, or more per week, according to their circumstances, and deposit it as a fund for the propagation of the gospel, much might be raised in this way . . . for propagating the gospel amongst the heathen.[24]

This is the language of traditional support.

Moreover, in a section of *Enquiry* addressing the impediments that potentially stand in the way of missions, Carey first writes that ministers of the gospel are to be wholly devoted to the ministry and not to engage in other employment. Carey states:

> A Christian minister is a person who in a peculiar sense is not his own; he is the servant of God, and therefore ought to be wholly devoted to him. By entering on that sacred office, he solemnly undertakes to be always engaged, as much as possible, in the Lord's work, and not to chase his own pleasure, or employment.[25]

---

24. Carey, *Enquiry*, 50.
25. Carey, *Enquiry*, 42.

Then even more specifically in regards to overseas missionaries, he states:

> It might be necessary, however, for two, at least, to go together, and in general I should think it best that they should be married men, and to prevent their time from being employed in procuring necessaries, two, or more, other persons, with their wives and families, might also accompany them, who should be wholly employed in providing for them.[26]

Carey discouraged Christian missionaries from seeking any secular employment while ministering in the field. We can state confidently that, at least in 1792, Carey's vision for missions did not include tentmaking as a purposeful missiological method, nor did he recommended self-support for missionaries.[27]

What have we learned from this limited tour through church history? I would argue that the most obvious takeaway is the lack of people engaging in tentmaking among those Wilson identifies as engaging in tentmaking. Considering that all of the data cited above from Wilson is taken from his book *Today's Tentmakers* within the chapter titled "The History of Tentmaking," we should have seen numerous strong examples of people who were unquestionably utilizing tentmaking.[28] Instead, he pointed to people like Christopher Columbus, Marco Polo, and the paid chaplains from the East India Company. None of these examples meet the biblical qualifications for being a tentmaker; nor, I would argue, do they meet Wilson's own definition of a tentmaker.

Even more astounding, earlier in his tentmaking book, in an attempt to lay down broad biblical support for tentmaking, Wilson writes, "Many of the godly men and women in the Old Testament were self-supporting witnesses."[29] He then begins to list OT men and women and their occupations, "Abel was a sheep farmer, Abraham was a cattle raiser, Hagar was a

---

26. Carey, *Enquiry*, 43.

27. It should be noted that a year before his death, Carey wrote, "We have ever held it to be an essential principle in the conduct of missions, that whenever it is practicable, missionaries should support themselves in whole or in part through their own exertions." Wilson, *Today's Tentmakers*, 32. Nothing can be categorically deduced from this statement since Carey himself did not *go* to India as a self-supporting missionary, and since Carey certainly did not advocate for self-support when he wrote his *Enquiry*. It could reflect a philosophical change after experiencing life as a self-supporting missionary. Alternatively, it may reflect a difference between how he viewed mission financing at the end of his life compared to what he originally outlined, perhaps due to the ineffectiveness of asking people to set aside one penny or more a week. We do know that this view is the opposite of what he wrote in 1792.

28. Wilson, *Today's Tentmakers*, 26–37.

29. Wilson, *Today's Tentmakers*, 20.

domestic worker, Isaac was a farmer, Rebekah was a water carrier . . . Joseph was a premier, Miriam was a baby-sitter . . . Samson was a champion fighter, Ruth was a gleaner, Boaz was a grain grower," and this continues for over half a page listing almost every significant character in the OT.[30] Was Rebekah being paid to carry the water? He continues through the NT, "Joseph was a carpenter, Martha was a housekeeper, Zacchaeus was a tax collector, Nicodemus and Joseph of Arimathea were supreme-court councilors, Barnabas was a landowner," and on and on.[31] Does having a job serve as legitimate grounds for calling someone a tentmaking missionary? Does any believer engaged in unpaid labor of any kind make them a missionary who is utilizing tentmaking?

You may be asking if Wilson is really attempting to categorize all the people he mentioned as tentmakers. Yes. Notice at the beginning, before he started to list the biblical characters, how he subtly shifted from using the term tentmakers or self-supporting missionaries to self-supporting witnesses. At first, I thought he might be making some sort of fine-line distinction between a self-supporting witness and a self-supporting missionary. But that is not what he is doing, because later he refers to one of these biblical examples as an example of tentmaking service. He also writes this following statement after listing all of the biblical examples: "The greatest prototype of a self-supporting witness was the tentmaker Paul."[32] So he *does* see self-supporting witness and self-supporting missionary and tentmaker as synonymous terms, and he uses those terms interchangeably. He wants the reader to see all the people he mentioned as biblical tentmaking examples.

Perhaps his most puzzling statement of all is this: "Even our Lord, though he was Creator of the universe, humbled himself to become a self-supporting carpenter."[33] Jesus was a carpenter by trade, but he did not work to support himself during his public ministry. The context of the discussion is tentmaking ministry, or self-supporting ministry. Jesus did not support himself during his public ministry by working as a carpenter. That is just not true. Wilson even acknowledges this two sentences later when he writes, "But our Lord also set his seal of approval on full-time missionary work since during his ministry he was supported by his friends."[34] If Jesus was supported by others during his ministry, then why is he an example of a self-supporting tentmaker? The answer is because Wilson's understanding

---

30. Wilson, *Today's Tentmakers*, 20.
31. Wilson, *Today's Tentmakers*, 21.
32. Wilson, *Today's Tentmakers*, 21.
33. Wilson, *Today's Tentmakers*, 21.
34. Wilson, *Today's Tentmakers*, 21.

of tentmaking is so imprecise that practically anyone, anywhere, qualifies as a tentmaker. In the end, Wilson's teaching on the topic of tentmaking is misleading, contradictory, and relies heavily on an ill-defined understanding of tentmaking.

I greatly appreciate Wilson's personal and professional contributions to the church. And anyone reading his work will immediately detect his love for Christ and his dedication to missions. I engage Wilson's work first with respect and then with trepidation, but if we are going to bring clarity to the subject of tentmaking then we are going to have to examine the existing scholarship with a critical eye. We never want to reach the point where we start to avoid challenging the work of others because we fear we might breach some unwritten code of social or professional politeness. As a general rule, robust interactions carried out with mutual respect for one another should be embraced, not shunned, when seeking truth and clarity.

TENTMAKING ON THE UNITED STATES FRONTIER

The use of Wilson as a tour guide was helpful, but he could only take us so far, and since it is not possible, considering the limited scope of this book, to look at every period of church history, we need to be somewhat selective. I thought it would be appropriate to briefly consider a period of church history in the United States, specifically the frontier expansion of the United States during the nineteenth century. Since Paul's tentmaking was yoked to the establishing of new churches, and the frontier expansion period was a time when many new churches were established, there seems to be a higher chance of finding some examples of tentmaking being utilized by the church. What do you think—will we find tentmaking, as modeled by Paul in the Bible, being implemented by the church during this period of frontier expansion?

When examining the United States' frontier expansion from a church planting and missiological perspective, this particular epoch can be divided into two phases. The first phase was from the formation of the Federal Constitution until approximately 1815, and the second phase was from 1815 and beyond, although there was some overlap between these two phases. What we are going to see is that during the first phase of the United States' frontier expansion, there is evidence that at least some ministers engaged in bivocational ministry. But, in the second phase of United States' frontier expansion, the overwhelming majority of ministers who were sent westward were paid a salary and did not utilize tentmaking.

The first phase of United States' frontier expansion for the church began at the close of the Revolutionary War. Prior to gaining independence, the church, for the most part, was contained within the first American colonies and a good portion operated under British and European ecclesiastical authority. William Sweet, who has researched historical Christianity in the United States extensively, provides an assessment of this time period before the United States' independence:

> Thus the Episcopalians had been subject to the Bishop of London; the Roman Catholics to the Vicar Apostolic of London; the Methodists were under the control of John Wesley; the Reformed Churches had connections with the Classis of Amsterdam, while the Presbyterians, Quakers, and Lutherans were not so specifically tied to Old World organizations. The Congregationalists and Baptists were, of course, indigenous American churches with each congregation theoretically independent.[35]

Before America became independent, there was not a significant amount of the colonial population exiting the original colonies. After the Federal Constitution was in place, and with the opening of land in Ohio and parts of Indiana from 1787 to 1794, the population began to move westward. This initial frontier expansion was relatively unorganized. Sweet comments, "The Ohio river was the great highway westward, people floating down the river in great flatboats."[36] Sometimes settlers brought along a minister, other times they did not. Sweet describes the scene:

> Some of the settlers went on foot, drawing their small belongings in carts while during this winter (1817) a train of sixty wagons carrying one hundred and twenty souls, men, women, and children journeyed to Indiana, carrying their minister with them, where they planned to buy a township. These are but examples of the many thousands who set their faces westward during the years between 1808 and 1820.[37]

During this first phase of westward expansion, three Protestant denominations are recognized for making an effort to send ministers to the frontier. The Presbyterians would sometimes appoint a minister to go and serve beyond the Alleghany Mountains, but these paid clergy were few. Sweet writes, "Thus occasional ministers visited the region over the mountains

---

35. Sweet, *Story of Religion*, 280.
36. Sweet, *Story of Religion*, 300.
37. Sweet, *Story of Religion*, 302.

for a number of years before regular ministers removed to the West."[38] The Baptists and the Methodists were also represented in this first phase of frontier expansion.

The Baptists, for whatever reason, commonly attracted people with an independent spirit. The Baptist Church was democratic in its form of government and generally did not place a high value on formal education. They were, however, far closer to utilizing a tentmaking and bivocational model than the Presbyterians or Methodists when it came to planting churches on the frontier. Sweet describes the Baptists during this first phase of westward expansion:

> The typical Baptist preacher on the frontier was a settler who worked on his land five or six days each week, except when called upon to hold weekday meetings or funerals. He was generally without much formal education, for there was a deep-seated prejudice against educated and salaried ministers, though some of the preachers received some support, which in the early days was paid in kind.[39]

While the Baptists appeared to have bivocational ministers working on the frontier, it seems they were motivated by a distaste for salaried ministers in general rather than by a desire to follow Pauline tentmaking. However, the Baptist model did appear to be working from a practical standpoint. While the Presbyterians were sending an inadequate amount of ordained and educated clergy, these bivocational Baptist ministers were moving out with the population and were responsible for planting churches. Sweet writes, "The initiative in the formation of a frontier Baptist Church came generally from a licensed or ordained farmer-preacher settled in a new community."[40]

The Methodists also participated in the first phase of westward expansion. In a discussion of the Methodist Church and their success in the first phase of the westward moving frontier population, Sweet comments on the introduction of the Wesley-inspired itinerant circuit system to America: "All the early Methodist preachers were itinerants, that is, they had no one place or congregation to which they ministered, but traveled circuits varying in size according to the number of settlements."[41] The Methodist Church encouraged an intentional search for young men with public-speaking skills. Once identified, these young men were recruited to become lay circuit

---

38. Sweet, *Story of Religion*, 304. Sweet states that there were only four regular Presbyterian ministers in the southwestern corner of Pennsylvania between 1776 and 1781.

39. Sweet, *Story of Religion*, 314.

40. Sweet, *Story of Religion*, 315.

41. Sweet, *Story of Religion*, 316–17.

preachers. These laymen often had existing jobs and would have been ideal candidates for purposeful tentmaking. Yet within the Methodist Church, even their lay ministers received traditional financial support. Sweet writes, "The early bishops moved about the country, from north to south, from east to west; stayed in the same rude cabins on the frontier, preached at camp-meetings and received the same salary as the humblest circuit rider."[42] All of the Methodist frontier ministers from bishops to lay circuit-riding preachers received a salary.

The second phase of United States frontier expansion began approximately in 1815. The Federal Constitution had marked the beginning of an increased sense of nationality, and the publishing and distribution of Carey's *Enquiry* marked a turning point in the church's missiological mindset. These factors, combined with a growing sense of interdenominational calling to reach the lost, sparked an effort not only to meet the demand of vacant frontier pulpits, but also to reach the American Indians with the gospel. This second phase was more organized than the first phase, and missionary societies dominated United States church planting and missionary efforts.

When the English organized a society and sent William Carey to India, they were soon followed by other denominations that formed missionary societies for the purpose of reaching people they referred to as heathen. In 1795, the London Missionary Society was formed. Other similar missionary societies began to be organized in the Netherlands and Scotland. These European missionary societies did not go unnoticed in the newly independent America. New England churches began to follow their brothers and sisters on the other side of the Atlantic. Sweet writes, "A like movement began at about the same time in America influenced by their English brethren, and numerous missionary societies were formed in the New England and middle states, and among Congregationalists, Presbyterians, Baptists, Dutch Reformed, and finally the Methodists."[43]

Many of these United States based missionary societies were formed to reach the American Indians, but many also supported ministers who were willing to plant and serve churches on the frontier. For example, one of these missionary societies was the New York Missionary Society. It was formed in 1796 and "was made up of representatives of Presbyterians, Dutch Reformed and Baptists and its immediate object was to carry the gospel to the southern Indians."[44] Another missionary society formed at this time was the Missionary Society of Connecticut, a Congregationalist society, organized

---

42. Sweet, *Story of Religion*, 319–20.
43. Sweet, *Story of Religion*, 351.
44. Sweet, *Story of Religion*, 351–52.

in 1798. Their purpose was to "Christianize the heathen in North America, and to support and promote Christian knowledge in the new settlements within the United States."[45] In 1800, the Missionary Society of Connecticut "sent its first missionary, David Bacon, 'afoot and alone, with no more luggage than he could carry on his person,' to the region south and west of Lake Erie."[46] The Missionary Society of Connecticut financially supported these ministers and, "by 1807, it had a permanent fund of $15,000."[47]

In a discussion of the Methodist Church and their success in the second phase of the westward-moving frontier population, Sweet comments on Francis Asbury, who introduced the Wesley-inspired itinerant circuit system to America. Sweet wrote that toward the end of his life, Asbury "collected money wherever he could to supply the wants of the frontier preachers and their families."[48] Methodist frontier preachers were not expected to support themselves with supplemental or secondary employment.

All of these early missionary societies, whether they were Congregationalist, Methodist, Presbyterian, Dutch Reformed, or interdenominational in composition, financially supported their missionaries and paid them some sort of salary. The prevailing assumption among these missionary societies appeared to be that if the gospel was going to reach the American Indian population and the unsettled frontier, missionary societies would need to send out paid clergy.

It also appears that the prevailing assumption among frontier residents was that the only way to secure a minister of the gospel was to negotiate through the missionary societies. In a letter to the Missionary Society of Connecticut dated 1799, five towns in Ohio had banded together and requested that a missionary be sent to them. They wrote, "Entertaining a hope that it will not be inconsistent with the original design of the Society in Connecticut, for extending the means of religious instruction in the interior parts of the United States, to send Missionaries to this part of the country."[49] In unsettled wilderness areas of America where churches were not established, the residents relied heavily on mission societies to send qualified ministers to plant churches and preach during this second phase of frontier expansion.

Surprisingly, even after a church had been planted and established in a region, the New England-based missionary societies often continued to

---

45. Sweet, *Story of Religion*, 352.
46. Sweet, *Story of Religion*, 352.
47. Sweet, *Story of Religion*, 352.
48. Sweet, *Story of Religion*, 355.
49. Sweet, *Religion on the American*, 71–72.

provide financial support. Sweet states, "Both Congregationalism and Presbyterianism in early Wisconsin were subsidized by the American Home Missionary Society, as was true everywhere else throughout the West. Up to 1851, the society had aided 121 ministers in Wisconsin, out of a total of 135."[50] Sweet's research indicates that during this second phase of frontier expansion, several other societies, like the Missionary Society of Connecticut, were formed in the New England states. All of them appeared to raise support for their missionaries, send out their missionaries, and supervise the work of their missionaries. This does not mean that there were no examples of bivocational ministry or tentmaking, but the majority of frontier pulpits were filled with ministers sent and supported by missionary societies during this period.

Sweet's research is corroborated by the church historian Kenneth Scott Latourette, who writes that 1815 marks a transition point for the spread of Christianity during United States' frontier expansion.[51] He notes that in regards to missionary channels and agencies, "Some were in existence before 1815. Others came into being after that year."[52] When discussing the United States' frontier Christian expansion prior to 1815 Latourette notes:

> Here and there a group organized a church before leaving their home in the older states and, settling together, already possessed a Christian nucleus. Much more numerous were laymen and women who took the initiative in the new communities in gathering others together in Sunday Schools and prayer meetings which grew into churches.[53]

Of course, these Christian nuclei and churches that were organized by laymen still had the onerous task of finding qualified ministers to fill their pulpits.

Latourette also describes activity prior to 1815, which corresponds to the Baptist bivocational work during the first phase of frontier church planting:

> Many clergymen moved West and, without support from the East, took up farms, worked on them six days a week for a livelihood for themselves and their families, and preached on Sundays. Eventually voluntary gifts from those to whom they

---

50. Sweet, *Religion on the American*, 36.
51. Latourette, *History of Christianity*, 1230.
52. Latourette, *History of Christianity*, 1230.
53. Latourette, *History of Christianity*, 1230–231.

ministered made it possible for numbers of these clergymen to give a larger proportion of their time to the church.[54]

This is noteworthy because it seems to be the closest example of tentmaking during frontier church planting and missional activity, and it matches Sweet's findings regarding the first phase of frontier expansion. Although we could assume that the Baptist bivocational farmer-preacher model continued in phase two of the United States' frontier expansion, we also have to wonder how many qualified clergy would have continued to work at a labor-intensive job six days a week in order to support themselves so they could preach free of charge to frontier churches after 1815 when there was a proliferation of missionary societies dedicated to sending ordained clergy into the frontier with a salary.

Latourette describes these farmer-ministers decreasing their time behind the plow and increasing their time behind the pulpit only when local financial support began to be available. This suggests pragmatic reasons for these frontier congregations' initial choices, rather than the more philosophical reasons suggested by Sweet, such as a distaste for educated and salaried ministers.

After a brief look at frontier expansion in the United States, we did *not* find evidence of the church implementing tentmaking as modeled by Paul in the Bible. The majority of ministers who planted or served frontier churches during the early to mid-nineteenth century were paid by missionary societies, their congregations, or a combination of both. While there is evidence of bivocational ministry during the United States' frontier expansion, especially among the Baptists, these ministers appeared to have practiced bivocational ministry for practical reasons or for reasons unrelated to Paul's example. There does not seem to be any evidence that indicates churches, ministers, or missionary societies purposefully chose tentmaking for didactic or evangelistic reasons based on the ministry context.

---

54. Latourette, *History of Christianity*, 1231.

8

Roland Allen

Before turning to contemporary church planting literature, we need to consider and reflect upon the writings of Roland Allen. Allen is someone on the church's historical landscape who has studied Paul's tentmaking and concluded that it was more than just background scenery on the set of a biblical play. Allen viewed Paul's financial-support choices as missiologically significant and advocated for the integrated use of Paul's apostolic missionary methods both on the mission field and in the contemporary church. His work needs to be both recognized and taken into account as we seek to form a sound biblical understanding of tentmaking.

Another reason why it is important for us to look at Allen and his writings on this topic is because he was the quintessential practical theologian. He identified correct biblical practice, or what *ought to be*, and sought to bring the contemporary church in line with that practice. Even more remarkable was his willingness to do so regardless of who agreed with him or what the church had historically practiced. This type of bold leadership is something the church is in desperate need of today. Steven Rutt quotes Allen as he pursued this simplistic yet increasingly forgotten path that should be common within the church, but disappointingly is not:

> . . . as I studied the method of the Apostle I entered into a large liberty, difficulties were smoothed away, doubts removed, and

> I began to understand what the establishment of the Church might be... At first I was horrified and dismayed. I thought that I must be quite mad, because I could not imagine how other men wiser than I had not seen what I saw. I wrote down what I saw in St. Paul's work. I simply wrote: "The Apostle did this; we do that." Then men like Bishop Gore and Father Waggett read it, and they said that it was illuminating. That dismayed me all the more because I could not understand how wise men could see what I saw and not change their whole manner of action.[1]

Before we interact with what Allen said about Paul's support choices, it will be helpful to understand who Allen was and what shaped his views. It appears that Allen was called by God for missionary work, shaped by God through varying experiences to produce a specific missiological and ministry philosophy, and guided by God as a prolific writer on the subject of missionary methods.

CALLED BY GOD

Allen was born in Bristol, England, in 1868 and eventually became a priest in the Anglican Church.[2] Apparently, Allen's desire to bring the gospel to unreached people groups had been placed on his heart at a young age. Hubert J.B. Allen, Allen's grandson who wrote a biography of Allen's life, describes one of Roland's memories, "*When I was about four years old and heard that there were men who had never been told the Gospel*, recounted Roland in his old age, he had cried out: *Then I shall go and tell them.*"[3]

Further evidence of an early missionary calling on Allen's life can be found in an excerpt from his application letter to the Society for the Propagation of the Gospel: "I am simply thirsting to go to the Foreign Mission Field, and I am ready to go wherever and whenever the Society has a vacancy... From my earliest years I was as firmly convinced of my vocation as I was of my existence."[4]

The principal of Leeds Clergy Training School, named Winfred Burrows, knew Allen as a student and described his as "a refined intellectual

---

1. Rutt, *Roland Allen: A Theology*, 27.

2. Roland Allen was "ordained as Deacon (1892) and Priest (1893) by Bishop Westcott of Durham." Rutt, *Roland Allen: A Missionary*, 21.

3. H.J.B. Allen, *Roland Allen: Pioneer*, 21. Please see the rest of H.J.B. Allen's, *Roland Allen: Pioneer, Priest, and Prophet* for an extended and detailed biography of Roland Allen's life. For a biographical summary of Roland Allen's life, see J.D. Payne, *Roland Allen: Pioneer of Spontaneous Expansion*, 11–21.

4. Paton, *Roland Allen: The Ministry*, xx.

man, small not vigorous, in no way burly or muscular."[5] Despite Allen's unimpressive physique, he would prove to be a courageous champion on the mission field.

SHAPED BY GOD

Missionary in China

Allen possessed a strong desire to serve as a foreign missionary. In 1892, he applied to an Anglican missionary organization, which at that time was called the Society for the Propagation of the Gospel (SPG). After a few setbacks, Allen was eventually sent to China in 1895 and spent most of his time as Legation Chaplain in Peking (Beijing).

Allen was in Peking during the Boxer Rebellion in 1900. The Boxers were an anti-European movement that was quasi-religious and sought to rally indigenous Chinese people around ancient hero worship. The Boxers were natively known as the *Fist of Righteous Harmony* and had remained dormant for several decades, but had been aroused and revived by what Allen himself described as the "aggressive attitude of foreign nations and the semi-political propaganda of the Roman Catholic Church," as well as "the tyrannical way in which the foreigners acted towards the natives in places taken by them."[6] This dislike of the Roman Catholic Church and foreigners in general was not without reason. The Boxers found sympathy with many Chinese nationals who increasingly saw "the uprooting of their most cherished customs and beliefs, and the enforced adaptation of habits and laws which were utterly strange and abhorrent to them."[7]

Allen was in Peking while it was under Boxer siege and remained steadfast under combat conditions. In June of 1900, a surviving Christian sought refuge within the Anglican mission and reported what was happening in the city as "the most horrible sight he had ever seen," and stated that the Boxers were "going about from house to house cutting down every Christian they could find, and the place was running with blood."[8] Allen described one of his memories: "Life there was becoming dangerous. Several bullets had found their way in: one had pierced a hat hanging on a peg a foot or two above on of the missionaries beds, and some of the people were

---

5. Rutt, *Roland Allen: A Missionary*, 21.
6. Allen, *Siege of the Peking Legations*, 1.
7. Allen, *Siege of the Peking Legations*, 1.
8. Allen, *Siege of the Peking Legations*, 85.

feeling nervous."[9] Elsewhere, Allen recounted standing at a funeral for two of his fallen missionaries: "At that moment there was a furious attack going on, and bullets were whistling through the trees."[10]

Allen arrived in Peking, China, in 1895 and was assigned to open a clergy school for the diocese of North China. Allen's grandson states, "Roland at once made friends with the Chinese, and . . . he began to learn Mandarin quickly and well: in only a few years he was already distinguished as a 'three-thousand-character man' and was preaching in Chinese."[11]

During his time in China, Roland's eyes began to see things on the front lines of missionary service that would influence his missiological thoughts and later writings. For example, he saw the gospel message being hindered by the missionaries who were bearing it because the missionaries were not Chinese. The indigenous population had a tendency to place all foreigners into the same basket. That meant that the Anglican Christian missionaries were viewed through the same lens as the foreign merchants and businessmen who traveled to China. As H.J.B. Allen states, "To the vast majority of Chinese *all foreigners were Christians, and all Christians were to be judged by the actions of those whom they happened to meet.*"[12]

It was during this time in China that Allen also saw faith that could remain firm and bold in the face of death. At the outset of the Boxer unrest in Peking, Allen describes two Christian missionaries as they went out to encourage and pray for some of the people they had led to Christ: "These two men went alone, armed with revolvers, into the heart of a district seething with Boxer agitation, in order to encourage their converts."[13] After providing some additional details, Allen reflectively writes, "It was no wonder that missionaries like these ready to lay down their lives for their people, exercised a great influence and won converts to the fold."[14]

After the Boxer rebellion and the siege of Peking, over thirty-thousand Christians had died in China, "including 135 missionaries of various denominations, together with over 50 of their children."[15] Of course, Allen had survived and returned to England on furlough, but he had been changed. His grandson writes, "By now his experiences in China were

---

9. Allen, *Siege of the Peking Legations*, 142.
10. Allen, *Siege of the Peking Legations*, 210.
11. H.J.B. Allen, *Roland Allen: Pioneer*, 27.
12. H.J.B. Allen, *Roland Allen: Pioneer*, 35.
13. Allen, *Siege of the Peking Legations*, 23.
14. Allen, *Siege of the Peking Legations*, 25.
15. H.J.B. Allen, *Roland Allen: Pioneer*, 55.

leading him to face several *fundamental questions in connexion with the propagation of the Church*."[16]

Allen's experiences as a missionary in China had prompted him to examine traditional cross-cultural missiological methods with a critical eye. His next set of experiences in parish ministry would cause him to turn that same analytical and questionable gaze toward the Church of England's ecclesiastical practice.

Parish Ministry

From 1904 to 1907, Roland Allen was the vicar in a rural Buckinghamshire parish called Chalfont St. Peter. Over the course of those few years, Allen became increasingly unsettled and disturbed over the fact that he was bound to perform weddings, baptisms, and funerals for people in the community who were notorious unbelievers. At that time, the Church of England mandated that all clergy perform these duties for anyone who requested them, even if they led openly immoral and unrepentant lives. Allen had shared these concerns with his congregation but tolerated the circumstances until his resignation in 1907.

Allen had seen what real faith looked like in China. He had seen men willing to endanger themselves and even die for Christ. Allen saw his Chinese converts possess a stout unwavering faith in Christ. To come back to England and see the contrasting cheap grace and nominal Christianity was too much. His conscience would not allow him to continue, and he made the decision to resign. Allen's grandson biographer writes, "He did this because he found himself unable conscientiously to carry out his legal duty, as a priest in the established Church of England, to perform solemn religious ceremonies even for undeserving persons who *habitually neglect their religious duties, or openly deny the truth of the Creeds, or by the immorality of their lives openly deny the laws of God.*"[17] Perhaps Allen's own words can best communicate his disillusionment with the laws and practices of the Church of England. In his resignation letter, Allen writes:

> For no one can justify these things. They undermine the fundamental principle that the Church stands for morality of life; they suggest the horrible doctrine that the Church does not regard morality as an essential part of religion. They embolden men to go on living in sin in the hope that they will not be rejected at the last. Ignorant men speak as if Christ and His Church had

16. H.J.B. Allen, *Roland Allen: Pioneer*, 58.
17. H.J.B. Allen, *Roland Allen: Pioneer*, 78.

nothing to offer which is not the natural inheritance of every Englishman, nor any right to lay down rules and conditions on which those gifts may be obtained; because they see every man, whatever his belief or his character, admitted without question to the highest privileges which the Church can bestow.[18]

Even though hundreds of supporters turned out to say their goodbyes at Allen's farewell gathering and several newspapers wrote sympathetic articles, this was a turning point for Allen.[19] He would no longer minister under the auspices of the Church of England. He stated that he had no quarrel with his bishop or with his church. He resigned with regret and asked for prayers. At the time, many stated that it was sad that Allen resigned and ended his ministry. Conversely, Roland Allen's grandson reports a Reverend H. Boone Porter remarking that *"those who are interested in Allen will believe that his resignation from the parish was really the beginning of his ministry, and not the end of it!"*[20] Allen moved into a house on Primrose Hill Road in north London where he began to concentrate heavily on study and writing.

Roland Allen's service as a missionary in China and his time serving Chalfont St. Peter were two experiences that significantly contributed to forming his missionary theology. While those experiences served as the tinder to start Allen's fiery reassessment of the church's missionary, evangelistic, and ecclesiastical practice, it was Scripture that continued to fuel his investigation and caused it to burn hot.

GUIDED BY GOD

Despite Allen's missionary service to China and his service to the church as an Anglican priest, he is most remembered for his writings. Allen's influential books and publications have made such an impact that he has been referred to as a prophet.[21] Unfortunately, this modern prophet was not recognized as such during his lifetime. In an introductory essay to one of David

---

18. H.J.B. Allen, *Roland Allen: Pioneer*, 184.

19. Newspapers such as the *Daily Telegraph, Daily Chronicle,* and *Liverpool Evening Press* published headlines such as, "A Manly Vicar," "Vicar's Sacrifice," and "Good Man Weary." H.J.B. Allen, *Roland Allen: Pioneer*, 79. One can only imagine what kind of headlines would appear in the local news today if a pastor resigned over his refusal to marry couples who were living together before marriage and fornicating.

20. H.J.B. Allen, *Roland Allen: Pioneer*, 82.

21. Roland Allen's grandson, H.J.B. Allen, wrote, "I was more than a little startled, when introduced to a Bishop in the early 1960s, to be swept into a warm episcopal embrace, accompanied by the remark: *I hear you are the Grandson of the Prophet!*" H.J.B. Allen, *Roland Allen: Pioneer*, vii.

Paton's books on Allen, Lamin Sanneh writes, "The writings of Roland Allen . . . suffer from a fault that would be the envy of most writers: they are a casualty of their own farsighted brilliance."[22] Similarly, in the foreword to Allen's biography written by his grandson, Leslie Newbigin writes, "Roland Allen was, in his time, a lonely prophet. His ideas seemed to most of his contemporaries eccentric and unrealistic."[23]

Allen's mind had been impacted by his Chinese missionary experience. After he returned he wrote his first book in 1901 titled, *The Siege of The Peking Legations*. The vast majority of the book is a rather detailed account of the day-to-day events he experienced during his time in China. However, there are already quiet whispers of Allen's dissatisfaction with traditional missionary methods. In the opening pages of the book, Allen writes that, "The labours of the missionaries have gained a wonderful measure of success, and that their Chinese converts can and sometimes do display those virtues which are peculiar to the Christian saint and martyr," but he also states, "Many faults may be found in the present methods by which missionaries seek to attain their object."[24]

Allen's change in missionary philosophy was not something he kept to himself. In March of 1901, Roland was the principal speaker at an SPG bicentenary meeting for young people, where he proclaimed, "*Western teachers can never preach the whole Gospel to Eastern minds.*"[25] Allen now believed that the theological schools like the one he had been assigned to establish in Peking were no longer appropriate because they did not produce Christians who went and made disciples. He also believed that the traditional missionary methods of the church were a hindrance to multiplication. In a 1927 quote from Allen, who was looking back and commenting on his time in China, he stated, "*I saw that if the Church in North China was to have no clergy at all except such as could pass through my little theological school and then be financially supported, Churches could not multiply rapidly.*"[26]

Allen and Voluntary Clergy

Allen has written powerfully on many topics, but we must limit the discussion here to the topics that most closely touch on tentmaking as a purposeful

---

22. Paton, *Roland Allen: The Ministry*, iii.
23. H.J.B. Allen, *Roland Allen: Pioneer*, xiii.
24. Allen, *Siege of the Peking Legations*, ix.
25. H.J.B. Allen, *Roland Allen: Pioneer*, 59.
26. H.J.B. Allen, *Roland Allen: Pioneer*, 59.

missiological method. Therefore, we will consider his writings on the topic of voluntary clergy and nonprofessional missionaries.

First of all, Allen must be given credit for noticing that the Bible actually has quite a bit to say about Paul's missionary strategy and his methods of support. Allen states, "By modern writers this is often overlooked, and the finance of St. Paul's journeys is treated as an interesting detail of ancient history, not as though it had anything to do with his success as a preacher of the Gospel. St. Paul himself does not so treat it."[27] Modern writers are still overlooking Paul's purposeful choices regarding missionary support and finances.

One of the concepts that Allen sought to define and develop in the church was something he called *voluntary clergy*, which he defines as "men who earn their living by the work of their hands or of their heads in the common market, and serve as clergy without stipend or fee of any kind."[28] In contrast, he described *stipendiary clergy* as traditional pastors and ministers who are supported by the church through traditional means. He also outlined additional differences such as the intangible elements of association and socialization. Allen's experience in China had shown him that the laity need to be able to relate to their priest, minister, or pastor. Allen states:

> Among our own people also the church sorely needs clergy in close touch with the ordinary life of the laity, living the life of ordinary men, sharing their difficulties and understanding their trials by close personal experience. Stipendiary clergy cut off by training and life from that common experience are constantly struggling to get close to the laity by wearing lay clothing, sharing in lay amusements, and organizing lay clubs; but they never quite succeed. To get close to men, it is necessary really to share their experience, and to share their experience is to share it by being in it, not merely to come as near to it as possible without being in it. The church needs clerics who really share the life of their people.[29]

Allen saw voluntary clergy being ordained, yet fulfilling a different role that was able to bridge the gap between clergy and laity. Allen describes the difference between stipendiary clergy and voluntary clergy as:

> A distinction between one form of service and another. Both stipendiary and voluntary clergy ought to be serving God and the Church all the time in all they do; but the service which the Church needs that each should do for God and for her is not

---

27. Allen, *Missionary Methods*, 49.
28. Paton, *Roland Allen: The Ministry*, 147.
29. Paton, *Roland Allen: The Ministry*, 150.

the same. The voluntary cleric carries the priesthood into the market place and the office. It is his work not only to minister at the altar or to preach, but to show men how the common work of daily life can be done in the spirit of the priest.[30]

Voluntary clergy, according to Allen, are pastors who do not take any money or stipend from the church, but instead are completely self-supported by secular employment. In addition, according to Allen, voluntary clergy are ministers who work in both the church and among people engaged in daily life. This is in contrast to traditional stipendiary clergy, who are ministers who work exclusively in the church and receive all their pay from the church. Notice that Allen's description of voluntary clergy, as given above and without comparing motivations, reasons, or rationales for practicing self-support, sounds similar to what the Apostle Paul practiced.

Allen cites bridging the relational and experiential gap between clergy and laity as one of the major reasons for the utilization of voluntary clergy, but he also lists practical reasons. For example, Allen writes:

> There are countless small groups of Christians needing pastors, which cannot afford to maintain clergy nor to provide them with sufficient occupation to save them from the temptations of idleness. There are also many large town parishes where the church needs assistant priests of varied capacity, drawn from many classes of the people, who can speak, each to his own class, in the language familiar to it, understanding by experience the difficulties and temptations of that class. It is also important that many services and sermons should not be heaped upon one man: the stipendiary ought to be able to leave his parish at proper intervals for rest and refreshment without feeling that his people are neglected and his work left undone; he ought also to be relieved from a pressure which drives him to minister when he is sick and unfit. It is in such cases that the assistance of voluntary clergy would be invaluable.[31]

Notice that Allen is, on a primary level, saying that voluntary clergy are needed to bridge the relational and experiential gap between clergy and laity. Then, on a secondary level, he identifies pragmatic reasons to argue for voluntary clergy: small groups of believers who need a part-time pastor, churches that need assistant pastors who can relate to the differing socioeconomic classes, and relief for full-time stipendiary clergy.

---

30. Paton, *Roland Allen: The Ministry*, 149–50.
31. Paton, *Roland Allen: The Ministry*, 147–48.

Although Allen's description of voluntary clergy is a close match to Paul's practice as a self-supporting tentmaker, the reasons that Allen cited to make his case for voluntary clergy do not seem to directly mirror the Apostle Paul's reasons. We do not see Allen, in these excerpts, referencing the need for voluntary clergy to support themselves in order to teach a specific biblical principle by example (didactic), or to set themselves apart from false teachers (evangelistic).[32]

I suppose someone could argue that Allen is advocating for voluntary clergy on the basis of evangelistic reasons, to which I would have to concede, yes. Sure, I can see how Allen may have thought that voluntary clergy would have a positive impact on the evangelistic efforts of the church and increase the overall spiritual harvest. Obviously, that is why he is ultimately proposing the concept of voluntary clergy. But that line of thinking jettisons the reasons Allen actually provided in his writings (both primary and secondary reasons identified above), and substitutes a general overarching goal that is true of any believer proposing an innovative idea to be utilized by the church. There is no *direct* connection between Allen's reasons for promoting voluntary clergy and Paul's self-disclosed reasons for his tentmaking in specific ministry contexts. It is just too much of a stretch. It should be satisfying enough that Allen proposed and described voluntary clergy in a way that so closely reflected Paul's practice, even though his underlying reasons and rationale for laboring as voluntary clergy do not align with Paul's self-disclosed reasons.

Allen and Nonprofessional Missionaries

In order to accurately comprehend Roland Allen's view of how Pauline apostolic methods should dictate contemporary missionary practice, we need to examine Allen's understanding of *nonprofessional missionaries*, which Allen sometimes called unofficial missionaries. Allen first wrote *Nonprofessional Missionaries* in 1929, and it is available now through various books that have reprinted collections of his writings. It remains the best source of information for understanding what Allen meant when he used the term nonprofessional missionary.

Allen defined professional missionaries using what most people would agree are conventional missionary hallmarks. *Professional missionaries* are called by God to impart what Allen described as "The secret of life in Christ"

---

32. If you remember from chapter 4, Paul's self-disclosed reasons for supporting himself in some ministry contexts and not others were either didactic or evangelistic in nature.

and are eager to communicate it to others.[33] Allen believed that all missionaries are evangelists. In addition, professional missionaries are formally trained and are sponsored by a missionary society or agency, and they do receive payment, or a stipend, for their work.

Nonprofessional missionaries, according to Allen, are people who have "no connection with a society which sends out professional missionaries."[34] Allen described these nonprofessional missionaries as going about their evangelistic work quietly behind the scenes without recognition so that they can retain the boast of openly earning their own living by some means other than missionary work. Allen hints that he may view nonprofessional missionaries in higher regard than professional missionaries:

> They [nonprofessional missionaries] see that the communication of a secret of life is not a proper subject for payment . . . They cannot let it appear that they are even seeking to increase the numbers of their own flock, or working for the aggrandizement of their own church, much less that they themselves are making a living. They feel that there is something nauseous in offering to others a way of life in Christ except on terms which wholly preclude any possibility that they are seeking anything whatsoever except the other man's salvation.[35]

Allen does more than hint at his favorable bias toward nonprofessional missionaries when he states, "They [nonprofessional missionaries] are doing the real missionary work, and it is they who prove that Christians do not only try to give their gospel to others when they have made that work their profession."[36]

Allen acknowledged that there will always be professional missionaries at work, and they are not to be judged. At the same time, Allen made it fairly clear that in order to most closely follow apostolic methods in the footsteps of Paul, he believed a person should become a nonprofessional missionary.

The advantages of nonprofessional missionaries are predictably similar to the advantages that Allen stated voluntary clergy have over stipendiary clergy. Allen noted that professional missionaries do not normally or easily associate socially with the people they are trying to reach. Allen elaborated by saying that professional missionaries are "around them but

---

33. Paton, *Roland Allen: The Ministry*, 65.
34. Paton, *Roland Allen: The Ministry*, 74.
35. Paton, *Roland Allen: The Ministry*, 74.
36. Paton, *Roland Allen: The Ministry*, 75.

they are not 'of' them; there is always a certain restraint, and constraint, in the intercourse."[37]

We need to slow down and review what Allen has said so far about nonprofessional missionaries. He has stated two cardinal features associated with nonprofessional missionaries. The first one is that nonprofessional missionaries are not sent out by, or associated with, any official missionary sending agency. The second feature is that they earn their living by something other than missionary work. This means they are self-supporting independent missionaries. The primary reasons Allen is advocating for the existence and use of nonprofessional missionaries is so that those whom they are trying to reach with the gospel, and all others who are watching, will in no way be under the impression that the missionary is motivated by financial compensation or reward.[38] Then, secondarily, he is saying that nonprofessional missionaries have the advantage of assimilating into their target people group better than traditional professional missionaries. Nonprofessional missionaries are able to bridge the social and relational gap between clergy and laity. Interestingly, bridging the social and relational gap between clergy and laity appeared to be Allen's primary reason for voluntary clergy, but avoiding the appearance of seeking worldly wealth through missionary work emerges as the primary reason for working as a nonprofessional missionary.[39]

Like voluntary clergy, Allen's portrait of a nonprofessional missionary looks similar to Paul's practice as a self-supporting tentmaker. But, once again, Allen's underlying reasons for advocating the use of nonprofessional missionaries do not match Paul's self-disclosed reasons for tentmaking. Paul did not make tents to dissuade others from thinking that he was greedy or *in it for the money*, nor did he support himself in some ministry contexts because he wanted to fit in better with the people he was trying to reach. He was not attempting to break down the division between clergy and laity. None of Allen's reasons for making use of voluntary clergy or

---

37. Paton, *Roland Allen: The Ministry*, 75.

38. I would group not receiving pay for missionary work and not belonging to a missionary society together since the missionary receives pay from the missionary society. Allen does not seem to be emphasizing a nonprofessional missionary's independent authority to go and minister in places of their own choosing and to be free to make their own administrative decisions so much as he is stressing the need for the general public and the target people group to know that the nonprofessional missionary is not receiving pay for missionary work.

39. Despite the respective placement of emphasis on the relational and financial motivations for voluntary clergy and nonprofessional missionaries in Roland Allen's initial descriptions, it seems as if both reasons may serve as equally motivating factors for proposing the use of both voluntary clergy and nonprofessional missionaries.

nonprofessional missionaries are "bad" or wrong, they are just not the same reasons supplied by Paul.

Another reason that Allen argued for the use of nonprofessional missionaries was that paying missionaries both modeled and created unwanted financial dependence upon outside support within the target people group. Allen believed that in order to achieve spontaneous expansion of the church under the power of the Holy Spirit, it was unreasonable and unbiblical to require new converts to quit their secular jobs and devote themselves to full-time ministry. He viewed the prevailing missionary method of financially supporting overseas clergy and paying them to lead local indigenous churches as detrimental to the missionary goal. Allen writes, "A Christian community which has learned from the very beginning that their ministers depend upon the foreigner for support and guidance are not prepared to support native priests."[40]

The bottom line for Allen, as he made his argument, was that he did not want fledgling Christian communities to rely on foreign aid because that would hinder the spontaneous expansion of the church. He also did not want new Christians to neglect their individual responsibility to proclaim the gospel. His concern was that if the only people new converts ever witnessed engaging in evangelism were paid missionaries, the unintended byproduct would be a lack of evangelistic responsibility and zeal among the newly reached people. Allen did not want new believers to adopt the belief that the only people who should be engaging in gospel proclamation or ministry work were paid professionals. These are valid concerns from a man who spent time on the frontlines of cross-cultural missions. Allen describes the field converts who were won and taught by stipendiary clergy: "They learn to receive, they learn to rely on paid and trained men. The more teachers they have, the less they feel the need for exerting themselves to teach others. That is perhaps quite natural, but it is disastrous."[41]

Finally, Allen charged that professional missionaries absorbed too much of the missionary spirit out of the church, which he believed was a hindrance to gospel progress. What he meant by that was that when a lay person in the church feels an impulse to make a missional contribution to the kingdom of God, they are left with the two options of either making a financial donation to an existing mission society or applying to a mission society to become a professional missionary. Therefore, Allen recommended that anyone who sensed a missionary call should proceed as nonprofessional missionary and refuse to join any missionary society or

---

40. Allen, *Spontaneous Expansion*, 133.
41. Allen, *Spontaneous Expansion*, 33.

receive payment. Allen suggested government service, trading, and farming as viable employment options for the nonprofessional missionary in an overseas cross-cultural missionary context.

In summary, Allen's descriptions of voluntary clergy and nonprofessional missionary both resemble Paul's self-support practice. And, while Allen's reasons for proposing these two types of positions are not the same as Paul's reasons for supporting himself with tentmaking, they are nonetheless valid reasons birthed from a desire to correct what Allen perceived as hindrances to his contemporary missionary practices and the spontaneous expansion of the church.

THE BIBLICAL BASIS FOR ALLEN'S CONVICTIONS

It is refreshing to see someone like Allen, at the beginning of the twentieth century, prompting and prodding the church to re-evaluate her missionary methods in light of the biblical account of Paul and his activity. Allen not only asked the church to follow in the footsteps of Paul, but Allen proposed the use of what he called voluntary clergy and nonprofessional missionaries based on Paul's support choices. Both voluntary clergy and nonprofessional missionaries were to be completely self-supportive.

What exactly did Allen base his thinking on? How did he arrive at the concepts of voluntary clergy and nonprofessional missionaries? It is clear that Allen was influenced by his experiences in China and as a parish minister, but what exactly did Allen believe about Paul and his support choices as revealed in Scripture? Allen believed that God has given us a prescription for missions and not just a description of Paul's missionary journeys. Perhaps one of the best summaries of Allen's desire for the church and her mission is provided by Rutt:

> Allen's vision for the Church encased a combination of *Spirit* and *Order*—that is, pneumatology and ecclesiology. He believed that the Holy Spirit empowers Christians to apply *apostolic principles* in any given situation through the one, holy, catholic and apostolic Church. His contribution to missiology stemmed from a Pauline understanding of an indigenously-led Church with its faith and practice rooted in the Bible, creeds, ministry and the sacraments and was, therefore, "fully equipped" with ministry to function as a "permanent and charismatic" Church. He proposed the restoration of an apostolic order to enhance

evangelism, particularly through the laity, by reaching out to pioneer regions where the Church had no current witness.[42]

Allen insisted that everything he was proposing in the theater of missionary methods was grounded in Scripture and apostolic principles. That's fine, but if we leave it at that, it is not unlike a church claiming to base everything it does on Scripture alone without any confessional statements, creeds, or summary statements of belief. "No creed but the Bible," works adequately until someone asks, "What does the Bible mean right here in this passage?" Just because two people read the same Scripture passages that describe Paul and his missionary journeys, that does not mean they are going to agree on the meaning of those passages, Paul's motivations for his methodological choices, what constitutes apostolic practice, or how to apply Pauline practices in a contemporary context.

To truly understand Allen's view, we need to know how he dissected Paul's missionary passages and, specifically, the conclusions he reached from studying Paul's ministry and financial support choices. At this point, we know that Allen believed that finances were more than an interesting detail in the Bible. We also know that he advocated the use of ministers and missionaries who did not receive a stipend of traditional support. Now we need to unpack and examine Allen's views much in the same way we analyzed Harris, Barnett, Thrall, and others in earlier chapters.

Navigating through Allen's thoughts on finances can be challenging. Payne has observed, "In all of Allen's missiology, his understanding of who should receive compensation and who should not receive compensation is possibly the most difficult concept to understand. Even within the same publication, at times he seemed to contradict himself."[43] The place where Allen provides his most lucid writing on this subject is from one of his first publications, *Missionary Methods: St. Paul's or Ours?*

In this book, Allen articulated his understanding of Paul's approach to finances succinctly: "There seem to have been three rules which guided his practice: (1) That he did not seek financial help for himself; (2) that he took no financial help to those to whom he preached; (3) that he did not administer local church funds."[44]

I want to be sure I am accurately representing and communicating Allen's views, so let us look at the last two rules first. Allen's second and

---

42. Rutt, *Roland Allen: A Theology*, 60. Rutt's scholarly work, published in 2018, is the most comprehensive resource on Roland Allen available at this time, and I do not think it will be displaced with research of higher quality at any point in the near future.

43. Payne, "Evaluation of the Systems," 80.

44. Allen, *Missionary Methods*, 49.

third rules are both correct and astute observations. It is true that Paul did not personally provide formal financial aid for the people he ministered to in the sense of supporting the church as a whole, and he did not, as far as we can tell from Scripture, administer local church funds while on site or after he left a church. However, these two rules are tangential to our topic and while they may deserve further study by those interested in general church and church planting finances, they are not relevant to the subject of tentmaking as a purposeful missiological method. Therefore, they will not be explored any further.[45]

Allen's first rule, however, deserves a closer examination. If by "he did not seek financial help for himself," Allen means that Paul did not *seek out* any acceptable form of financial support from the churches he ministered to, but welcomed it if they voluntarily offered or gave it to him then we might be able to agree with Allen and call his first rule valid. For example, in Acts 16:15, Lydia urged Paul, and he agreed to accept local support in the form of staying in a host household. Paul did not ask her for that support, she offered it to him so we could say he did not technically *seek* it. And, in Phil 4:16–17, where Paul is thanking the Philippians for their partnership, he writes, "Even in Thessalonica you sent me help for my needs once and again. Not that I seek the gift, but I seek the fruit that increases to your credit." Someone could argue that Paul was not seeking financial assistance from the Philippian church, but they gave it to him anyway. On the other hand, we have to wonder what "entered into partnership with me in giving and receiving" means in Phil 4:15. The phrase suggests some sort of agreed upon relationship involving financial support, but we really do not know what that means or if Paul initiated the partnership with them or if they approached him with a desire to partner. And of course in 2 Cor 11:8, he tells the church in Corinth, "I robbed other churches by accepting support from them in order to serve you." It could be argued that Paul simply *accepted* unsolicited support from the other churches and did not seek it out.

Once again, if Allen intended the phrase *he did not seek* to mean that Paul did not intentionally seek out support from the churches to which he ministered, we might be able to agree with his first rule. But upon closer examination of Allen's own expanded explanation of his first rule, we can see that this is not what he meant. Allen writes, "He refused to receive anything from those who listened to him . . . Heathen religion, the Jewish law, Christ's directions all alike insisted on the right of the minister to receive support.

---

45. Allen's last two rules are, for the most part, already present in the majority of churches because the deacons are the church officers biblically responsible for the collection and distribution of church funds.

But he himself did not receive it, and he was careful to explain his reason."[46] And later Allen states, "He received money; but not from those to whom he was preaching."[47] After a statement like that, we no longer have to wonder what exactly Allen was intending in the phrase, "he did not seek financial help for himself." Allen means that Paul was not paid by those to whom he was preaching.

By stating his first rule, Allen is saying that he believes Paul refused to accept any support from the churches he served. But as we discovered earlier, Paul did receive support from those to whom he preached when he stayed with Lydia and accepted congregational support from the beginning of his ministry at Philippi. This means that Allen's first identified rule is not true.

How then did Allen arrive at that rule? He fell into the familiar trap of lumping all of Paul's individual missionary contexts together, and then attempting to find a set of principles, or rules, that governed all of Paul's behavior when it came to his financial support. Under his expanded explanation of his first rule, Allen cites Scripture passages referring to the Corinthians (1 Cor 9:12), the Thessalonians (1 Thess 2:9), and the Ephesians (Acts 20:33–34). He, like many modern NT scholars, scooped all of these ministry contexts together and attempted to come up with a set of rules that governed them all. Not surprisingly, Allen had to make an exception to his rule by acknowledging that Paul did accept gifts, "Yet St. Paul did receive gifts from his converts . . . He does not seem to have felt any unwillingness to receive help; he rather welcomed it."[48] The idea that there is one set of bedrock principles that guided Paul's support choices is a fallacy that has been decisively dismissed in previous chapters. Paul did not have a hard set of rules or principles that dictated his support choices in all ministry contexts. He tailored his support choices based on the unique and individual needs of each church and region.

When Allen states that Paul was willing to accept gifts from his converts, it appears that he is drawing a distinction between gifts and support similar to Barnett back in chapter 5. Allen opens himself up to this possibility when, on the one hand, he writes that Paul "did not receive financial aid from his converts," but also states, "Paul did receive gifts from his converts."[49] Even with these two statements and the surrounding context, it is unclear if Allen views a substantial difference between financial aid and gifts. But those two statements are taken from his work in 1912. By the time

---

46. Allen, *Missionary Methods*, 50.
47. Allen, *Missionary Methods*, 51.
48. Allen, *Missionary Methods*, 51.
49. Allen, *Missionary Methods*, 51.

he wrote *Nonprofessional Missionaries* in 1929, we can easily see that Allen did, in fact, believe there was a difference between gifts and support:

> The distinction between gifts and a stipend opens our eyes; for there is a distinction, and a real distinction. Gifts are given to a man who is doing a work to which he feels called, a work he would do, gifts or no gifts; the stipend is a regular payment agreed upon before the man begins to do the work.[50]

Notice that so far with his 1929 work, Allen is clarifying that he *does* see a difference between support and gifts. But after drawing this distinction between gifts and support (or gifts and a stipend), Allen strangely says that Paul refused gifts as a way of combating charges from his enemies that he was motivated by financial gain to preach the gospel. Allen writes:

> The charge was brought against him [Paul] that he did not preach the gospel for nothing, that he was not wholly disinterested. How did he answer it? . . . It was not his acceptance of gifts which proved his disinterestedness but his refusal of them.[51]

Allen appears to be contradicting his early writing, where he stated that Paul did accept gifts.

Perhaps we will never know if Allen believed Paul accepted or refused gifts, or if Allen's understanding of whether or not Paul accepted gifts as a means of support changed over time. Regardless, we have already dealt with the topic in chapter 5. There is no reason to differentiate between monetary gifts and financial aid and financial support. The primary reason anyone would want to do that would be to make a case for Paul refusing support but accepting gifts, but remember that Paul said he accepted support ὀφώνιον [*opsonion*] from the other churches when he was ministering in Corinth: "I robbed other churches by accepting support from them in order to serve you" (2 Cor 11:8). And Paul clearly states that he received gifts δόμα [*doma*] in Phil 4:17–18. The Bible teaches us that Paul accepted both gifts and support, not one or the other.

There are two other remarkable aspects to Allen's understanding of the Pauline missionary passages about finances that stand out. First, even though Allen fell into the familiar trap of attempting to find one overarching set of principles that regulated all of Paul's financial support choices, Allen did grasp the underlying fact that Paul made purposeful choices based on individual missionary contexts. Allen writes, "It is of comparatively small importance how the finances of the Church are organized . . . its importance

---

50. Paton, *Roland Allen: The Ministry*, 70.
51. Paton, *Roland Allen: The Ministry*, 70–71.

lay wholly in the way in which it might affect those to whom he preached, never as though it made any personal difference to him."[52]

Allen understood that Paul approached his financial support choices with the same attitude as every other facet of his life that was not otherwise commanded by Christ. Paul followed a *become-all-things-to-all-people* pattern (1 Cor 9:19–23) when it came to financial support choices. Paul was not following some sort of apostolic code of honor or operating out of fear that the gospel might somehow be cheapened if he accepted payment for his ministry. He was leveraging everything at his disposal to reach people with the good news. It is curious that Allen both assigned a set of three overarching rules to Paul's financial choices *and* at the same time asserted that Paul made financial choices based on how it might affect those to whom he preached.

Second, Allen identified some of the same determining reasons for Paul's choices that Paul himself gives us in Scripture. Remember, Paul offered two didactic reasons and one evangelistic reason for choosing to support himself in certain ministry contexts and not others. The evangelistic reason Paul gave for his choice to support himself in Corinth was, "Nevertheless, we have not made use of this right, but we endure anything rather than put an obstacle in the way of the gospel of Christ" (1 Cor 9:12). Allen states, "What is of supreme importance is how these arrangements, whatever they may be, affect the minds of the people, and so promote, or hinder, the spread of the Gospel."[53] Likewise, even though Allen believed Paul "refused to receive anything from those who listened to him," he explains, "But he himself did not receive it [pay], and he was careful to explain his reason. He saw that it would be a hindrance to his work."[54] There it is, Allen identified a similar evangelistic "obstacle-to-the-gospel" reason that Paul provided for choosing to support himself in Corinth. Allen stated that accepting support would have been a hindrance, or an obstacle, to the gospel.[55]

---

52. Allen, *Missionary Methods*, 49.
53. Allen, *Missionary Methods*, 49.
54. Allen, *Missionary Methods*, 50.
55. As I have elucidated earlier in the book, the reason accepting traditional support from the believers in Corinth would have put an obstacle in the way of the gospel is because Paul would then be indistinguishable from the false apostles who were proclaiming another Jesus. It is true that Allen does not cite exactly *how* Paul's choice to support himself would alleviate hindrances to gospel ministry, but since Allen's work on Paul represents such a nascent stage of tentmaking research and discovery, we should be content and pleased that he was able to identify Paul's self-disclosed reasons for self-support directly from Scripture. Allen's observations were groundbreaking for his time and continue to elude many modern writers.

What is more, even though Allen lumped all of Paul's ministry contexts together, he still identified another one of Paul's self-disclosed reasons for choosing to support himself in certain ministry contexts. One of Paul's didactic reasons was to teach a strong work ethic by example and combat the problem of idleness. This was his self-disclosed reason for self-support in Thessalonica. As Allen lists the reasons why Paul did not accept support, he quotes 1 Thess 2:9 and observes, "He [Paul] was anxious to set them an example of quiet work."[56] There it is again, Allen identified a second one of Paul's reasons for self-support. Allen falls short of identifying Paul's third reason for choosing to support himself in Ephesus, which was to teach the church that they should be willing to go to great lengths in order to be in a position to give to the poor.

Allen was a pioneer thinker who challenged the conventional wisdom of his day. His experiences from front line cross-cultural missions and local parish ministry raised numerous internal concerns with the way missionaries and missionary societies operated. This prompted him to turn to the Bible for a period of study and consideration. In that way, Allen was the model of a practical theologian. He searched Scripture to determine what the normative missionary methods *ought to be*, he answered the descriptive question of what was going on within the missionary methods of his day, and then he proposed changes to bring contemporary practice into alignment with biblical methods.

---

56. Allen, *Missionary Methods*, 50.

9

Contemporary Church Planting Literature

In chapter 1, I noted that the contemporary church planting literature was divided when it came to an understanding of tentmaking. I cited a few examples and said we would examine several contemporary church planting authorities in more detail later in the book. Now that we have identified Paul's own self-disclosed didactic and evangelistic reasons for self-support, and have had an opportunity to review NT scholarship, a limited survey of church history, and Roland Allen, it is time to circle back to the contemporary church planting literature for a closer look. The purpose of conducting a brief review of contemporary church planting literature is similar to the reason we spent time interacting with the NT scholarship that has been written on tentmaking and Paul's self-support choices. It is important to recognize the overall lack of consensus on this topic.

The reason for identifying this lack of agreement will become clear later. For now, try to mentally take note of the wide-ranging opinions that appear within the contemporary literature review. Definitions vary greatly from one another and are occasionally found drifting completely unsecured from biblical moorings. Some authors make it all about the money, others all about the people, others all about gaining access to closed- or limited-access countries. Some authors advocate for the use of tentmaking, while one author argues against the use of tentmaking and implies that Paul made a mistake when he supported himself.

From an aerial view the whole scene looks rather chaotic, kind of like a circus. There are some exceptions of course, but instead of the church presenting a united front on the topic of tentmaking, we see fragmentation. My guess is that the reader will be surprised to find the total inattention (or mere obligatory mention) given by some of the authors to Paul's apostolic practice of self-support.

In order to help us sort through the material, the following information will, when possible, be gleaned from each author as they are considered:

1. Whether or not the author mentions tentmaking.
2. The author's definition of tentmaking and/or bivocational ministry.[1]
3. The author's understanding of how to appropriately use tentmaking.

J. CHRISTY WILSON

The first contemporary author to be considered is J. Christy Wilson Jr. Interestingly, Wilson's *Today's Tentmakers* is a book about tentmaking missionaries rather than a book about tentmaking as a church planting strategy. In other words, while Wilson dedicates the entire book to the subject of tentmaking, he does not directly connect tentmaking with church planting. He does frequently describe tentmaking as a method to intentionally reach the unreached which, most people would agree, would include planting churches. And some of his examples depict tentmaking missionaries who plant churches.

Wilson's definition of tentmaking was provided earlier in the book, but it is listed here again:

> But the Scriptures say that there are two types of cross-cultural witnesses. The first are those who receive full support from churches. This is the way the Apostle Peter was supported. On the other hand, the Apostle Paul earned his own salary by making tents. Even today, cross-cultural witnesses or "missionaries" fall into these two categories. Some are funded by the

---

1. Bivocational ministry and tentmaking are two different concepts and they will each be clearly defined later. However, at this point I recognize that many authors use these terms interchangeably, and so I will accept definitions of either one in this portion of the review. I do not want to exclude any author from the tentmaking discussion just because they do not distinguish between tentmaking and bivocational ministry and, for whatever reason, favor one term over the other.

contributions of fellow Christians, while others support themselves through various professions.²

We could summarize Wilson's definition by stating that he views tentmakers as cross-cultural missionaries who support themselves through various professions. Wilson believes that tentmaking missionaries should be used primarily in overseas cross-cultural missions. He further identifies two types of tentmakers:

> The first type, like the Apostle Paul, are principally motivated to go overseas to be witnesses for Jesus Christ, and their job is a means to this end. The second category are those who may suddenly find themselves assigned abroad by their company without having planned to go as a self-supporting missionary. Both types can render great service to the Lord.³

The problem with Wilson's definition of tentmaking, is that it is too broad to be useful. His definition would include just about any Christian who happens to be working outside of the United States, and every chapter of his book is written with the assumption that tentmakers are people who are working overseas and witnessing. According to Wilson, if someone is a Christian and is assigned to work on a project overseas, that means they have unintentionally stumbled into tentmaking without even realizing it.

In the next-to-last chapter of his book, Wilson waters down the definition of tentmaking so much that a person engaging in tentmaking is indistinguishable from an average lay Christian. Wilson states, "Just as the term 'missionary' can mean either a Christian in general or a special cross-cultural witness, in the same way the term 'tentmaker' can refer to many different categories of believers."⁴ This is followed by a discussion of how all Christians belong to the priesthood of believers and are called to witness to other people. It is baffling why Wilson attempts to stretch the meaning of this concept so thin. Wilson's understanding of tentmaking suffers from focusing exclusively on overseas missions, and his definition

---

2. Wilson, *Today's Tentmakers*, 15.
3. Wilson, *Today's Tentmakers*, 68.
4. Wilson, *Today's Tentmakers*, 141. I disagree with Wilson's belief that a missionary can refer to a general Christian. I find that particular understanding and definition of the term *missionary* unconvincing, unbiblical, and unhelpful. I believe it also devalues and disrespects the work that genuine missionaries do. The Bible makes distinctions between the various functions performed by different members of the church body, likewise we are not to dilute the definition of missionary until it reaches a point where all Christians and spiritual gifts are viewed with undifferentiated sameness. See 1 Cor 12:27–30.

ultimately disappoints because, by the end of the book, it has morphed into an overly broad and meaningless collection of generic life situations and ministry contexts.

JONATHAN LEWIS, TETSUNAO YAMAMORI, AND DON HAMILTON

The next contemporary author to be considered is Jonathan Lewis. Lewis edited a book titled, *Working Your Way to the Nations: A Guide to Effective Tentmaking*, which was autonomously touted as "the first-of-its-kind book of essays on effective tentmaking by experienced and knowledgeable missions specialists from around the world."[5] Yamamori provides a detailed definition of tentmaking:

> Tentmakers are what the Apostle Paul describes as "Christ's ambassadors" (2 Cor. 5:20). These ambassadors must be (1) physically, emotionally, and spiritually self-reliant; (2) adaptable; (3) biblically literate; (4) alert to the emerging mission context; (5) trained in meeting needs vital to the people group they seek to penetrate; (6) trained in long-term and low-profile evangelistic skills; (7) equipped with broad new strategic thinking; and (8) prepared with a special strategy for responding to opportunities presented by need.[6]

A perusal of the above definition shows that there are some points that could be said about any believer; for example, point number three: biblically literate. I would hope all pastors, missionaries, and lay Christians would be biblically literate. Another interesting observation about the above definition is that it says absolutely nothing about means of financial support. That seems odd, especially in light of the fact that the word "tentmaker" finds its etiological origin in the Apostle Paul who made tents to provide purposeful self-support. It would have been easy to include the phrase "financially self-supporting" in point number one. Perhaps the phrase *physically self-reliant* is supposed to communicate financial self-support, but if that is what Yamamori was trying to communicate, then why did he not just say so? Definitions, by nature, should be clear and precise. Physically self-reliant communicates the idea of being able to perform the various activities of daily living without assistance from others, especially when the phrase is combined with the traits of being emotionally and spiritually self-reliant.

5. Lewis, *Working Your Way*, v.
6. Lewis, *Working Your Way*, vi.

There also seems to be at least one point that does not match the example of Paul the tentmaker. Point number six says that tentmakers should be trained in low-profile evangelistic skills. Is this included because it was the way of Paul or the way of Christians who want to avoid persecution in hostile environments? Paul did *not* keep a low profile when he evangelized.

I think it is also worth pointing out that Yamamori cites 2 Cor 5:20 and says that when Paul uses the phrase *Christ's ambassadors* in that verse, he is describing tentmakers. But is that what Paul had in mind in that passage—tentmaking?[7]

Despite the questionable definition of tentmaker offered above, an alternative definition is offered by a separate contributor to Lewis' book. Don Hamilton acknowledges that some people have defined tentmaking so loosely that the label could be applied to anyone who is a Christian and working. He cites this definition and comments:

> "As long as you're living for Christ and earning your own living rather than being supported, then you're a tentmaker." There is probably some value to a loose definition like this. By and large, however, such a definition tends to confuse rather than clarify the concept . . . the following definition applies: *A "tentmaker" is a Christian who works in a cross-cultural situation, is recognized by members of the host culture as something other than a "religious professional," and yet, in terms of his or her commitment, calling, motivation, and training, is a "missionary" in every way.*[8]

I appreciate the way Hamilton resists the urge to water down the definition until it is meaningless, but his definition could be summarized as an undercover missionary. The NT does not present Paul as an undercover missionary who was recognized by his target group as something other than an apostle. Paul's custom was to enter the local synagogue and immediately engage the Jews. Paul's reputation among his target group was that of a passionate proclaimer of the gospel, and he often stirred up crowds and whole cities with his bold proclamation of Jesus Christ.

The reason, I believe, we see these types of clandestine phrases work their way into modern tentmaker definitions is because a tentmaker is viewed as a type of missionary who can penetrate closed-access, limited-access, or

---

7. In 2 Cor 5:18–20, Paul writing to the church in Corinth and explaining how, as an ambassador for Christ, he has been entrusted with the ministry of reconciliation. Followers of Jesus continue to act as Christ's ambassadors, not as apostles, but as representatives of Christ nonetheless who are entrusted with the gospel and sent to a spiritually dead world in need of reconciliation to God. The intent in 2 Cor 5:20 has absolutely nothing to to with self-support or tentmaking.

8. Lewis, *Working Your Way*, 2.

creative-access countries. Lewis' book mirrors Wilson's understanding of tentmaking as something a missionary does in overseas contexts. While Wilson mentions the advantage of reaching closed- or limited-access countries through tentmaking, Lewis' book is written with the presupposition that a tentmaker's sole purpose is to be a missionary to a closed- or limited-access country. Lewis writes, "To enter creative-access countries, Christian witnesses must use *tentmaking* strategies."[9] The obvious problem, or course, is that Paul did not make tents in order to gain access to closed- or limited-access countries. We do not have to go as far as saying this is a misuse of tentmaking, but we can confidently state that this was not Paul's motivation for making tents and purposefully choosing to support himself in certain ministry contexts and not others.

Lewis' book fails to see Paul accepting traditional support in some contexts and purposefully choosing to support himself in other ministry contexts. Instead, it seems to be written from the perspective that Paul never accepted support. As a result, the reasons the book suggests for why Paul made tents are askew. Some come close to identifying Paul's self-disclosed reasons, others do not. For example Detlef Bloecher, who is another contributing author to Lewis' book on tentmaking, cites modeling a work ethic.[10] But he also lists Paul wanting to avoid any accusations of wrong motives (such as greed), Paul not wanting to be burden on anyone, and that Paul made tents so he could be an example for new believers.[11] But that begs the question, what kind of an example, or, an example of what? Bloecher writes, "A tentmaker displays a harmonic merger of professional work and personal walk with the Lord as a suitable model for young believers."[12] The problem with offering that reason for tentmaking is that Paul never said that he was supporting himself in order that he could model the merger of professional work and personal walk with the Lord for young believers. Paul did give other reasons, which we have identified in chapter 4.

Lewis' book hits the bull's-eye in one respect. Tentmakers are presented as missionaries who are setting out to intentionally plant churches and start church planting movements. Yamamori writes, "The strategic shift required in today's mission context is to focus on mobilizing, training, fielding, and monitoring an army of men and women *called* to serve

---

9. Lewis, *Working Your Way*, 15.
10. Lewis, *Working Your Way*, 19.
11. Lewis, *Working Your Way*, 18–20.
12. Lewis, *Working Your Way*, 20.

as tentmakers, to plant a pioneer church movement in the midst of every unreached people group.[13]

Likewise, "The main goal of tentmaking is not evangelism but the establishment and growth of local churches."[14] It is always refreshing to see a link between tentmaking and church planting. Paul certainly linked the two together.

STUART MURRAY

Stuart Murray has contributed to the body of church planting literature, but has relatively little to say concerning tentmaking. Murray does not define bivocational ministry and he does not refer to bivocational work as tentmaking. However, slightly more than a page and a half on bivocational ministry from his book, *Church Planting: Laying Foundations*, supports the idea that a bivocational minister is a minister who is supporting himself through a secular job while at the same time providing leadership to a church plant.[15]

Murray states that church plants with bivocational ministers are "freed from the onerous financial commitment of supporting a full-time leader."[16] He sees other advantages of combining bivocational ministry and church planting such as churches becoming less dependent on professional leaders and an opportunity for the bivocational ministers to "escape an immersion in church culture that arguably hinders effective teaching, pastoral care, and spiritual leadership, as much as it reduces evangelistic impact."[17]

In his 2001 book, Murray devoted slightly over a page and a half to bivocational ministry out of a nearly three-hundred page book. In the concluding paragraph, he writes, "Bivocational leadership has too often been regarded as second class, suitable only for churches unable to afford a 'proper' minister, and for leaders lacking the skills to be full-time ministers. Perhaps it is time to reconsider the advantages of such leadership."[18] In his 2010 book on church planting, he only allocates a single paragraph to bivocational ministry, in which he says much of what he had to say in 2001, except with more brevity.[19] Ironically, the single paragraph on bivocational ministry is located six pages after a chapter subheading titled, "Learning

13. Lewis, *Working Your Way*, v.
14. Lewis, *Working Your Way*, 21.
15. Murray, *Church Planting*, 224–25.
16. Murray, *Church Planting*, 224.
17. Murray, *Church Planting*, 225.
18. Murray, *Church Planting*, 225.
19. Murray, *Planting Churches*, 170.

from the New Testament."[20] Sadly, no connection is made between apostolic practice and bivocational ministry or tentmaking. Paul is not mentioned in Murray's bivocational discussions.

ED STETZER

Ed Stetzer has received praise for the insight he has brought to the church planting table. One of his more prominent works, *Planting Missional Churches*, devotes an entire chapter, titled, *The Biblical Basis of Church Planting*, to examining what the Bible has to say about church planting.[21] Stetzer concentrates his analysis of NT church planting by focusing on the example of the Apostle Paul.

Stetzer includes an outline created by John Worcester that identifies nine primary characteristics about Paul the church planter. There are thirty-six bullet points under those characteristics and not one of them mentions tentmaking. In fact, throughout Stetzer's entire chapter devoted to analyzing apostolic and NT church planting methods, there is not one single reference to Paul's finances. There are no references to tentmaking. None. This is shocking, especially when Stetzer posed such questions as, "What did Paul do that was worthy of imitation? What did he want his readers, including us, to imitate?"[22] Tentmaking did not even warrant a footnote. This is incredible considering how often Paul wrote about his finances and how he went to great lengths to ensure his readers understood *why* he chose the support methods that he utilized. What is perhaps even more astonishing is that at the end of Stetzer's chapter, "The Biblical Basis of Church Planting," he listed Roland Allen's *Missionary Methods: St. Paul's or Ours?* as the first entry under "Resources for Further Reading."[23]

Bivocational ministry does surface later in Stetzer's 2006 book under the chapter titled, "Finding and Handling Finances."[24] He dedicates a few pages to self-supporting ministry under a chapter subheading called, "Get a Job."[25] Stetzer does not provide a formal definition of bivocational ministry or tentmaking, and his understanding of bivocational ministry appears to be grounded in practical reasons rather than on theological conclusions or apostolic methods. Stetzer quotes heavily from Steve Sjogren and Rob Lewin

20. Murray, *Planting Churches*, 164.
21. Stetzer, *Planting Missional*, 37.
22. Stetzer, *Planting Missional*, 44.
23. Stetzer, *Planting Missional*, 52.
24. Stetzer, *Planting Missional*, 220.
25. Stetzer, *Planting Missional*, 226.

and calls their book *Community of Kindness* an "excellent church planting book."[26] He advocates the use of bivocational ministry when planting missional or house-church communities, or when it is used as a temporary stepping stone toward full-time ministry. Stetzer also discloses a personal rationale for choosing bivocational ministry early in his career, "When I was unable to find adequate funding at my first church plant, I took a job insulating houses."[27]

In *Viral Churches*, Stetzer and Bird offer an entire chapter on church planting finances titled, "Funding: Partnerships Matter."[28] Within this chapter, they list several chapter subheadings that introduce and discuss various means of church planting support. Some of the subheadings include: "Money from Denominational Sources," "More Parent Churches," "Money from Church planting Networks," and "Money from Church Planting Churches."[29] Finally, near the end of the chapter they cover all of the other church planting funding options in a catch all chapter subheading titled, "Additional Funding Sources."[30] Within this section, there are seven paragraphs. Within one of those paragraphs, there is a sentence that lists all of the funding sources that have not already been named. Within that one sentence, bivocational work is listed within a series of several options separated by commas, "Whether the source is the denomination, a network or organization, a mother church, a partner church, bivocational work, the early launch team, or other individuals, the key to soliciting support is through authentic relationships."[31] The apostolic method that Paul purposefully and strategically chose to use in some of his missional church planting contexts is relegated to two words, mentioned almost as an afterthought, in a book on church planting.

Then, surprisingly, in Stetzer's 2016 revised edition of *Planting Missional Churches*, there is a noticeable shift in his presentation of bivocational ministry. The chapter titled "Finding and Handling Finances" was updated so that the subheading previously titled "Get a Job" now appears as "Bivocational/Tentmaking."[32] While much of this section remained unchanged, and

---

26. Stetzer, *Planting Missional*, 227. Steve Sjogren and Rob Lewin and their book, *Community of Kindness*, will be reviewed next.
27. Stetzer, *Planting Missional*, 229.
28. Stetzer and Bird, *Viral Churches*, 149.
29. Stetzer and Bird, *Viral Churches*, 150–55.
30. Stetzer and Bird, *Viral Churches*, 158.
31. Stetzer and Bird, *Viral Churches*, 158.
32. Stetzer and Im, *Planting Missional*, 170.

while he continues to quote generously from Sjogren and Lewin, there is the prominent inclusion of this fresh statement:

> Planters should not view bivocational planting as a penalty but as an opportunity. The Apostle Paul certainly viewed his bivocational position this way. Although he had the right to be compensated for gospel ministry (1 Cor 9:3–18), Paul, for the sake of effectively advancing the gospel, chose to build tents.[33]

This same section on bivocational ministry in the 2006 edition of *Planting Missional Churches* did not mention Paul by name—at all. Why is Stetzer suddenly talking about how Paul viewed his own self-support? Even more baffling, what caused Stetzer to start describing Paul's tentmaking as a purposeful choice, as I have been arguing throughout this book?[34]

Despite the fact that Stetzer's understanding of tentmaking appears to have, for whatever reasons, matured in the right direction between editions, he is still missing the big picture and presents conflicting messages about bivocational church planting by comparing Pauline tentmaking to inaccurate modern examples. For example, immediately after (correctly) saying that Paul chose to make tents in order to advance the gospel, he provides an example of a church planter turning to bivocational ministry due to the high cost of living in his target community:

> This is precisely what Cisco Cotto, lead pastor of the Village Church at Oak Park in Oak Park, Illinois, has done. Cisco made the decision early on—given the high cost of living associated with Oak Park—not only to be bivocational but also to have every leader at the Village Church be bivocational.[35]

But this is *not* precisely what Paul did. Paul did *not* decide to support himself because it was expensive to live in Corinth.

Another modern example of bivocational planting, new for the 2016 edition, portrays bivocational work as something that a planter can turn to when faced with desperate financial necessity. Stetzer writes:

> Seth Shelton also had to seek bivocational employment when planting The Way in Springfield, Missouri. Although his home

---

33. Stetzer and Im, *Planting Missional*, 173.

34. It is worth mentioning that one possible explanation for this change in Stetzer's thinking and writing on the topic of bivocational planting in his 2016 edition of *Planting Missional Churches* is because during the course of my DMin work at Reformed Theological Seminary in 2014, my faculty advisor shared my unpublished research on tentmaking with Ed Stetzer.

35. Stetzer and Im, *Planting Missional*, 173.

church affirmed his going to plant The Way, he had no money, no supplies, and few people. As a result, during the first five years of planting The Way, Seth worked as a full-time production manager at an aircraft repair station.[36]

Do you see the word *had* at the beginning of the above quote? So, on the one hand Stetzer tells us that Paul chose to make tents, but on the other hand he tells us that Seth Shelton *had* to turn to self-support. Which is it? Is tentmaking a purposeful choice or a financial backup plan that planters have to reluctantly turn to when forced into a corner?

Although Stetzer mentions bivocational ministry in his earlier literature, he fails to make any type of connection between tentmaking and apostolic method. He also appears to have understood tentmaking and bivocational ministry as funding options that could be selected when other, more traditional methods of support are unavailable or have been exhausted. In his later writing, he precipitously states that Paul chose to support himself. And while this is true, he leaves that isolated statement underdeveloped and anemic. Did Paul always make this choice to support himself? If not, what influenced his choices? How, exactly, did Paul's choice to support himself contribute to gospel advancement? Stetzer does not tell us. There is no follow-up discussion or supporting explanations about Paul the tentmaker. And lastly, the examples of bivocational ministry provided by Stetzer in 2016 actually communicated *contradictory* messages that conflicted both with the biblical model of tentmaking and with Stetzer's abrupt and minimalist statement that Paul made a purposeful choice. The Oak Park, Illinois, and Springfield, Missouri, examples present tentmaking/bivocational ministry as an option that could either help offset the high cost of living or act as a financial backup plan when traditional funding and support were unavailable.

STEVE SJOGREN AND ROB LEWIN

Steve Sjogren and Rob Lewin's *Community of Kindness* is another resource offered to those interested in planting and growing churches.[37] They do not supply a definition of tentmaking or bivocational ministry, but they do recommend that church planters take an outside secular job. Their rationale is not theologically based or linked with Paul's apostolic methods. They advocate working in the secular world while planting a church in order to

36. Stetzer and Im, *Planting Missional*, 171.
37. Sjogren and Lewin, *Community of Kindness*.

"destroy the sacred-secular conflict," and to "interact with the people in the market-place" so that the church planter is viewed by others as "functioning in the role of a 'normal' person outside the rank of pastor."[38] They also mention that working at another job in addition to church planting prevents the leader from avoiding the workplace and communicates the message that the leader is not "trying to live off other people."[39]

While Sjogren and Lewin offer various reasons for working, they view bivocational ministry as a temporary step in the church planting process. Their primary reasons for engaging in secular work while planting a church include community immersion and sending a type of *I'm-one-of-you* message to those inside and outside of the church being planted. They state, "Work in a nonchurch environment until the church grows larger. Work even if you don't need the extra income. You desperately need to get into the community. You need to work no matter what your financial backing looks like."[40]

It is curious to note that Sjogren and Lewin do not advocate tentmaking as a support option, nor do not link bivocational ministry with Pauline methods. It does seem as if they view secular work as something that could be discarded after a congregation reaches two-hundred.[41]

C. PETER WAGNER

C. Peter Wagner's book, *Church Planting for a Greater Harvest*, has been around since 1990.[42] Wagner does not attempt to define bivocational ministry or tentmaking, although he uses both terms.[43] Within a presentation of twelve ways to plant a church, Wagner offers the "Founding Pastor" as one of the valid models for planting churches.[44] Within the Founding Pastor model, the possibility of bivocational ministry and tentmaking is raised: "Frequently, the founding pastor is bivocational or a tentmaker. This is one of the major ways of cutting the costs of new church development, and I highly recommend it."[45]

---

38. Sjogren and Lewin, *Community of Kindness*, 173–74.
39. Sjogren and Lewin, *Community of Kindness*, 173.
40. Sjogren and Lewin, *Community of Kindness*, 172.
41. Sjogren and Lewin, *Community of Kindness*, 172–73.
42. Wagner, *Church Planting*.
43. Wagner, *Church Planting*, 72.
44. Wagner, *Church Planting*, 71. For all twelve of Wagner's models, see Wagner, *Church Planting*, 60–73.
45. Wagner, *Church Planting*, 72.

Wagner classifies tentmaking and bivocational ministry as a possibility for one particular church planting model, and also indicates that it has a practical side benefit of reducing costs. Wagner understands tentmaking as something that some church planting pastors do in order to get started: "Most plan to quit their job and give full time to the church as soon as they possibly can."[46]

E. ELBERT SMITH

I had not heard of E. Elbert Smith before researching tentmaking, but I was drawn to his work largely because of the title of his book, *Church Planting by the Book*.[47] It has a unique format that systematically walks through nine churches that appear in the book of Acts. As the title of the book suggests, Smith is interested in drawing church planting insights and conclusions directly from Scripture. Amen to that.

The first thing worth mentioning from Smith's work is that he correctly identifies the Philippian Church as one of the poorer churches that Paul established. When commenting on what he calls the "direction of the money flow," Smith writes, "This new Macedonian church, noted for its poverty (see 2 Cor 8:1–2), did not receive money from the missionary but gave money for the missionary's work in other places."[48] I agree with Smith's observation that the church in Philippi was one of the poorest, and yet Paul chose not to support himself in the Philippian ministry context. The significance of this fact indicates, as we discussed in chapter 2, that Paul's support choices were not based on whether or not a local church had the financial resources to support him by traditional means.

In Smith's chapter on the church in Corinth, there is a chapter subheading called, "Tentmaking."[49] Unfortunately, Smith misunderstands Acts 18:5 and concludes that Paul had been forced to work in Corinth as a tentmaker out of financial necessity, but promptly quit working once Timothy and Silas arrived from Macedonia with burden-relieving money. Smith states, "Paul worked during the week as a tentmaker until he received the offering from the Philippians. As soon as he received that economic support, he dedicated himself full time to the ministry."[50] However, this is not true. In chapter 3, we discussed how Acts 18:5 has served as the main wooden

---

46. Wagner, *Church Planting*, 73.
47. Smith, *Church Planting*, 73.
48. Smith, *Church Planting*, 111.
49. Smith, *Church Planting*, 132.
50. Smith, *Church Planting*, 133.

support board for the tentmaking background scenery that has been in place for so long. The prevailing view that understands Paul's tentmaking as a financial backup plan leans heavily upon translating Acts 18:5 in a way that suggests Paul had to wait for outside support before he could start devoting himself completely to full-time ministry. However, as was shown decisively in chapter 3, that is not what the Bible is saying in that verse.

But Smith has adopted the prevailing view and therefore concludes, "It appears that the reason Paul worked as a tentmaker, and one reason people do so today, was out of economic necessity. He supported his church planting with secular work, using his skill in a trade. One reason for tentmaking is economic need."[51] I would agree that one reason church planters turn to self-support *today* is out of economic necessity, but I would strongly disagree that Paul turned to tentmaking out of economic necessity. Is Smith forgetting about 1 Cor 9:1–12 and 2 Cor 11:1–15, where Paul explicitly tells us why he chose to support himself in Corinth? Paul plainly tells us why he purposefully chose to refuse Corinthian support, and none of his reasons have anything to do with financial necessity.

Smith provides one other rationale, or basis, for someone to engage in tentmaking, and that is to gain entrance into a city or country. Smith writes, "Another reason for tentmaking is to provide a worker entrance to a city."[52] I was surprised to see that Smith never specified what *type* of city, because other writers have recommended that tentmaking should be used to gain access to limited-, restricted-, or closed-access countries. The idea is that once a tentmaking missionary has gained entrance into a hostile environment under the guise of a legitimate worker, they can secretly carry out their missionary and evangelistic objectives. Tentmaking missionaries, then, are able to serve in politically restricted nations that traditional missionaries are unable to enter.[53] But Smith never mentions hostile environments or closed-access nations. He simply states that tentmaking is a way to gain entrance into a city or country—presumably any city or any country. Later, Smith summarizes his two reasons for tentmaking, "So the first reason for tentmaking is economic; the second is for an entrance into a city or country."[54]

There is nothing in his discussion about using tentmaking to gain entrance into a city that would indicate he has closed- or restricted-access nations in mind. That seemed off to me, or maybe negligent. Perhaps he

---

51. Smith, *Church Planting*, 133.
52. Smith, *Church Planting*, 133.
53. We saw this when we examined Jonathan Lewis' work, and we will see this understanding of tentmaking surface again later under our analysis of Ruth E. Siemens.
54. Smith, *Church Planting*, 134.

expects his readers to be so familiar with tentmaking as a strategy used to gain entrance into hostile environments that he did not feel the need to mention it? We cannot be sure, but if that was Smith's expectation, then readers have to fill in a lot of blanks on their own.

In order to back up his conclusion that tentmaking should be used to provide entrance to a city, he offers up an OT reference to Samuel offering a sacrifice at Bethlehem. Here is the full quotation:

> Another reason for tentmaking is to provide a worker entrance to a city. We see an example of such a motive in 1 Samuel 16. The Lord had commanded the prophet Samuel to go to Bethlehem and anoint one of the sons of Jesse as the next king. Samuel asked how he could do that since Saul would kill him when he heard of it. The Lord told him, "Take a heifer with you and say, 'I have come to sacrifice to the LORD'"(16:2). Sacrificing a heifer provided Samuel a secondary, legitimate reason to be in the city while he obeyed the Lord's primary command.
>
> The Lord has commanded sent-out ones to go—and sometimes getting a legitimate job is an excellent means of gaining entrance into the place God has sent a worker. Tentmaking provides a legitimate reason to be in a city.[55].

I re-read this section numerous times, until I finally realized that, yes, Smith is citing 1 Sam 16 as biblical grounds to support his belief that tentmaking, as modeled by the Apostle Paul, is to be used as a strategy to gain entrance to cities.

First, we should observe that there is no direct correlation between Samuel being commanded by God to anoint David as king and Pauline tentmaking. Is Samuel working to support himself while establishing a church? No. Is Samuel working to support himself for any reason? No. Is Samuel being paid wages in this passage? No. Samuel's actions in the 1 Sam 16 passage are completely and totally unrelated to Paul's tentmaking.

Second, Smith is attempting to point to 1 Sam 16 as biblical grounds for using tentmaking as a way of entering a city. But is Samuel working in order to gain access to a closed city? No. Is Samuel bringing a heifer to sacrifice so he can gain access to a city? No. In fact, the city is not *closed* to him. Samuel was not barred from entering the city and could have just walked into Bethlehem at any time. The passage is not, in any way, about gaining city entrance. It is about God commanding Samuel to anoint David. Samuel is fearful for his life and God describes what he wants Samuel to do, but this passage is not about Samuel trying to figure out how he will gain

---

55. Smith, *Church Planting*, 133–34.

entrance to Bethlehem. The city is not closed and Samuel is not working, or planting churches, or performing missionary work. The passage in 1 Sam 16 does not lend support to the idea that tentmaking should be used to gain access to cites.

What we *do* see in the 1 Sam 16 passage is God allowing the purpose of anointing David to be concealed behind the action of offering a sacrifice. God allowed Samuel's primary purpose for going to Bethlehem to be concealed behind a secondary and legitimate reason. I think this is what Smith ultimately is struggling to convey with his reference to 1 Sam 16. Smith is, I believe, attempting to show us a passage in the OT where God allowed someone to go about their real business while concealing it behind a secondary, yet still legitimate, action. Therefore, according to Smith, the church can and should use tentmaking to conceal their primary reason for being in a city, which is gospel proclamation, church planting, and general mission work, by working a legitimate and helpful job. But the problem with this line of thinking is that Paul never utilized tentmaking in that manner. The church does that today, but Paul did not. Smith has *started* with the church's modern misunderstanding of tentmaking, and then gone back into the OT to find a passage that is completely unrelated to tentmaking in order to find support. He has cited a passage that has absolutely nothing to do with tentmaking, and attempts to pull out an example that does not align with tentmaking.

1 Sam 16 does teach us something, but it does not teach us to use tentmaking like a crowbar to open up stubborn ministry contexts. It teaches us that God allowed Samuel's primary purpose for going to Bethlehem to be concealed behind a secondary and legitimate purpose. It was not yet time for David's anointing to be made public. But Paul never hid his primary purpose of preaching the gospel and evangelizing behind a secondary purpose. Paul spoke boldly and publically. God did not want Paul's identity or the preaching of the gospel to be concealed from public knowledge.

I realize that there are people who are able to penetrate restricted-access nations with the gospel because they are allowed entrance as secular workers. There is nothing wrong with that. What I am saying is that it is not tentmaking. Maybe the church can call it *heifering*, but it is not tentmaking. Paul never made tents to gain access to a ministry context.

Finally, if we are going to develop a proper biblical understanding of tentmaking, it makes sense to go to the NT passages that are most directly related to the topic. I do not understand why anyone would try to precariously set one of their reasons for tentmaking on the foundation of 1 Sam 16.

AUBREY MALPHURS

Aubrey Malphurs was one of the first authors I was directed to when I was considering church planting, so I picked up a copy of his 2004 book.[56] In this work, Malphurs views tentmaking and bivocational ministry as a final recourse that should be avoided if at all possible:

> It should be stressed that except in unusual circumstances any outside employment on the part of the church planting team must be viewed as temporary. Like most other ministries, church planting is a full-time responsibility. Anything less will hinder the work of this ministry.[57]

Even though Malphurs discourages church planters from utilizing an apostolic missionary method, and despite only dedicating slightly over a half page to the topic, he does connect tentmaking with Pauline practice and he does differentiate between tentmaking and bivocational ministry.[58] Malphurs defines tentmaking by linking it to Pauline example:

> In this [tentmaking] situation, church planters turn to a particular trade or profession only when there aren't enough funds available for their support. They may work one week and be off the next. The advantage is that they can determine when and how long they work. Paul is a good example of this. Periodically, he used his talents as an actual tentmaker to provide for his personal needs. He was able to schedule work around his ministry. (This is how we got the term tentmaker.)[59]

A couple of observations should be made about Malphurs' understanding and definition of tentmaking. First, he views tentmaking as a fallback strategy for financial support when "there aren't enough funds available."[60] But, we have looked at the biblical record and have seen that Paul did not make tents out of desperation or expediency when funding was unavailable. Second, although he links tentmaking with Paul and states that Paul was an example of tentmaking, Paul was not an example of someone who intermittently turned to tentmaking when funds were not available in a particular ministry context. Remember, Paul's boast to the Corinthians was that he, "refrained and will refrain from burdening you in any way" (1 Cor 11:9).

---

56. Malphurs, *Planting Growing Churches*.
57. Malphurs, *Planting Growing Churches*, 53.
58. Malphurs, *Planting Growing Churches*, 52.
59. Malphurs, *Planting Growing Churches*, 52.
60. Malphurs, *Planting Growing Churches*, 52.

This was followed by a solemn oath and the reason why he refused to accept support in Corinth. Paul was not an example of a minister who worked one week and then was off the next week when the tithes and offerings at the church in Corinth met budget. Paul was purposeful and goal-oriented with his support choices. Malphurs also defines bivocational ministry: "In this [bivocational] situation, church planters find regular employment that occupies a certain portion of their time every week. The disadvantage of a bivocational ministry is that the ministry has to be scheduled around the hours of the other job."[61]

In his more recent book, *The Nuts and Bolts of Church Planting*, Malphurs reveals a personal experience that sheds some light on why he possesses such a negative view of tentmaking and bivocational ministry: "During my first church plant, I attempted to work and found my second job most distracting and time-consuming."[62] Malphurs continues with these startling comments:

> I believe that having a second job can also give others the idea that you aren't completely committed to the new work. I realize that the Apostle Paul was a "tentmaker." However, I would say the same to him, and I believe he made tents only as a last resort. Keep in mind that for various reasons some people refused to support him. Therefore he made tents to provide for himself and a number of the churches he started.[63]

At least three things stand out from this excerpt from Malphurs. First, the unqualified readiness of Malphurs to correct and admonish the Apostle Paul is extremely off-putting and pregnant with hubris. I think we can all agree that Paul knew what he was doing and, by extension, that God rightly and sovereignly called and guided Paul to simultaneously proclaim the gospel and work as a tentmaker in certain ministry contexts. Second, as the biblical record testifies, Paul did *not* make tents only as a last resort. That statement by Malphurs is untrue. Third, who is Malphurs referring to when he instructs his readers to remember that there were people that refused to support Paul? That statement is also untrue. Paul did *not* make tents because people refused to support him, it was Paul who purposefully refused to accept support from some of the churches. In the immediate context of defending his right to receive support, but choosing not to, Paul writes in 1 Cor 9:12, "Nevertheless, we have not made use of this right, but endure anything rather than put an obstacle in the way of the gospel of Christ." In

---

61. Malphurs, *Planting Growing Churches*, 52.
62. Malphurs, *Nuts and Bolts*, 43.
63. Malphurs, *Nuts and Bolts*, 43.

1 Cor 9:15, Paul states, "But I have made no use of any of these rights, nor am I writing these things to secure any such provision." It is obvious that Malphurs is not a fan of tentmaking, but when he draws the conclusion that Paul made tents because the people he ministered to refused to support him, he is allowing his personal opinion to eclipse what is written in God's word.

Malphurs defines tentmaking and bivocational ministry, but his definitions are flawed and lack biblical support. He is one of the few authors to make the connection between tentmaking and Pauline missionary methods, but suggests that Paul was misguided in his missionary practices and could have benefited from Malphurs' advice. In the end, Malphurs' understanding of tentmaking contains echoes of his personal bias and is also unpleasantly contradictory to Scripture. Additionally, how should we react to a church planting authority who discourages leaders from using a missionary method described in the Bible?

RUTH E. SIEMENS

Ruth E. Siemens served as a missionary for twenty-one years in Latin America and Europe. She wrote an *International Journal of Frontier Missions* article titled, "The Vital Role of Tentmaking in Paul's Mission Strategy."[64] Siemens obviously views Paul's tentmaking as a purposeful part of his overall missionary strategy. Siemens writes, "He [Paul] would not have dedicated the better part of many days making tents had it not been a vital part of his mission strategy."[65] She correctly concludes that Paul made a purposeful choice to support himself. This is evident from the opening question in her article, "Why did Paul spend so much time doing manual labor when he did not have to do it?"[66] She correctly observes that Paul did not turn to tentmaking as a financial backup plan, "A major reason [why Paul's tentmaking example and teaching are largely ignored] is the common belief that Paul usually had church support, and only made tents during financial emergencies. I hope to show that this is a myth based on proof-texts taken out of context."[67] And, Siemens offers her own preliminary definition of tentmaking early in the article, "I will use the term *tentmaker* to mean missions-committed Christians

---

64. Siemens, "Vital Role."
65. Siemens, "Vital Role," 129.
66. Siemens, "Vital Role," 121.
67. Siemens, "Vital Role," 121–22. Later in her article, she cites Acts 18:5 and *correctly* points out that Paul did not quit working in response to Timothy and Silas arriving from Macedonia with funds.

who support themselves abroad, and make Jesus Christ known on the job and in their free time."[68] Later she writes that Paul's strategy gives definition to tentmaking:

> Tentmakers are mission-committed people who support themselves, and integrate work and witness, doing cross-cultural evangelism on the job and other ministries in their free time. If the definition omits the financial aspect—self-support, or the on-the-job evangelism, or the cross-cultural nature of that ministry, then it is not Pauline tentmaking![69]

Siemens' definition of tentmaking includes the element of cross-cultural evangelism. Did Paul engage in cross-cultural evangelism or was he reaching evangelistically pristine groups of people who had never heard the gospel but shared a similar cultural identity? I would argue the latter. All of the cities of Ephesus, Corinth, Thessalonica, and Philippi were part of the Roman Empire. All of them had been Hellenized and spoke Koine Greek as the *lingua franca*. All of them were located around the Aegean Sea and were port cities or near port cities. All of them had diaspora Jews and established synagogues, and all of them were able to support a traveling tentmaker who spoke their languages and could blend in on a cultural level with ease. The cities where Paul established churches were not dissimilar enough to necessitate a cross-cultural evangelism element in a biblical definition of tentmaking, as Siemens insists. In fact, the opposite is true. They were all very similar in nature.[70]

68. Siemens, "Vital Role," 121.
69. Siemens, "Vital Role," 128.
70. I am not arguing against the Great Commission mandate to take the gospel to all people groups. I am saying that the people groups that Paul was proclaiming the gospel to and establishing churches in, although in different geographic locations, all shared a similar cultural ethos. In addition, although there were diverse ethnicities represented in each of these cities, that does not mean that every time Paul traveled to another city around the Aegean Sea he was crossing into a completely novel and distinct ethno-linguistic ministry context. Thessalonica and Philippi were less than one-hundred miles away from each other. Paul himself was a Roman citizen born in Tarsus which was itself a Hellenized city located on the mouth of a river which emptied into the Mediterranean Sea. Tarsus was a junction point of land and sea routes and exceedingly similar to the cities where Paul planted churches. If anyone believes that Paul was participating in cross-cultural missions in the sense that we would normally think of them today, I would entertain an intelligent and documented rejoinder that could substantiate such a claim. Was Paul bringing the gospel to people who had not heard it? Yes. In that sense he was penetrating new people groups with the gospel. Unless someone brought the gospel to them, they were not going to hear it. Was Paul engaging in cross-cultural evangelism? No. Was Paul bringing the gospel to closed-, limited-, or creative-access ministry contexts? No. If the idea is to define tentmaking using only

Siemens' insistence on including a cross-cultural component to her definition of tentmaking does not reflect the biblical and historical record; instead, it exposes her desire to see tentmaking missionaries gain acceptance as legitimate missionaries. She writes, "Tentmakers are often made out to be second class."[71] Siemens describes tentmakers as a group of missionaries who are misunderstood by the larger missionary community, but who should be validated and supported: "They [tentmakers] receive little help or encouragement from their churches or the mission community because these do not understand the tentmaker approach to which the tentmakers are called by the Lord."[72] Elsewhere she writes, "The mission community is not even sure whether to accept tentmakers as valid workers."[73]

Siemens understands a tentmaker as a separate type of missionary who is well-suited for cross-cultural closed-access, limited-access, or creative-access countries. One of her key observations is that "Paul gives us a complete pioneering strategy for hostile environments."[74] But does he? Additionally, she writes, "Regular missionaries cannot do a better job in those countries since they cannot enter at all."[75] That may be, but does the biblical record portray Paul entering restricted areas? Did he have to pass through customs under the aegis of a tentmaker in order to pass a border checkpoint? The answer is no, Paul was able to travel freely to each of the cities where he established churches and walked unhindered into the local synagogue or public gathering place to speak. The Bible never portrays Paul's tentmaking as a strategy to gain access to restricted regions.

Although Siemens connects Paul and his tentmaking with the concept of purposeful missionary methods, her definition contains contemporary missional elements that are, I am convinced, unmaliciously imported for her convenience. She also views tentmaking as a subset or an elite corps of missionaries who are striving, or at least were striving in 1997, for acceptance and recognition among traditional missionaries, churches, and missionary societies.

---

biblically based elements from Paul's experience, then a cross-cultural component is not necessary, nor should it be included.

71. Siemens, "Vital Role," 128.
72. Siemens, "Vital Role" 128.
73. Siemens, "Vital Role," 128.
74. Siemens, "Vital Role," 129.
75. Siemens, "Vital Role," 128.

DAVID J. HESSELGRAVE

David J. Hesselgrave places emphasis on Pauline missionary methods in his book, *Planting Churches Cross-Culturally: North America and Beyond*.[76] In his chapter titled "Church Planting Strategy—The Pauline Cycle," Hesselgrave carefully walks through the biblical model laid out for us in Scripture.[77] He also makes a direct and unapologetic appeal to Paul's missionary practices as a guiding template for the contemporary church. Hesselgrave states:

> It would be foolhardy for us to disregard the Holy Spirit-inspired record of the way in which the early Christians, and especially Paul and his cohorts, actually built up the churches of their day as it would have been for Paul to disregard the Holy Spirit's guidance received in Arabia and Antioch . . . We must ask whether or not Pauline strategy is applicable in our day. To that question we answer yes.[78]

Hesselgrave stresses the importance of following Pauline principles and says that "church planners and planters should always be faithful to biblical principles, and they should always be attentive to biblical precedents."[79]

The rest of the chapter unpacks the Pauline method of evangelism and church planting. The cycle is described in detail with an accompanying illustrative model that displays this cycle as a wheel that repeats itself. Tentmaking is absent throughout the discussion. Toward the end of the chapter, Hesselgrave writes, "It is of vital importance that the Pauline Cycle strategy be applied to existing churches as well as to pioneer situations."[80] The reader is left to assume that tentmaking and Paul's methods of support are not strategically significant enough to be included in the Pauline cycle of evangelism and church planting.

Interestingly, Hesselgrave quotes Roland Allen later in his book.[81] Hesselgrave highlights Allen's three rules that we examined previously near the end of chapter 8. He also notes that Allen "was not hard-pressed to find certain exceptions to these rules."[82] But the conclusion that Hesselgrave reaches is that church planters need to be cautious about bringing too many

---

76. Hesselgrave, *Planting Churches*.
77. Hesselgrave, *Planting Churches*, 42–51.
78. Hesselgrave, *Planting Churches*, 44.
79. Hesselgrave, *Planting Churches*, 46.
80. Hesselgrave, *Planting Churches*, 50.
81. Hesselgrave, *Planting Churches*, 73, 76.
82. Hesselgrave, *Planting Churches*, 76.

resources to bear on the target area because it might inhibit indigenous local initiative. At the same time, planters should not burden the target area by withholding resources and expecting too much too soon.[83] That is all Hesselgrave has to say about church planting finances in a book that underscores the importance of following Pauline missionary methods.

Hesselgrave does not provide a definition of tentmaking or bivocational ministry. He also fails to make a connection between Paul's missionary methods and tentmaking. Due to the complete lack of tentmaking or bivocational material, Hesselgrave's understanding of this Pauline missionary method is indeterminable. It should be noted that Hesselgrave's research and presentation of the Pauline church planting cycle is exceptionally well done.

DARRIN PATRICK

Darrin Patrick delivers a work on church planting that places more emphasis on the spiritual formation of the church planter than church planting methods, but he is included in this study because many potential church planters have this type of book shoved into their hands by well-meaning denominational officials. *Church Planter: The Man, the Message, the Mission* communicates the belief that Paul's methods and biblical precedents are important enough for the church today to pay attention to and follow: "Because the New Testament church is centered on the life and work of Christ, it takes the commands of Christ seriously. Consequently, gospel-centered, missional churches in the twenty-first century will imitate churches in the book of Acts."[84]

Patrick quotes 1 Cor 9:19–23 and suggests that churches today should become all things to all people: "Paul was so zealous to win people for Christ that he was willing to adapt his methods and lifestyle in order to be as winsome as possible."[85] Patrick lists sermon style, seeking out new speaking venues, and naming well-known philosophers as examples of Paul contextualizing his methods in order to become all things to all people, so that by all means, he might save some.[86] Financial support is not listed as an example of contextualization or as a purposeful methodological choice.

Patrick does not mention or define tentmaking, nor does he connect tentmaking with Pauline missionary methods. Like Hesselgrave, the absence of a tentmaking discussion in Patrick's work prohibits us from drawing any

83. Hesselgrave, *Planting Churches*, 76–77.
84. Patrick, *Church Planter*, 190.
85. Patrick, *Church Planter*, 205.
86. Patrick, *Church Planter*, 204–07.

conclusions. In his defense, he did not discuss church planting finances anywhere in his book. However I suppose, at a minimum, that in itself makes a statement about Patrick's understanding of how important financial support choices are within a book intended to prepare church planters for the task of planting Acts-like churches.

TIM KELLER AND ALLEN THOMPSON

The Redeemer Church Planting Center *Church Planter Manual,* written by Timothy J. Keller and J. Allen Thompson, is regularly used to train international church planters.[87] The manual recommends authors such as Hesselgrave, Malphurs, and Roland Allen as resources for further study. There is no section of the manual dedicated to finances, but it is written with the expectation that finances, which presumably include the lead planter's support, will be raised.

Tentmaking is brought up briefly within a case-study examination of Paul in Ephesus. Paul's tentmaking is viewed as having value because it promoted community involvement and provided unbelievers access to Paul. The application for church planters was not that they should use self-support as a purposeful missionary method, but that they should be "fully engaged in the civic life of the city" and "accessible and engaging."[88]

Keller and Thompson do not provide a definition of tentmaking. They do make a connection between tentmaking and Pauline missionary methods, but it is unclear if they view tentmaking as a purposeful choice by Paul, or if was partially or wholly motivated by financial need. Their understanding of tentmaking is that Paul lived and worked in the communities he was ministering to, and his tentmaking work shows contemporary church planters that they, too, should become involved in their target communities and find a way to be accessible and engaging.

J.D. PAYNE

J.D. Payne is an associate professor at Samford University and has written extensively on missions and evangelism. The first thing that stands out about Payne is that in his 2009 *Discovering Church Planting: An Introduction to the Whats, Whys, and Hows of Global Church Planting,* he dedicates an entire chapter to tentmaking called, "Tentmaking and Church Planting."[89] Payne

---

87. Keller and Thompson, *Church Planter Manual.*
88. Keller and Thompson, *Church Planter Manual,* 236–37.
89. Payne, *Discovering Church Planting,* 361–79.

clearly states his definition of tentmaking, or tentmaker, in more than one source.[90] Payne writes that a tentmaker is, "*A missionary who is focused on evangelism that results in churches and who is financially supported by a marketable skill, trade, and/or other nonministerial source of income.*"[91] Payne successfully resists the temptation to follow so many other missiologists and place cross-cultural language in his definition of tentmaking. Moreover, he includes a church planting element in his definition. I applaud Payne's courage to define tentmaking solely on the basis of the biblical record, even though it means narrowing the definition.

He also distinguishes tentmaking from bivocational ministry and provides a definition of a bivocational missionary: "A bivocational missionary is someone who receives a portion of his or her salary from a church and/or denomination and another portion of salary from a non-clergy type of employment."[92] Clearly, Payne views tentmakers and bivocational missionaries as types of missionaries.[93]

Before providing his reasons why church planters should consider tentmaking when planting churches, Payne offers a summary statement that accurately captures how tentmaking has been utilized for practical reasons in overseas cross-cultural missionary contexts, but relatively ignored by those in Western nations unless they have no other options:

> Because traditional missionary approaches are prohibited in certain countries, the Church needs a legitimate way to minister within those nations, and tentmaking provides a means of gaining entrée. In contrast, Western nations have been more open to missionary activities, and so tentmaking is rarely on anyone's

---

90. Payne defines tentmaker with almost identical language in "Tentmaking and North American Church Planting," a paper presented to the Southeastern Regional EMS (March 18–19, 2005) Louisville, Kentucky, and in *Discovering Church Planting: An Introduction to the Whats, Whys, And Hows of Global Church Planting* (Colorado Springs, CO: Paternoster, 2009), 363–64.

91. Payne, *Discovering Church Planting*, 363–64.

92. Payne, *Discovering Church Planting*, 364.

93. This should prompt us to ask if Payne views pastors as a type of missionary, since pastors plant churches and sometimes utilize tentmaking. Payne devotes an entire chapter to explaining his view on whether or not church planters are pastors or missionaries, and suggests that church planters fall into one of two categories: "apostolic missionaries" or "missional pastors." Apostolic missionaries most closely resemble the NT model of Paul. Missional pastors are those who plant a church and remain pastoring the church after it has been established, and are the most commonly found church planter type in Western nations. Payne argues that church planters should, in most cases, be apostolic missionaries, with missional pastors being allowed as the exception. For a more thorough understanding of his views on this topic, see Payne, *Discovering Church Planting*, 381–91.

mind unless there is a financial crisis facing a denomination or mission agency. When this happens, the Church considers tentmaking or bivocational options out of pragmatic, rather than theological and missiological, convictions.[94]

Payne follows this opening explanation by listing eight reasons why tentmaking should be utilized. Keep in mind that his eight reasons for using tentmaking are part of a larger argument he is making for the legitimate use of tentmaking by Western nations which are not considered evangelistically closed- or creative-access nations. Having said that, Payne refreshingly lists "biblical support" as his number one reason to utilize tentmaking in places like the United States.[95] He adds, "If the concept of tentmaker is going to be supported by biblical evidence, then the textual evidence requires the tentmaker also to be involved in church planting."[96]

The rest of Payne's reasons for using tentmaking as a legitimate missiological church planting method are practical in nature. For example, he references Sjogren and Lewin's instructions for church planters to work even if they do not need the income as a strategy to break down the wall between clergy and laity. Payne also advocates tentmaking because self-support would enable planters to gain credibility with the people they are attempting to reach. He states that it would decrease church planters' dependency on denominational support, while at the same time relieve the general financial strain that plagues so many church planters. He notes that tentmaking church planters would be freed from restrictive guidelines and benchmarks placed on them by denominations or supervising multiplication teams that often provide funding with strings attached. Finally, Payne notes that tentmakers may enjoy a level of satisfaction from their secular jobs that may offset ministry discouragements or periods of fruitlessness.[97]

Payne insightfully provides this reason for Paul's tentmaking: "Partly as a way to become all things to all people so he could win some."[98] I would of course ask the follow-up question: How did Paul's refusal to accept payment remove any hindrance to the spread of the gospel? The answer was explained in chapter 4; it was how Paul distinguished himself from the other "false apostles."

Payne provides a *biblically* grounded definition of tentmaking. He also provides a clear definition of bivocational ministry. Payne understands

---

94. Payne, *Discovering Church Planting*, 366.
95. Payne, *Discovering Church Planting*, 366.
96. Payne, *Discovering Church Planting*, 367.
97. Payne, *Discovering Church Planting*, 367–70.
98. Payne, "Tentmaking and North American," 16.

tentmaking as something that must lead to the establishment of new churches and he convincingly promotes tentmaking as a viable missiological method for North American church plants. Finally, he rightly perceives that tentmaking should not be a fallback option for desperate times: "I do not agree with those who have advocated that tentmaking should only be the option 'in the absence of another means of full support' and that 'self-support is legitimate as a temporary option.'"[99] Among contemporary authors, Payne stands out as one who has spent some serious time exploring tentmaking and, as a result, consistently reaches solid biblically based conclusions.

CONCLUDING REMARKS

Several contemporary authors and missiologists have been presented in order to summarize their understandings and definitions of tentmaking and bivocational ministry. What we have found is that within the contemporary literature, the definitions of tentmaking vary widely. Some authors do not provide a definition or description of tentmaking. Some authors do not mention tentmaking even when they are discussing Paul's missionary methods and church planting finances. Among those that do offer tentmaking definitions and recommendations, there is inconsistency and disagreement over what it is and the role it should play in missionary and church planting efforts. The primary reason for the confusion over how to properly define and implement tentmaking, in this author's analysis, is due to a lack of understanding and agreement on how and why *Paul* selectively used tentmaking. In other words, the problem originates further upstream. Should we really expect everyone to be on the same page regarding how to apply and use tentmaking if not everyone agrees with what the Bible has to say about Paul's tentmaking and support choices?

Before we can move toward any type of tentmaking recommendations or models for sound implementation as a purposeful missiological method, it will be beneficial to evaluate the similarities and differences between biblical Pauline tentmaking practice (chapters 2 and 4), and how tentmaking has been understood and implemented by the church in both historical and contemporary contexts (chapters 3, 5, and 7–9). We need to compare Paul's understanding of tentmaking with the church's understanding of tentmaking. We have laid each of these garments out on top of the bed side by side, but now we need to put them on at the same time and stand in front of the mirror to see if they match—or clash.

---

99. Payne, "Tentmaking and North American," 16.

10

Business as Mission

Before we compare the way Paul understood and practiced tentmaking to how the church has historically understood and practiced tentmaking, there is one additional area of contemporary missiology that needs to be examined. Business as Mission (BAM) is a relative newcomer to the missions table, and it will be helpful for our overall understanding of tentmaking if we can determine how BAM and tentmaking are related. Are BAM and tentmaking eating off of the same plate, or do they each deserve their own chair at the missions table? If they are related, or even synonymous as some insinuate, then why coin a new term? Why not just call BAM, tentmaking? And if that is the case, then we could assume we are automatically including BAM whenever we discuss tentmaking. If they are not related, then BAM should not be taken into consideration when discussing tentmaking. We need to take a look at what people are saying about BAM. But be warned: the world of BAM may very well be more confusing than the contradictory and fragmented contemporary church planting literature we just finished reviewing in chapter 9.

PATRICK LAI

Patrick Lai and Neal Johnson have both offered weighty four-hundred plus page tomes that introduce, describe, and attempt to promote BAM. Remarkably, Lai uses BAM and tentmaking synonymously throughout his writing. The title of Lai's book, *Tentmaking: The Life and Work of Business as Missions*, reveals his understanding that if someone is engaging in tentmaking, then they are engaging in BAM.[1]

Lai references the Tentmaking Task Force of the Lausanne II Congress and suggests that in order to develop an accurate definition of tentmaking (and ostensibly BAM), the Lausanne Task Force considerations should be taken into account.[2] These considerations include: called to minister, religious ministry, secular identity, intentionality, training, cross-cultural, closed country—RAN, CAN, resident visa, and source of salary.[3] But if we are determined to allow the Bible to define tentmaking, can elements such as *resident visa* and *closed country* be permitted? Paul never obtained a resident visa or visited a closed country.

Lai notes, "The Lausanne Tentmaking Task Force failed in its assignment to define what a tentmaker is."[4] Nevertheless, Lai ends up incorporating the Lausanne Tentmaking Task Force recommended considerations into his definition of tentmaker:

> Tentmakers, as missionaries, are called to minister the gospel of Jesus cross-culturally. Tentmakers are intentional in serving God. To that end, tentmakers pursue appropriate training, which equips them for a measurable religious ministry while living among the people they are called to reach. Tentmakers have a non-missionary identity. Some tentmakers are supported wholly by their jobs, while others receive support from churches and Christian friends.[5]

Lai expands his definition by developing an elaborate tentmaking taxonomy that intentionally mirrors Ralph Winter's evangelism classification system.

1. Lai, *Tentmaking*.
2. The Lausanne II Congress was an international congress, or conference, on world evangelization held in Manila, Philippines, from July 11 to July 20, 1989 with over four-thousand church leaders in attendance. It is sometimes simply called "Lausanne II." The first international conference on world evangelism took place in Lausanne, Switzerland, in 1974; hence the name, "Lausanne."
3. RAN stands for *restricted-access nations*, and CAN stands for *creative-access nations*.
4. Lai, *Tentmaking*, 20.
5. Lai, *Tentmaking*, 21.

Lai identifies five groups of tentmakers that he labels alpha-numerically: T-1, T-2, T-3, T-4, and T-5.[6] While interesting, an in-depth analysis of Lai's tentmaking taxonomy is unnecessary for the purpose of this book. It is enough to note that Lai attempts to advance the definition of tentmaking by breaking it down into even smaller subcategories of what is already viewed by many as an offshoot and specialization of traditional missionary work. Lai also defines a bivocational worker as

> a cross-cultural missionary who utilizes his or her "secular" skills as a means to gain entry/residence to serve in an area where "missionary" visas are restricted or not issued. The bivocational individual (also referred to as a "tentmaker") has two vocations (one being a missionary, the other being a job in business or NGO, teaching, etc.). This individual prepares for and is accountable to both vocations.[7]

Like many others, Lai attempts to identify the reasons Paul made tents: "First he sometimes worked to supplement his income so as not to burden those to whom he was ministering (1 Cor 9:12; 1 Thess 2:9). Second, he worked to identify with people and make friendships through which he could share his faith (Acts 18:2–3)."[8] As discussed in chapter 4, Paul's self-disclosed reasons for purposefully choosing to support himself in some ministry contexts and not others were not to earn burden-relieving income or to make friends. Lai needs to ask and answer the next logical question: Why did Paul refrain from burdening the churches where he intentionally refused their traditional support? Incidentally, how can Acts 18:2–3 legitimately demonstrate that Paul turned to tentmaking in order to identify with people and make friends? Paul was adept at proclaiming the gospel in all settings and to all people. He did not need to set up shop as a tentmaker in order to share his faith.

Lai summarizes his understanding of related tentmaking terminology by writing, "After reading hundreds of articles on ministry, missions, the marketplace, and work, I believe tentmaking is a subset of mission work. Thus, I have chosen to use the terms *worker*, *missionary*, and *tentmaker* interchangeably. The term *tentmaker* is used because of its historical and biblical implications."[9] This, coupled with his definition of bivocational worker and his synonymous use of BAM and tentmaking, leads to the conclusion

---

6. For a complete explanation of Lai's tentmaking classification system, see Lai, *Tentmaking*, 21–29.

7. Lai, *Tentmaking*, 383.

8. Lai, *Tentmaking*, 11.

9. Lai, *Tentmaking*, xii.

that Lai sees very few differences between the meanings of tentmaking, bivocational ministry, BAM, and missionary work in general. For Lai, the differences that do exist appear to be subtly nuanced and overlapping, not clearly defined and separated.

C. NEAL JOHNSON

We saw that Lai makes almost no differentiation at all between tentmaking and BAM. Johnson on the other hand does *not* present the two as interchangeable. In fact, Johnson takes great care to distinguish tentmaking from BAM by stating: "BAM is broadly defined as a for-profit commercial business venture that is Christian led, intentionally devoted to being used as an instrument of God's mission [*missio Dei*] to the world, and is operated in a crosscultural environment, either domestic or international."[10] However, Johnson is not confident enough of his definition of BAM to leave it unqualified. He adds, "I am compelled to state that any definition of BAM—including my own working definition on the previous page—is by its nature limiting and therefore inadequate."[11]

Likewise, the 2004 Lausanne Working Group 30 on BAM composed of sixty-eight BAM activists from twenty-eight different countries could not arrive at a consensus on how to define BAM. Johnson comments on this 2004 Lausanne work group, "After a week of meetings, our group concluded that it was virtually impossible to achieve a universally satisfactory definition of BAM."[12] Let that sink in for a moment. An international team of sixty-eight experts on BAM met for a week, and they, the global authorities on BAM, could not even define it.

Despite the inability of Johnson or the 2004 Lausanne work group on BAM to arrive at a definition of BAM, Johnson remains undeterred and charges ahead by drawing lines of distinction between BAM and tentmaking. At the same time, he simultaneously maintains that BAM and tentmaking are related because they both belong to what Johnson calls the Marketplace Mission Movement (MMM), which he immediately admits is "quite young and ill-defined."[13] This young and ill-defined MMM, itself a form or subcategory of missions, is nonetheless "dividing into four distinct, self-selected camps: tentmaking, marketplace ministries, enterprise development, and Business

---

10. Johnson, *Business as Mission*, 27–28.
11. Johnson, *Business as Mission*, 28.
12. Johnson, *Business as Mission*, 28.
13. Johnson, *Business as Mission*, 112.

as Mission."[14] So, Johnson understands tentmaking as one of four different types of distinct camps within the MMM. He does not view tentmaking and BAM as equivalent, but they are related, and he does not consider tentmaking the same thing as what he calls, "regular missionaries."[15] Are you confused yet? In the end, Johnson describes BAM as a tool to improve local social and economic conditions, "This cycle is the heart of BAM's business-development component: creating businesses that create jobs that put money in the hands of marginalized people and thereby allows them to climb onto the bottom rung of the economic development ladder."[16]

Here is a question that should be posed to Johnson and others: Since there is no consensus to what BAM or tentmaking means, is this pursuit of new terminology and descriptive labeling helpful? Does it bring clarity to missional activity, or does drawing divisions and imposing additional niche classifications between similar and overlapping activities actually exacerbate the confusion? I would argue the latter.

When Johnson attempts to describe why Paul supported himself by making tents, he states:

> Paul understood the vital importance of the marketplace to himself, to the gospel and to mission. It not only helped him to make a living but, in so doing, illustrated the reality and relevance of Jesus and his message in the real world.[17]

Johnson continues to explain tentmaking to his readers:

> No matter where he [Paul] went, it helped him financially while he preached the gospel . . . In the popular mind it quite simply means making your money in your business so that you can afford to do ministry outside of the business . . . making money *here* so that he or she can preach the gospel *out there*.[18]

In response to Johnson, I would point out that Paul did not make tents everywhere he went, and when he did make tents, it was a choice. Paul purposefully and intentionally refused traditional payment. Paul did not make tents because he needed the money to finance a preaching mission that would otherwise grind to a halt. Paul never *had* to make tents so he could go and preach the gospel.

---

14. Johnson, *Business as Mission*, 112.
15. Johnson, *Business as Mission*, 125.
16. Johnson, *Business as Mission*, 35.
17. Johnson, *Business as Mission*, 115.
18. Johnson, *Business as Mission*, 115.

OTHER BAM VOICES

Let's go ahead and take a brief look at a couple of other BAM perspectives. Michael R. Baer writes about BAM with the motivation of eliminating the division that he perceives exists between the sacred and the secular, specifically between business and missions. Baer believes that there are many genuine believers who "simply don't see any connection between their Christianity and their business lives."[19] Instead of being Christians who run businesses, Baer's desire is to see Christians seamlessly integrate their businesses and the Great Commission. Business owners will accomplish this integration by discovering and living out what he calls their unique, "kingdom purpose."[20] Much of his book on BAM is devoted to helping the reader take steps to discover their particular kingdom purpose, and then guiding them through the process of transforming their business so that it holistically serves that unique kingdom purpose.

Now, notice that Baer does not present BAM in a way that aligns with Lai or Johnson. Baer does not view BAM as being synonymous with tentmaking, and he does not see BAM as a way to create jobs and help marginalized people climb up the socioeconomic ladder with the end goal of improving the overall well-being of a society. According to Baer, BAM is all about getting Christian business owners to "set aside their own purposes and submit fully to God's purposes for their enterprises."[21] Baer continues, "It is this action, more than any other, that distinguishes a kingdom company from a company run by Christians. Kingdom business is intentional."[22]

Unfortunately, this conception of BAM is neither novel, nor something that deserves to be recognized as a distinct missional entity. What Baer is describing is average spiritually regenerate business owners genuinely living out their faith. It has been said that one definition of revival is the church doing what she ought to be doing. The church *ought* to be engaged in fervent prayer and aggressive evangelism. She *ought* to be gathering frequently for Spirit-filled worship where Scripture is powerfully and unapologetically proclaimed, and so forth. Except often times the church is not doing all these things. Therefore, when the church actually does do everything she ought to be doing, it seems so unusual that we exclaim that there must be some sort of a revival going on. In the same way, Christian business owners *ought* to "set aside their own purposes and submit fully to God's purposes

---

19. Baer, *Business as Mission*, 140.
20. Baer, *Business as Mission*, 50.
21. Baer, *Business as Mission*, 50–51.
22. Baer, *Business as Mission*, 51.

for their enterprises."[23] They *ought* to be doing this all the time. Baer provides a vision of what it would look like if business owners embraced his understanding of BAM:

> Imagine what could happen if every Christian businessperson recognized that God had a purpose for his or her company that was greater than profit, employment, or customer satisfaction. Imagine if the vast number of believing business owners and operators were to turn their companies over to God to use for his glory. Imagine the power and joy of integrating business and faith for God's kingdom. Think of the financial, technological, and human resources that would come into play. Think of the ways in which entire societies could be transformed for Christ.[24]

See what I mean? If you are a Christian who owns a business, then you should already recognize that God has a purpose for your company. You should already have turned your company over to God to use for his glory. Consider the alternative for a moment. What if we encountered a professing believer who stated that they had thought about it and decided not to allow their business to serve God's kingdom purposes? After much reflection, they decided that they did not want to seek the glory of God in all that they do, and that they thought it would be best if they compartmentalized their faith and their work life. What would we say to that? We would say that they are a nominal believer—not really a Christian.

Much of the book follows this same pattern. For example, Baer states that one of the characteristics of a kingdom business is operational excellence. Operations, according to Baer, "refers simply to the how of running a business. I am using the term in its broadest sense to describe all the various functions of business—strategy, HR, financial management, IS, technology, sales, and service."[25] One of the defining characteristics of a kingdom business is that the business operates with excellence? Should not all Christian-owned companies operate with excellence? Do not many purely secular businesses pursue operational excellence? Baer attempts to make his point for operational excellence as a defining characteristic of kingdom businesses by giving the example of how no one would respect a pastor who demonstrated a lack of excellence in his preparation, study habits, or administration. But by making this comparison, Baer shows that operational excellence *is* a universal trait that all Christians should pursue no matter who they are, regardless of vocation. Operational excellence is not something that belongs

---

23. Baer, *Business as Mission*, 50–51.
24. Baer, *Business as Mission*, 9–10.
25. Baer, *Business as Mission*, 119–20.

to the business world, let alone a unique characteristic belonging to *kingdom companies*. We all ought to be pursuing excellence in all we do, all the time.

Some other areas of his BAM presentation are straw man polemics. For example, he spends an entire chapter defending business as a "good thing from God."[26] Baer starts with this presupposition, "In much of the world there is a fundamental conviction among sincere Christians that there is something intrinsically wrong with business and that no serious follower of Christ would go into business, much less consider it a calling."[27] I am not sure where all these people are that think business is evil. I have yet to meet one person who espouses this view. I think most people realize that there can be evil people who are involved in business without believing that *business* itself is inherently evil. By the same token, Bible-believing Christians understand that there can be evil people involved in politics, but that does not necessarily lead to the conclusion that all Christians philosophically think that all civil government is evil. Yet, Baer seems to think that many in the church believe business is evil, and it is within the chapter on defending the non-evil nature of business that he cites Paul and tentmaking. Baer argues that since Paul engaged in a tentmaking business, this means that business is not evil.

Although Baer's presentation of BAM is different than Lai and Johnson, it suffers from being indistinct from what Christian business owners already *ought* to be doing, and it ultimately goes too far. In his attempt to break down the dividing line between secular and sacred, business and mission, Baer writes:

> There is no difference between doing a deal and serving communion. Life is a whole and is holistically submitted to God's authority. Wherever they are and whatever they are doing, they are serving and worshiping the Master. There is no sacred and secular, no dichotomy. There is no business and ministry. All is sacred. All is ministry.[28]

Except there is a difference between doing a deal and serving communion. The Lord's Table is one of two sacraments instituted by Jesus Christ and is, among other things, the nonverbal proclamation of the gospel and an ordinary means of grace. A business deal is not a sacrament, and the faithful church, as well as the faithful business owner, will want to keep that division between the secular and sacred firmly in place.

---

26. Baer, *Business as Mission*, 25–34.
27. Baer, *Business as Mission*, 25.
28. Baer, *Business as Mission*, 142.

Rundle and Steffen will be the last BAM perspective we review before ultimately deciding how BAM compares with tentmaking. I appreciate how Rundle and Steffen quickly describe the kind of BAM they are *not* advocating, "This is not a book about microenterprise development. As valid as helping poor people start their own businesses may be, what we are describing is a fundamentally different approach to economic and spiritual development."[29] If you recall, this is essentially how Johnson viewed BAM—starting businesses to improve the economic and social conditions of a people and a society, so Rundle and Steffen are not portraying BAM as something used to fight poverty and move a society up the socioeconomic ladder.

They describe BAM as having a "humanitarian and transformational purpose" through the establishment of Great Commission Companies (GCC).[30] Rundle and Steffen believe that the Bible's overall message is that good triumphs over evil, and that by establishing GCCs that exemplify and model the freedom and life that Jesus brings, humanitarian and spiritual transformation will occur. Great Commission Companies are defined by six characteristics, including being socially responsible, being an income-producing business, managed by kingdom professionals, bringing glory to God, promoting the growth and multiplication of local churches, and placing its main focus on the least evangelized and least developed parts of the world.[31] They state, "That is the purpose of a GCC: to bring good news in word and deed to the neediest parts of the world. The good news about globalization is that the barriers that once prevented people from hearing this message are falling and the missions baton is being handed to a new breed of messenger."[32] Rundle and Steffen appear to want to mobilize business people and *send* them out with missionary purpose because they view them as the ones who have been handed the baton of missions responsibility. Over half of their book, *Great Commission Companies*, is dedicated to highlighting some existing GCCs in an overview-and-example type of format.

Interestingly, they point to the Apostle Paul as an example of someone who worked to add "credibility to his message," and to "set a pattern of lay witness and ministry by regular working Christians."[33] According to Rundle and Steffen, Paul was a regular working Christian who made tents to

---

29. Rundle and Steffen, *Great Commission Companies*, 20.
30. Rundle and Steffen, *Great Commission Companies*, 29.
31. Rundle and Steffen, *Great Commission Companies*, 45–47.
32. Rundle and Steffen, *Great Commission Companies*, 29.
33. Rundle and Steffen, *Great Commission Companies*, 22.

demonstrate that "missions is the responsibility of all Christians."[34] First, I would not call Paul a regular Christian, because he was not a *regular* Christian. He never presented himself as a regular Christian. He had a direct commission from the resurrected Jesus Christ. He was an apostle. As Paul himself stated in 1 Cor 12:28, "Are all apostles?" No. Paul was not a *regular guy*. Second, as has been argued throughout this book and shown definitively from Scripture, Paul did not make tents to show people that regular Christians should be engaged in missional activity. Regular Christians *should* be engaged in "missional" activity, but that was not why Paul made tents and it was not among his self-disclosed reasons.

In the end, Rundle and Steffen set forth their view of BAM with enough differentiation from Lai, Johnson, and Baer to carve out their own unique understanding of BAM. If you are keeping count, we have looked at four different BAM proponents and we have heard four distinctly different descriptions of BAM.

THE VERDICT

We began this chapter by asking if tentmaking and BAM were synonymous. According to some, such as Lai, yes. According to others, like Johnson, no. But we can do better than merely compare contradictory opinions. Let's figure this out with what we know to be true about tentmaking based on the biblical evidence.

First, BAM contains too many non-Pauline elements to qualify as tentmaking. For example, Johnson states, "BAM must be about job making, never about job taking. In that sense BAM distinguishes itself from the classical concept of tentmaking."[35] I am unsure what Johnson means by the *classical* concept of tentmaking, since there has never been any sort of agreed-upon definition of tentmaking.[36] Regardless, Paul was not motivated to make tents because he wanted to create jobs for, or take jobs from, others.

Likewise, Johnson's view of BAM fails to align with Pauline tentmaking when it comes to the duration and permanency of self-support. Johnson states, "By their very nature, businesses are designed to be long-lasting, even

---

34. Rundle and Steffen, *Great Commission Companies*, 43.

35. Johnson, *Business as Mission*, 33.

36. Similarly, Rundle and Steffen state, "As with earlier debates about the definition of 'tentmaker,' there is a fierce tug-of-war taking place about the definition and goals of BAM." Rundle and Steffen, *Great Commission Companies*, 7. I do not know what they mean by *earlier debates* since there is still no consensus regarding the definition of tentmaking.

perpetual institutions that have a permanent presence in the community."[37] Paul supported himself selectively and his ministry was itinerant in nature. There is no indication that Paul was attempting to set up a permanent business.

Furthermore, Paul was not a business tycoon with an eye to transform the society through his tentmaking business. His goal was *not* to create jobs and funnel money into the community so that the overall standard of living improved. Paul was an apostle who sought to proclaim the gospel of Jesus Christ. It was the transforming power of the gospel that Paul wanted to see spread outward from the churches he established, not economic growth. This is a fundamental difference between Paul's missionary activity and BAM. We also saw that neither Baer nor Rundle and Steffen communicated an understanding of BAM that came anywhere close to biblical tentmaking.

Unfortunately, BAM is precariously close to stepping outside of *any* distinctively Christian missionary activity. Johnson states:

> This cycle is the heart of BAM's business-development component: creating businesses that create jobs that put money in the hands of marginalized people and thereby allows them to climb onto the bottom rung of the economic development ladder. Once on the ladder, the free-market economic engine begins to move, allowing them to slowly ascend upward from one rung to the next. With each higher rung the economic engine moves at a faster pace and allows the people and their communities (and nations) to develop the capacity to realize better, fuller, healthier, richer lives. It also gives these people a stake in the stability of the society and, collectively, can begin raising their hopes, aspirations, and expectations.[38]

Notice the absence of anything related to gospel proclamation in the above definition? The language is completely devoid of any reference to Jesus, the gospel, or the church. If this view of BAM is adopted, then BAM has left the missionary map. While good and humanitarian in nature, firing up a country's economic engine and raising people's hopes and dreams so they live better, fuller, healthier, and richer lives does not constitute Christian mission. All those things can be done by secular businesses run by hardhearted atheists. If this is what BAM is, then BAM is not mission. Or to put it another way, while a Christian could still engage in this type of BAM, this type of BAM is not inherently Christian mission.

---

37. Johnson, *Business as Mission*, 41.
38. Johnson, *Business as Mission*, 35.

At this point, we are prepared to make some conclusions about BAM. First, BAM is not clearly understood or grasped by the people most familiar with it. It is still too ill-defined to begin serious or fruitful evaluation. It seems like each author is competitively grasping at BAM by the reigns, eager to have it pull their own cart. And, if we adopt Baer's view, BAM really is not anything other than Christians being Christians. Why do we have to give a special name for the basic tasks of glorifying God, surrendering to God's will, and pursuing excellence and treat BAM like a brand new missional frontier that needs promoting and exploring? I wonder if Baer realizes that there are thousands of Christian business owners who are already doing everything he is advocating, and they have never heard of BAM.

Second and lastly, the verdict is in: BAM is not synonymous with tentmaking. We did see each of the authors energetically championing and promoting their own version of what they think BAM should be, and we did see a flurry of conflicting statements on Paul's tentmaking. But now that the dust has settled, we can confidently state that whatever BAM is or turns out to be, it is not the same thing as tentmaking.

11

Paul's Tentmaking vs. Tentmaking in the Church

In chapter 3, Paul's tentmaking was compared to an old set piece that has functioned as the static background for the more important and dynamic action occurring on the stage of Acts. Paul and the other characters that have lines go about their business traveling from port to port proclaiming the gospel, making new disciples, and establishing new churches, while tentmaking is part of the scenery that is always present but largely unnoticed. Biblical scholars and commentators often attempt to border Paul's tentmaking with neat linear pieces of trim called "principles" or "rules," but there are always a few curved sections that will not fit unless cut or allowed to extend beyond the framed edges as exceptions.

Now that we have examined the actual historical and contemporary church record, the situation has not improved. Pastors, missionaries, teachers, authors, and missionary organizations have approached Paul's tentmaking from a variety of directions. For some, tentmaking continues to be viewed as an anachronistic and insignificant detail that is either left out of church planting discussions completely or mentioned in passing. For others, it has been misunderstood or watered down to apply to just about any Christian who is alive and working. Still others see an opportunity to garner apostolic support for their particular philosophy of church planting or missions, so they have picked up Paul's tentmaking and shaped it like a wax nose until it complements their view.

Tentmaking does not have to continue to be the forgotten set piece or the misunderstood and malleable missiological oddity. There is a better way, but before a course for this better way can be charted, a side-by-side comparison of how Paul utilized tentmaking and how the church has used, and continues to use, tentmaking is necessary. In this chapter, the biblical and theological foundations of Pauline tentmaking will be compared and contrasted with the historical and contemporary church's understanding and application of tentmaking to see if they match and complement one another, or if they clash like a striped suit coat and plaid pants.

DISTINCTION #1: IMPORTANT VS. IGNORED AND INDIFFERENT

The first distinction that can be made when comparing Pauline tentmaking with the church's historical and current tentmaking is that Paul placed a high importance on the significance of his tentmaking, whereas the church has largely ignored the significance of Paul's tentmaking. The qualifying word *largely* is used because there are a few people, such as Roland Allen and others, who have recognized the importance of Paul's self-support and the significance it carries as a missiological method.

Paul placed great importance on his purposeful choice to make tents. Large portions of 1 Cor 9, 2 Cor 11, and 2 Thess 3 are devoted to Paul's careful and detailed explanation of his right to receive support as a minister of the gospel, and the reasons why he was choosing to refuse support. Paul *drew attention* to the topic of his financial support because he wanted his readers to understand its importance.

Conversely, the historical church has largely ignored or remained indifferent to the significance of tentmaking. With the notable exception of the Moravian missionaries who supported themselves as they made disciples and planted churches, most historical missionaries avoided self-support unless they were left with no other choice. William Carey's own writings indicate that he resorted to tentmaking only after his traditional support was withdrawn.

A brief overview of the United States' frontier expansion revealed that prior to 1815 some Baptist ministers were laboring as bivocational farmer-pastors, but the motivating factors behind that bivocational lifestyle were not associated with Pauline missionary methods. Historians state that the Baptists were motivated by distaste for formal training and preferred pastors who had not attained advanced degrees. Licensed laymen who plowed the ground six days a week were a better fit for Baptist congregations who were leery of ordained clergy. Other than these Baptist farmer-pastors, no other self-supporting clergy appeared to be moving westward during this first phase of frontier expansion, and even traditionally supported ministers were relatively scarce.

After 1815, missionary societies and denominations began to send more ordained and traditionally supported clergy westward. Tentmaking was ostensibly ignored by these organizations and the church sent out ministers only when the necessary funds had been raised and were available.

We need to remember that there was a much higher level of cultural respect for clergy during this period in America's history. This respect, coupled with a wider and more pronounced division between clergy and laity, contributed to the mindset that ministers should engage exclusively in ministry. While always on guard against extravagance and excess, it was understood that ordained clergy serving churches should be provided a living wage.[1] Churches and missionary societies were expected to provide financial support for ordained clergy.

Contemporary church planting authors also largely ignore or remain indifferent to Paul's tentmaking. There are exceptions in this group, as well; such as Roland Allen, Ruth E. Siemens, J.D. Payne, and others mentioned in chapter 9. But remarkably there are some church planting authors who have completely ignored tentmaking. David Hesselgrave, author of *Planting Churches Cross-Culturally*, wrote extensively on church planting and the importance of following Pauline principles as revealed in Scripture, yet he never mentioned tentmaking.[2] Darrin Patrick wrote *Church Planter* and instructed his readers to plant churches that look like the churches in Acts, yet he never mentioned tentmaking.[3]

It is not just published authors who are ignoring tentmaking. Bruce Finn wrote a dissertation titled, *Small Churches Can Plant Churches*, and

---

1. In a collection of church records and meeting minutes from frontier churches, the topic of clergy salary and subscription occurs frequently. For example, the 1839 records written by a clerk from a Congregational church in DuPage, Illinois, state, "Moved that the subscription for Mr. Porter salary for 1838 be made up by adding to our several subscription sums sufficient to make out the amount," and later at another meeting, salary was the only agenda item: "Church met at the house of Br. Rose. The Rev. Mr. Porter proposed to the church to furnish him with hay and wood & he would deduct 76 dollars on his salary. Church voted to accept his proposition." Sweet, *Religion on the American*, 150.

2. Hesselgrave, *Planting Churches*.

3. Patrick, *Church Planter*.

within this dissertation there is a section called, "Financial Support."[4] Finn discusses financial strategies recommended for small churches interested in church planting and does not mention tentmaking.

Someone could raise a hand of objection in defense of these authors and point out that it is possible that they were not interested in discussing tentmaking as a strategy, or that there were many other more important church planting topics to cover. Any paper, article, or book has a finite amount of space, so authors cannot be expected to cover all topics related to church planting in every written work. In response, I would point out that the Bible also has a finite amount of text and space, and within the NT passages that are written about Paul or by Paul describing his missionary journeys, his choice to support himself and his own explanation for those purposeful choices takes up a significant amount of space that is equal to or greater than other church planting topics that are consistently mentioned by authors who have ignored tentmaking—authors, I might add, who are championing and advocating apostolic methods.

For example, Hesselgrave identifies something he calls, "The Pauline Cycle," which he presents in figure form throughout his book.[5] The first section of the cycle is titled, "Missionaries Commissioned."[6] This component of Paul's missionary church planting and evangelism plan is supported by two Scripture passages, Acts 13:1–4 and Acts 15:39–40. I agree that being called and sent by the church is an important part of missions. I would agree with Hesselgrave's observation, "God calls and sends missionary-evangelists in and through the churches."[7] However, when we look at how many actual verses this principle is built upon, we come up with a total of six. When the total number of verses that address Paul's self-support choices are added up, the total number is thirty-eight.[8] The verses related to tentmaking and support choices outnumber the commissioning passages by more than six to one, yet tentmaking did not warrant inclusion in a book on church planting that advocates following Paul's apostolic methods.

Other popular church planting authors include tentmaking and bivocational ministry almost as an afterthought. If tentmaking is mentioned, it is discussed briefly and not always in a favorable light. Stuart Murray's 2010

4. Finn, "Small Churches Can Plant Churches," 162.
5. Hesselgrave, *Planting Churches*.
6. Hesselgrave, *Planting Churches*, 47.
7. Hesselgrave, *Planting Churches*, 96.
8. The verses I am including in this count are Acts 16:15; 18:3; 20:33–35; 1 Cor 9:6–18; 2 Cor 11:7–12; 12:13–16; 1 Thess 1:9; 4:11–12; 5:14; 2 Thess 3:7–12. A strong case may be made to include additional verses, but these are the verses that most directly address Paul's tentmaking and the explanation of his support choices.

book on church planting devotes one paragraph to bivocational ministry with no connection to Paul. Aubrey Malphurs includes a brief discussion of tentmaking but informs his readers that Paul made a mistake. Malphurs advises his readers against tentmaking. Tim Keller's church planting manual assumes that planters will need to raise support, but there is no mention of how that should be done and no mention of tentmaking as a purposeful method of support. As chapter 9 revealed, some authors will include discussions of tentmaking, but will rarely hit on Paul's self-disclosed reasons for self-support. Most writers point to the financial or practical benefits that accompany working while planting a church.

Why does the vast majority of church history and contemporary literature fail to pick up on the importance of Paul's tentmaking? Because the church has cast a casual glance at tentmaking and concluded that it is relatively unimportant. Consequently, a paltry amount of serious research has gone into Pauline tentmaking, and old assumptions and conclusions about Paul's tentmaking have remained unchallenged. The point is not that all people throughout church history and all contemporary church planting authors have ignored or remained indifferent to tentmaking. However, compared to the importance that Paul placed on his purposeful support choices, the church has predominately missed the significance and importance of tentmaking as a missiological method.

DISTINCTION #2: PURPOSEFUL VS. PRAGMATIC

The second distinction that can be made when comparing Pauline tentmaking with the church's historical and contemporary tentmaking is that Paul purposefully chose to make tents in certain ministry contexts and not others, whereas the church has almost always practiced tentmaking for pragmatic reasons. Paul made a purposeful choice, but the church has predominately turned to tentmaking only when she has lacked traditional support.

At the beginning of chapter 2, four primary means of financial support were identified as being available to Paul during his itinerant ministry. He could have accepted traditional support and direct pay, lived in a patron's house, begged, or worked. We also saw that Paul accepted support from some churches but not others, and that his choices were not dependent on the financial circumstances of the churches he served. Paul accepted a large amount of support from one of the least affluent churches, Philippi, and refused support from one of the most affluent churches, Corinth. Paul made a purposeful choice to support himself with tentmaking in certain ministry contexts and not others. In chapter 4, we concluded that Paul made tents for didactic and evangelistic reasons.

It is true that there were and are practical benefits associated with tentmaking. When Paul supported himself with tentmaking it functioned as a reliable and portable means of support and it allowed him to make local social connections that he *might* not have been in a position to make if he were not making tents. However, Paul did *not* support himself for these pragmatic reasons and, more importantly, he never pointed to practical benefits as the reason he made tents. Nowhere in the Bible does Paul provide us with pragmatic or practical reasons as the basis for his choice to support himself.[9]

We need to remember that it is not as if Paul failed to provide any reasons for his purposeful choice to support himself. We are not left to wonder why he made tents, or deduce that it must have been to supplement his income when times were tough, or that he did not want to place a burdensome financial strain on churches with limited economic resources. And, it certainly was not because people refused to support him, as Malphurs concluded.[10] Paul explicitly tells us why he made a purposeful choice to support himself in some ministry contexts and not others. It was for the didactic reasons of teaching against an idleness problem in Thessalonica, and to teach the Ephesian church to take radical steps in order to be in a position to give to the poor. In Corinth, Paul engaged in tentmaking in order to make a sharp distinction between himself and the other false teachers that were proclaiming another Jesus. By distinguishing himself from the false teachers through tentmaking and self-support, he was removing a potential obstacle that might prevent someone from hearing and believing the true gospel.

The bottom line is that Paul made a purposeful choice to support himself through tentmaking. Paul did not make tents out of desperation or as a pragmatic fallback strategy when traditional support was unavailable. It was not a financial backup plan. He did not make tents because some of the churches he ministered to were *unable to afford a pastor*. Paul *did* make tents as a carefully chosen missiological method for didactic and evangelistic reasons. Unfortunately, the church has bypassed the reasons Paul provides for tentmaking and has supplied her own reasons based on assumptions, presuppositions, and a puzzling widespread desire to prove that Paul acted consistently from church to church.

---

9. Pragmatic and practical reasons would include but are not limited to: relating to others, identifying with the common laborer, blending in with the artisan class, financial necessity, supplementing his traditional support, having a portable means of support, having a consistent means of support, removing socioeconomic barriers, making marketplace connections, or making friends.

10. Malphurs, *Nuts and Bolts*, 43.

As pointed out under distinction number one, the church has largely ignored or remained indifferent to Paul's tentmaking; and why not? If the church's understanding of Pauline tentmaking was that he did it to supply what was lacking, then why engage in tentmaking if the church is able to finance missionary activity? Among those in church history who have paid attention to Pauline tentmaking and who have engaged in it, most did so for practical reasons. Even one of the best historical examples of purposeful tentmaking, the Moravians, were motivated by a blend of practical and didactic reasons. C. Wilson states, "The practical aspect was the church would save money and could send out more missionaries . . . the theological reason for maintaining this policy was to show the heathen the biblical example of the responsibility to work diligently to support one's family."[11]

Virtually every other example in church history reveals the church engaging in tentmaking for practical reasons. Wilson attempted to lift up Christopher Columbus and Marco Polo as examples of tentmakers, but in order to do so the definition of tentmaker had to become semantically empty. William Carey turned to tentmaking only when his traditional support disappeared. The Baptist frontier farmer-pastors were motivated by practical and philosophical reasons such as a general denominational distaste for educated and salaried clergy, but not biblical or theological reasons.

The contemporary literature review revealed several who ignored or remained indifferent to tentmaking. When an author did take time to investigate tentmaking, the prevailing rationales for using tentmaking were pragmatic or invented by the author, not established by Paul. For example, Bloecher writes, "A tentmaker displays a harmonic merger of professional work and personal walk with the Lord as a suitable model for young believers."[12] Murray advocates tentmaking so that church plants can be "freed from the onerous financial commitment of supporting a full-time leader."[13] The problem with both of these reasons is that they are never provided by Paul. Paul did not engage in tentmaking to display a harmonic merger of professional work and personal walk, or to free the churches he ministered to from the onerous financial commitment of supporting him.[14]

Ed Stetzer views tentmaking and bivocational work as a solution to financing a church plant when no other way is available, when the cost of living in a target community is too high, or as something he himself did when

---

11. C. Wilson, "Evaluation of the Missiology," 5.

12. Lewis, *Working Your Way*, 20.

13. Murray, *Church Planting*, 224.

14. I maintain that it would *not* have been onerous for the Corinthian church to support Paul if he had decided to accept traditional support from them.

he was "unable to find adequate funding."[15] Sjogren and Lewin advocate tentmaking in order to "destroy the sacred-secular conflict."[16] Is that what Paul was trying to do? C. Peter Wagner recommends tentmaking as "one of the major ways of cutting the costs of new church development."[17] Ruth Siemens understands tentmaking as something to be practiced to gain access to closed countries. According to Siemens, tentmaking should be utilized for the pragmatic reason of gaining access to people groups who are inaccessible to traditional missionaries: "Paul gives us a complete pioneering strategy for hostile environments."[18] I fail to see how Pauline tentmaking exists in the Bible in order to provide us with a "complete pioneering strategy for hostile environments," when Paul never used his tentmaking as a strategy to gain entrance into hostile environments.[19] That purpose is completely foreign to the biblical record of Paul's missionary work. Siemens is guilty of importing a reason that does not exist in order to support her recommendation that tentmaking should be utilized for penetrating hostile environments. The use of tentmaking and self-support may very well assist missionaries in gaining access to hostile environments, but that purpose is not related to Pauline practice.

All of the above reasons are pragmatic and practical in nature and are not related to the purposeful choice that Paul made. Paul did not make tents to raise funds or to destroy the sacred-secular conflict, or to cut costs, or to penetrate hostile environments. None of those things are true.

Paul purposefully chose to support himself in selected ministry contexts, but the historic and contemporary church, with relatively few exceptions, has engaged in tentmaking for pragmatic reasons. When the church has voluntarily opted to utilize tentmaking, the reasons cited are usually unrelated to Paul's self-disclosed purposes.

DISTINCTION #3: METHOD VS. MISSIONARY

Two of the cardinal distinctions between Pauline tentmaking and the historical and contemporary church's practice and understanding of tentmaking have been discussed thus far. The third distinction is that Paul used tentmaking as a *missiological method*, whereas the church has almost universally understood tentmaking to be a *type of missionary*. This third

---

15. Stetzer, *Planting Missional*, 229.
16. Sjogren and Lewin, *Community of Kindness*, 173.
17. Wagner, *Church Planting*, 72.
18. Siemens, "Vital Role," 129.
19. Siemens, "Vital Role," 129.

distinction is possibly the *most significant distinction* between Pauline tentmaking and tentmaking in the historical and contemporary church, and it has an enormous impact on the definition, application, and use of tentmaking and self-support.

When Paul described himself, he used the word apostle. Rom 1:1 states, "Paul, a servant of Christ Jesus, called to be an apostle, set apart for the gospel of God." In 1 Cor 1:1, he states, "Paul, called by the will of God to be an apostle of Christ Jesus." In 2 Cor 1:1: "Paul, an apostle of Christ Jesus by the will of God." Gal 1:1 states, "Paul, an apostle." Paul's self-identification as an apostle of Christ Jesus continues throughout his epistles, and not just in the opening greetings. At the beginning of 1 Cor 9, Paul asks, "Am I not free? Am I not an apostle? Have I not seen Jesus our Lord? Are not you my workmanship in the Lord" (1 Cor 9:1)? There should be no doubt in anyone's mind that Paul was an apostle, that he viewed himself as an apostle, and that he publically identified himself as an apostle to others.

Paul's mission was to proclaim the gospel to the Gentiles. Gal 1:15–16 states, "But when he who had set me apart before I was born, and who called me by his grace, was pleased to reveal his Son to me, in order that I might preach him among the Gentiles." Gal 2:7 states, "On the contrary, when they saw that I had been entrusted with the gospel to the uncircumcised." In 1 Tim 2:7, Paul says, "For this I was appointed a preacher and an apostle (I am telling the truth, I am not lying), a teacher of the Gentiles in faith and truth." And of course, Acts 9:15 records Jesus telling Ananias what Paul's mission was: "But the Lord said to him, 'Go, for he is a chosen instrument of mine to carry my name before the Gentiles and kings and the children of Israel.'"

Question: Did Paul ever refer to himself as a tentmaker? The question seems ridiculous. Paul *never* identified himself as a tentmaker. Can we imagine Paul opening his letters with, "Paul, a tentmaker for Jesus Christ," or "Paul, a servant of Jesus Christ, called to be a tentmaker?" Does Scripture say that Jesus commissioned Paul to be a tentmaker to the Gentiles? Of course not. There is nothing in the NT that would lead us to believe that Paul viewed himself as a tentmaker, or a tentmaker for Christ, or, and this is *crucial*, a tentmaking missionary. Paul was an apostle of Jesus Christ, commissioned and sent to proclaim the gospel. The point is this: Paul never viewed his tentmaking as something that defined him. Tentmaking was not who he was; it was something he chose to do in certain ministry contexts. In other words, for Paul, *tentmaking was a missiological method, not a type of missionary.*

It is no coincidence that the 1 Cor 9:19–23 passage about becoming all things to all people falls immediately after an extended explanation of why Paul did not make use of his right to support as an apostle of Jesus Christ.

Paul was an apostle of Jesus Christ who used everything at his disposal to achieve his goal of saving as many people as possible. He told us this in 1 Cor 9:22: "I have become all things to all people, that by all means I might save some." This practice of becoming all things meant doing all things allowed by Scripture. This governed all areas of his ministry, not just some areas. He gave a couple of examples in 1 Cor 9:19–22, but the principle of becoming all things to all people extends beyond becoming a Jew to the Jews or becoming a Gentile to the Gentiles. The immediate biblical context (1 Cor 9:1–18) shows that it also applies to his support choices. When it came to nonessential practices and morally neutral strategic options, Paul was a chameleon for Christ.

Paul's tentmaking and support choices were like missiological tools in his tool belt. He would assess his ministry context and select the appropriate tool. Self-support was one of those tools and it came with a toggle switch. He either chose to support himself by tentmaking or not, depending on which would yield him the greatest harvest and gospel impact.

Tentmaking was a missiological method, and that is how Paul viewed it. However, it did not define who he was any more than going first to the Jews and then to the Gentiles defined him. In chapter 3, we examined Acts 13:44–47 and Acts18:4–7 and saw that Paul's custom and practice recorded for us in Scripture was to preach first to the Jews, then to the Gentiles. When first entering a city, he would go to the local synagogue and proclaim the gospel. That was a missiological method, but it did not define him. We do not think of Paul as a synagoguing missionary. No one refers to Paul as a synagoguer like people refer to him as a tentmaker. Similarly, none of the other methods that Paul employed contribute to the formation of his identity, nor should they. Yes, Paul did purposefully choose to make tents in some ministry contexts, but that choice was one component of a deliberate missionary strategy and it was only used when necessary. Tentmaking did not define him. Figure one illustrates where tentmaking fits into Paul's identity and missiological methods.

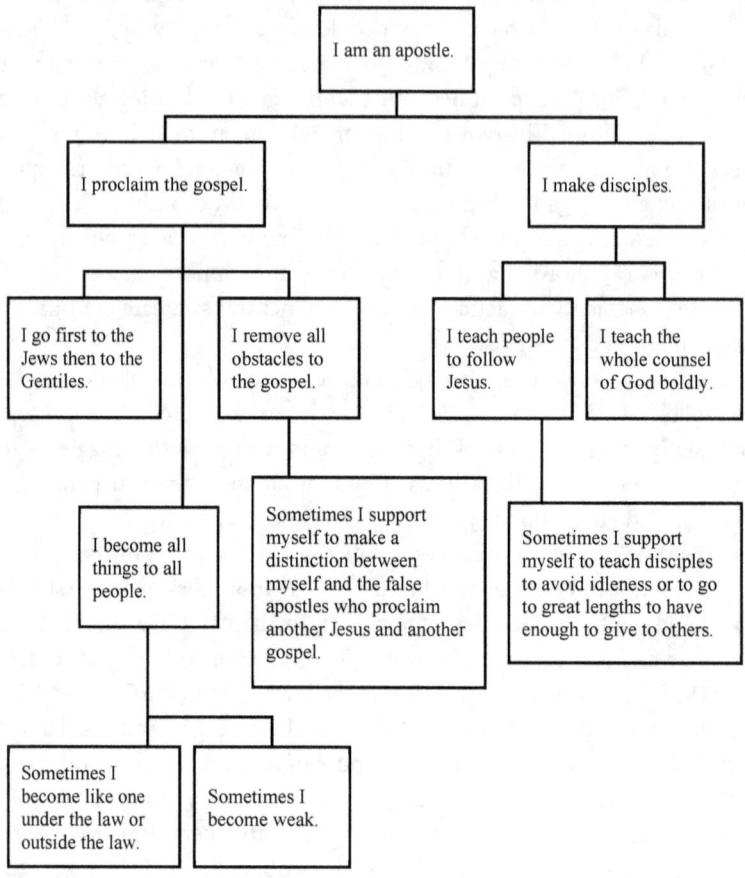

Figure 1—Paul's understanding of tentmaking.

We can only imagine how Paul might react if he knew that two thousand years later people would refer to him as a tentmaking missionary. The biblical record shows us that Paul did not view his purposeful choice to support himself by tentmaking in some ministry contexts and not others as something that should categorize him as a certain type of missionary, or a certain type of apostle. To use the word *tentmaking* as an adjective to clarify what kind of apostle or missionary or evangelist we are talking about is strangely out of touch with how the Bible describes tentmaking. Yet, strange as it seems, that is what the church does. Paul used tentmaking as a missiological method, but the contemporary literature overwhelmingly uses tentmaking to refer to a type of missionary.

The early church did not make a concerted effort to define tentmaking or to classify different types of missionaries. Interestingly, one of the closest examples of Pauline tentmaking is the example of the Moravian missionaries. Count Zinzendorf did not send out Dober and Nitschmaun with one gold coin because he wanted to send out tentmaking missionaries. He did it because he was sending out missionaries, and he understood that their self-support on the mission field would lead to humility which would be evangelistically advantageous. C. Wilson writes:

> Zinzendorf put much emphasis on the inner condition of his missionaries. He stressed that humility must be a key characteristic in their life and that this humility should lead to a distinct type of lifestyle. In turn, this distinct lifestyle would be a key element in winning the heathen to Christ.[20]

The Moravians were the missionaries who came the closest to mirroring Paul's purposeful choice to support themselves for evangelistic reasons, and they are also the closest historical example of correctly understanding tentmaking as a missiological method and not as a type of missionary.

The rest of the historical review that was covered in chapter 7 exposed the church utilizing tentmaking and self-support as a last resort when traditional finances were lacking. As the historical church utilized tentmaking for pragmatic and practical reasons, it is difficult to look back and determine if they viewed themselves using a missiological method when traditional support was unavailable, or if they viewed themselves as having to switch from being traditional missionaries to tentmaking missionaries when traditional support was unavailable.

There appears to be an absence of any sort of significant tentmaking discussions in the literature until Roland Allen's fresh examination, *Missionary Methods: St. Paul's or Ours?* in 1912.[21] At no time in any of Allen's writings does he refer to Paul as a tentmaking missionary. There is no indication that Allen viewed Paul's tentmaking as part of his identity, or as something that assigned him to a certain type or class of missionary. In fact, we have the opposite. Allen correctly perceived that Paul's choice to support himself was purposeful. Allen also correctly perceived that Paul's choice to support

---

20. C. Wilson, "Evaluation of the Missiology," 4–5.
21. Allen, *Missionary Methods*.

himself was intentionally designed to positively impact his missiological goals. Allen writes, "It is strange how often he refers to it, what anxiety he shows that his position should not be misunderstood; but he speaks as if its importance lay wholly in the way in which it might affect those to whom he preached, never as though it made any personal difference to him."[22]

What is more, Allen consistently viewed and referred to Paul's purposeful self-support choice as a practice. Allen believed Paul's self-support choice was a missiological method, not something that cordoned him off as a certain type of missionary. The very titles of Allen's writings reveal his understanding of Paul's self-support: *Missionary Methods* (1912), *Missionary Principles* (1913), and *Educational Principles and Missionary Methods* (1919). Allen is one of the few writers who correctly understood tentmaking as a missiological method rather than a type of missionary.

By 1923, Allen had developed the concept for something he called voluntary clergy. This was quite possibly the earliest reference to labeling any type of missionary or clergy based on the method of support they chose. Allen believed that there was a place for voluntary clergy and stipendiary clergy. Unfortunately, the reasons he cited in support of voluntary clergy were the same financial and pragmatic and practical reasons so many people cite today when recommending self-support.

The conclusion to be drawn from Allen's writings is that while he initially and continually viewed tentmaking and Paul's purposeful choice to support himself as a missiological method, Allen eventually distinguished traditional clergy and missionaries from voluntary clergy and nonprofessional missionaries based on the origins of their financial support. This opened the door for others to begin classifying ministers and missionaries based on their methods of support.

Approximately fifty years later, Wilson divided missionaries into two categories and concluded that tentmakers were missionaries who supported themselves. Wilson explains:

> But the Scriptures say that there are two types of cross-cultural witnesses. The first are those who receive full support from churches. This is the way the Apostle Peter was supported. On the other hand, the Apostle Paul earned his own salary by making tents. Even today, cross-cultural witnesses of "missionaries" fall into these two categories. Some are funded by the contributions of fellow Christians, while others support themselves through various professions.[23]

---

22. Allen, *Missionary Methods*, 49.
23. Wilson, *Today's Tentmakers*, 15.

I find Wilson's first sentence in the above quote somewhat unsettling. When he states that, "The Scriptures say that there are two types of cross-cultural witnesses," I want to ask, do they?[24] Because the Scriptures do not *say* that, anywhere. Nevertheless, Wilson sought to define and classify missionaries based on how he understood their methods of support. Others, in the wake of Allen and Wilson, have also attempted to define, organize, classify, and sort ministers and missionaries into varying categories and subsets based on support choices.

One of the problems that has haunted Wilson and others who have attempted to define tentmaking and classify ministers and missionaries based on their source of financial support is a lack of consensus. For example, in 1979, Wilson had to acknowledge that "different terms have been used to define and characterize 'tentmakers.' Since this is a new concept to many, it has been difficult to settle on an expression in our vocabulary that signifies what is really meant."[25] Wilson went on to mention several labels and understandings of who could qualify for being a tentmaker and what others considered a tentmaker to be. He listed such terms as nonprofessional missionary, the lay apostolate, tentmaker, lay pastor, self-supporting witness, and self-supporting missionary.[26]

Yet, over forty years later, missiologists are still struggling to find any consensus surrounding the definition and understanding of tentmaking. Payne writes:

> The word tentmaking stirs up a variety of images. For some the tentmaker is a missionary who travels land and sea to conduct mission work while supporting himself or herself by a skill or trade. Another person sees the tentmaker as a missionary doing covert activities in creative-access nations and thus compromising Christian integrity. For others a tentmaker is someone who ventures into a distant land to minister to others but is forced to earn his or her living through a secular occupation because of not being able to become a "real" missionary through a mission agency. Some may even understand the tentmaker to be someone who works for the Camping Superstore![27]

Payne continues by referring his readers to six different authors who all have their own definition and understanding of tentmaking.

---

24. Wilson, *Today's Tentmakers*, 15.
25. Wilson, *Today's Tentmakers*, 15.
26. Wilson, *Today's Tentmakers*, 15–16.
27. Payne, *Discovering Church Planting*, 363.

Many others have identified this ongoing lack of consensus surrounding tentmaking and tentmakers. Siemens writes, "Almost everything that is said today about tentmaking can be immediately contradicted because everyone uses a different definition—one of 20 that are floating around."[28] Johnson observes:

> One of the major problems facing the uninitiated in the tentmaking world is endless confusion over the label *tentmaker*, the definition of a tentmaker and the variables that comprise its essence . . . Even within tentmaking circles, there is widespread dissatisfaction, great confusion and seemingly endless wrangling over the term *tentmaker* and its meaning.[29]

Johnson provides a list of seventeen different terms that have and are being used to describe tentmaking.

Allen provided one or possibly two terms to describe tentmaking and self-support in 1923, Wilson provided six terms in 1979, and Johnson provided seventeen terms in 2009. The trajectory surrounding the understanding and definition of tentmaking is moving from being something slightly difficult to grasp to a disorderly pile of conflicting ideas, assertions, and conceptual understandings. Moving from unclear to even less clear is not a good thing.

Why is there so much disagreement among missiologists? Why are tentmaking definitions so divergent? The reason, I believe, is two-fold. First, there is a lack of understanding surrounding what the actual biblical texts say regarding tentmaking and how Paul viewed and utilized self-support. This is what I meant at the end of chapter 9, when I said the problem originates further upstream. Many NT scholars are imprisoned by their desire to prove that Paul was consistent in his support choices. This has led to the development of inaccurate theories to explain Paul's tentmaking. These erroneous theories with principles, rules, and exceptions have influenced the church and resulted in the subsequent varied definitions and understandings of tentmaking.

Second, the church has failed to recognize the distinctions outlined in this chapter. For many centuries, the church largely ignored or remained indifferent to Paul's tentmaking. And we have seen that there are still church planting authorities who continue to ignore or remain indifferent to Pauline tentmaking. When the church has paid attention to Paul's tentmaking, it has usually been within a scenario of first turning to self-support for pragmatic

---

28. Siemens, "Vital Role," 127.
29. Johnson, *Business as Mission*, 116.

and practical reasons, then in retrospect congratulating herself for following in the footsteps of Paul.

But by far, the most confusion stems from viewing tentmaking as a type of missionary instead of a missionary method. Compared to the biblical model of Paul's identity and understanding of tentmaking, the contemporary church's model looks more like this:

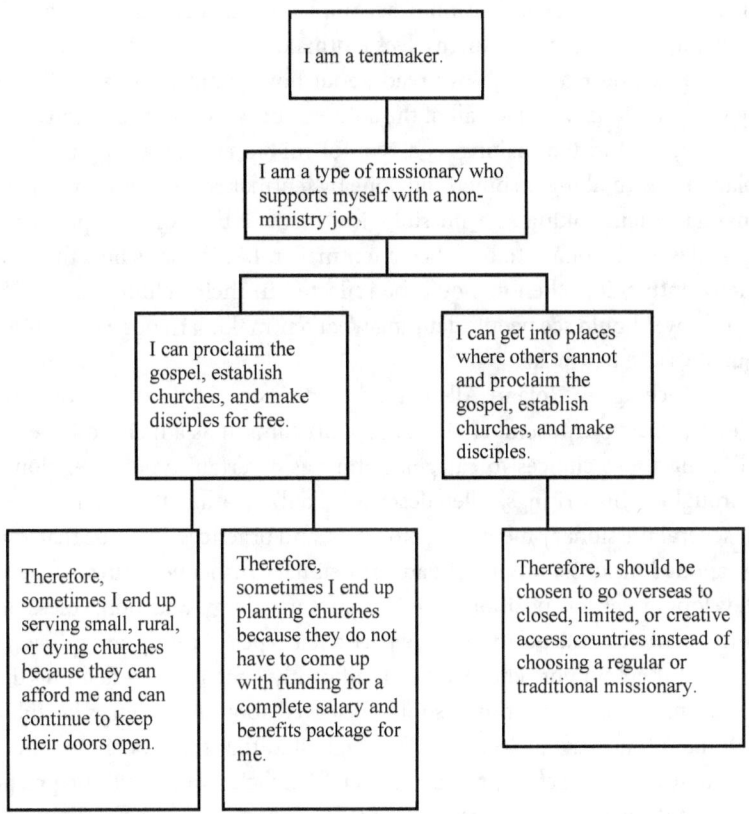

Figure 2—The contemporary church's understanding of tentmaking.

The contemporary church views tentmaking as a type of missionary, while Paul viewed tentmaking as a missiological method. In Figure 1, tentmaking appears at the bottom of the illustration because Paul understood it to be a missiological method. Tentmaking was not part of Paul's *identity*.

He was an apostle and referred to himself with that identifying label. In Figure 2, tentmaking appears at the apex of the model.[30] The contemporary church views a person utilizing self-support within a ministry context as a tentmaker, not as a missionary or a minister who is purposefully electing to use self-support as a missiological method. The contemporary church's understanding views a tentmaker as a type of missionary who, because they are or choose to be a tentmaker, can now accomplish certain tasks and goals that regular missionaries cannot accomplish. Ministers and missionaries utilizing self-support call themselves tentmakers.

Over and over again, we read about how tentmakers are a different type of missionary. In fact, all of the authors surveyed in the previous chapters understand tentmaking as a type of missionary or a type of church planter. Tentmaking is something done by tentmakers. At a minimum, they may view tentmaking as a missiological method that, once implemented, qualifies a missionary to be called a tentmaker. But if that is how they truly view tentmaking, then it should be reflected in their definitions. In other words, we should see people defining what tentmaking is, not who is or who qualifies as a tentmaker.

Once again, Roland Allen stands out as one of the few people who viewed Paul's purposeful choice to support himself as a method instead of allowing those choices to categorize him as a certain type of missionary. Throughout his writings, Allen described Paul's treatment of finances as one of several missionary methods, principles, and practices. It is true that when he applied his observations of Paul's missionary principles, Allen suggested developing certain positions called voluntary clergy and nonprofessional missionaries. These positions were particular types of clergy and missionaries, and their support choices did significantly contribute to defining their position. However, two things should be noted about Allen. First, he did not call them tentmakers. Second, Allen suggested that these positions should be pursued purposefully, not as financial fallback strategies to be grasped at like a drowning victim reaches out to a life preserver just before slipping under the water. Allen was an advocate of voluntary clergy and nonprofessional missionaries because they were based on apostolic practice.

---

30. Neither of these two illustrations that display Paul's and the church's understanding of tentmaking are intended to be comprehensive presentations of Paul's missiological methods and strategies. They are for illustrative purposes only and are designed to simplistically show the marked difference between biblical tentmaking and how the contemporary church understands tentmaking.

CONCLUSION

Three salient distinctions have been made after comparing the biblical and theological foundations of Pauline tentmaking with the historical and contemporary church's understanding and application of tentmaking. The first distinction revealed that tentmaking was an important missiological method that Paul intentionally called attention to in his letters, while the historical and contemporary church has largely ignored or remained indifferent to Paul's self-support. The second distinction revealed Paul's purposeful choice to support himself juxtaposed with the historical and contemporary church's pragmatic reasons for turning to tentmaking. The third distinction, the most significant, described how Paul understood tentmaking to be a missiological method, whereas the historical and contemporary church has understood tentmaking to describe a type of missionary.

Now that we can clearly see the mismatch between how the Bible portrays tentmaking and how the contemporary church understands tentmaking, we need to bring something helpful and constructive to the discussion. We do not simply want to point out the problem without offering a solution, so we are going to build an objective and biblical definition of tentmaking and illuminate a course that leads to the recovery of tentmaking as a valid and purposeful missiological method for the church.

12

Defining Tentmaking

When it comes to the task of defining tentmaking, it is much preferable to start from scratch rather than attempt to retool existing definitions. It is also important to identify the critical elements that must be included in a definition based solely on the biblical record and apostolic example. When that is completed, it is simply a matter of cobbling those elements together into a lucid declarative sentence. And of course, we do not want to forget that an accurate definition of tentmaking must take into account the three distinctions that were made in the previous chapter.

I want to emphasize that we are seeking a definition of tentmaking based on biblical principles alone instead of importing elements for convenience or to bolster support for an agenda. Statements that could be true of anyone or of any missionary or minister should not be included in a tentmaking definition. For example, within Yamamori's definition of tentmaking, an element called "biblically literate" was included.[1] We obviously want all ministers, missionaries, church planters, and followers of Jesus Christ to be biblically literate.

---

1. Lewis, *Working Your Way*, vi.

DEFINITIONAL COMPONENTS

The starting place for defining tentmaking is the word of God. If Paul had not made tents, then we would not be discussing the issue. Therefore, tentmaking is *biblically grounded*. The Bible also teaches us that Paul considered his choice to support himself as important. It was important enough for the Holy Spirit to breathe out several verses of Scripture dedicated to describing Paul's self-support. Paul went to great lengths in order to draw attention to his choice to support himself and to identify the underlying reasons for that choice.

Paul viewed himself as an apostle. That was his identity and calling in Christ Jesus. Self-support was one of the methods he used to accomplish his apostolic calling and mission to the Gentiles. It is supremely important to identify tentmaking as a *missiological method* and not as a type of missionary.

An accurate and faithful definition of tentmaking will remember that Paul did not use self-support as a fallback strategy when times were tough or when a particular church could not afford to compensate him for his missionary work. Paul *purposefully* chose to support himself, and that choice was divorced from the fiscal health of the churches he served. Tentmaking was a purposeful choice, but it was not a continual or consistent choice. Despite what so many authors have attempted to prove, there were no set of rules or principles that guided Paul's consistent use of self-support. He utilized this particular method *selectively* based on the missiological and evangelistic context. The specific reasons Paul provides in Scripture are *didactic* and *evangelistic* in nature.

A couple of other components will need to be included that have not received much attention so far. Earlier in the previous chapter, under the discussion of the first distinction ("Important vs. Ignored and Indifferent") it was noted that Hesselgrave considers commissioning, based on Acts 13:1–4 and Acts 15:39–40 an important process in what he calls the "Pauline Cycle."[2] I stated that I agree that being called and sent by the church is an important part of missions. It is so important that it should be included in a definition of tentmaking. Acts 9:1–19 could also be included to demonstrate that a Christian leader who utilizes the missionary method of tentmaking must have an *internal call* from God as well as an *external call* from their church.

Another defining tentmaking component that has not received much attention within the previous chapters is the fact that Paul was adequately

---

2. Hesselgrave, *Planting Churches*, 47.

trained. He was not an illiterate day-laborer with no training or preparation in the things of God or in the proper handling of Scripture. His encounter with the resurrected Jesus was not the only thing that qualified him to be a leader in Christ's church. In Acts 22:3, Paul described himself this way: "I am a Jew, born in Tarsus in Cilicia, but brought up in this city, educated at the feet of Gamaliel according to the strict manner of the law of our fathers, being zealous for God as all of you are this day." The point is that Paul was not a layman. He had received formal teaching and knew Scripture. Obviously, all of our church leaders cannot be held to the gold standard of paralleling the Apostle Paul's credentials before being allowed to serve, but we should and do require some training for people who are going to formally lead Christ's church. We train and examine elders before allowing them to lead. In a similar manner, we should not lower the bar for someone just because they have discerned that self-support is the best missiological method for a particular evangelistic and ministry context. Paul was *adequately trained* with an internal and external call, not some uneducated self-supporting maverick with a high degree of business acumen and a desire for missions.

Payne has made the following observation:

> Rare is the missiologist or New Testament scholar who would argue that Paul was not both a tentmaker as well as a church planter. If the concept of tentmaker is going to be supported by biblical evidence, then textual application requires the tentmaker also to be involved in church planting.[3]

I agree. A tentmaking definition must include something about *establishing or planting churches*.

Finally, what about the amount of self-support? Does someone following in the footsteps of Paul and practicing biblical tentmaking have to generate all of the necessary funding from their own non-ministry labor, or can they rely on a combination of self-support and outside assistance? Can they receive some of their income from the church they are serving and the other portion from secular employment? The best way to answer these questions is to go back and consult the Bible.

The latter question is the easiest to answer. No. If someone is going to be practicing biblical tentmaking, then they cannot earn or receive any part of their income from the church they are actively serving. That would defeat the whole purpose of tentmaking. Paul would not have been able to achieve any of his didactic or evangelistic goals if he had accepted anything from Corinth, Thessalonica, or Ephesus while he was ministering in those places.

---

3. Payne, "Tentmaking and North American," 8.

He was explicitly clear about not taking anything from them, remember? In 2 Cor 11:9, Paul says to the Corinthians, "And when I was with you and was in need, I did not burden anyone . . . So I refrained and will refrain from burdening you in any way." Remember, the *burden* language is used by Paul to describe his free-of-charge ministry. He is saying that he did not take any payment from them, in any way. In 2 Thess 3:7-8, Paul says to the Thessalonians, "We were not idle when we were with you, nor did we eat anyone's bread without paying for it, but with toil and labor we worked night and day, that we might not be a burden to any of you." And Acts 20:34 records Paul's parting words to the Ephesian elders, "You yourselves know that these hands ministered to my necessities and to those who were with me." If biblical tentmaking is going to be rightly practiced, then the minister may not accept payment, in any form, from the church where tentmaking is being utilized. Tentmaking must be practiced utilizing *complete self-support*.

We do know, however, that Paul accepted support from outside churches when he ministered to the churches in Corinth and Thessalonica. In 2 Cor 11:8, Paul states, "I robbed other churches by accepting support from them in order to serve you." And in Phil 4:16 we read, "Even in Thessalonica you sent me help for my needs once and again." Yet there is no biblical evidence that Paul received outside financial support when he was ministering in Ephesus. What does this tell us? It tells us that anyone practicing tentmaking must be completely self-supportive and not take any financial payment from those that belong to the church where the tentmaker is actively ministering, but that the tentmaker may or may not choose to receive outside gifts or support if it is offered. I would argue that Paul went out of his way to ensure that he was able to fully support himself in all situations, whether he received outside support or not. In this way, he did not depend on either the church he where he was ministering or on anyone else. The Macedonian gifts were welcomed, but it does not appear that he was counting on their financial assistance as part of his overall support strategy. Remember Phil 4:17, where he thanks the Philippians and says, "Not that I seek the gift, but I seek the fruit that increases to your credit." Paul was not seeking outside support, but welcomed it for his own benefit and for the benefit of the givers.

When we combine all of these components together, stating a definition of tentmaking becomes a rather straightforward task: *Tentmaking is the biblically grounded missiological method of complete self-support, which may be used purposefully and selectively by an internally (self) and externally (church) called and adequately trained Christian leader for evangelistic or didactic reasons when establishing churches.*

TENTMAKING ADVANTAGES

There are two advantages to a biblically accurate definition of tentmaking that should be highlighted. First, tentmaking does not have to be full-time employment; second, tentmaking is not geographically or culturally limited.

A biblically accurate definition of tentmaking shows us that although this missiological method must be the only source of on-site income for the church planter, it does not mean that the self-support has to be full-time. The self-support can be any type of job that provides enough to meet the needs of the church planter and any dependents. The Bible does not tell us that Paul worked forty hours a week. He may have worked seventy-two hours one week and thirty-three hours another week. Speculation is rarely profitable when it comes to what the Bible does not say, but we *can* conclude that Paul worked enough to meet his needs. Scripture tells us that he was driven by his apostolic mission and it would seem unreasonable to think that Paul would have remained confined to his workbench by some sort of predetermined salary threshold he wanted to meet for the week or the month that went beyond what he needed. Tentmaking does not have to be full-time employment, but it does have to be sufficient to completely meet the financial needs of the church planter and any dependents.

Earlier in the book, I remarked that one of the contributing factors to the confusion and misunderstanding around tentmaking is the propensity for well-intentioned Christians to import elements into the definition of tentmaking that are unsubstantiated by Scripture. For example, Wilson states that tentmaking has to include being an overseas witness for Jesus Christ.[4] Yamamori stated that the qualifications for tentmaking included being trained in "low-profile evangelistic skills."[5] Similarly, Siemens states, "Paul gives a complete pioneering strategy for hostile environments."[6] None of these elements (i.e., overseas witness, low-profile evangelistic skill, pioneering strategy for hostile environments) were part of Paul's experience. While it is true Paul traveled by boat, the cities of Corinth, Ephesus, Philippi, and Thessalonica were all situated around the Aegean Sea and were within a few hundred miles of each other, and everyone spoke Koine Greek. Philippi and Thessalonica are only seventy-four miles apart, and all of the cities were Hellenized. Paul was neither low-profile in his evangelism, nor was he attempting to gain entrance into politically restricted nations. It is true that

---

4. Wilson, *Today's Tentmakers*, 68.
5. Lewis, *Working Your Way*, vi.
6. Siemens, "Vital Role," 129.

some of the environments where he proclaimed the gospel became hostile environments, but that was not until *after* he had preached the gospel.

The point is that when tentmaking is correctly selected as a purposeful missiological method, it in no way has to be utilized across cultures, in closed- or limited-access countries, or overseas. It can, but none of these things are the *sine qua non* of tentmaking. Tentmaking can be used anywhere; it is not limited by geography, culture, or target-group receptivity. Tentmaking does not have to be used to cross ethno-linguistic barriers with the gospel in order to be considered valid.

WHAT TENTMAKING IS NOT

It should be noted that there are many brothers and sisters laboring in the Lord's fields that have served or are sacrificially serving Christ's church with different views, understandings, and definitions of tentmaking. By stating the above definition, I do not want to communicate disrespect to any of the writers mentioned. There are those who, undoubtedly, will object that this definition is not inclusive enough. I would remind them of two things, and leave them with a challenge.

First, the Bible is full of sharp distinctions and clear boundaries. Our God is a God of order. There is nothing inherently wrong with drawing lines and objectively stating who is inside and who is standing outside based on Scripture's teaching. In fact, as Christ's church, we *must* continually draw hard lines in order to maintain pure doctrine and rightly practice biblical ecclesiology. Making sharp distinctions should not be unfamiliar or uncomfortable for us.

Secondly, just because someone can no longer refer to themselves as a tentmaker does not mean that they are any less useful to God or to the church. There are many people who may have to take the *I am a tentmaker* patch off of their letterman's jacket, but that does not mean that they are being kicked off of God's team.

Finally, I would challenge those who may push back at this definition to go back and review the applicable passages and verses. Go back and review the varying definitions of tentmaking to see if they align with the Bible. Go back and look at how some of Wilson's examples of tentmaking do not even meet the threshold of his own definition. Go back and ask the tough questions, such as, "Was Paul consistent with his use of self-support?" or, "Was Paul attempting to penetrate closed- or limited-access countries?" In essence, my challenge to those who have enlarged and broadened the tentmaking definition beyond the Pauline example is to take another look at the biblical evidence, and then reflect on their own understanding of tentmaking while simultaneously asking, "Is this true?"

In order to add clarity to the definition provided above, it will be helpful to state a few examples of what does not qualify as tentmaking. For example, a church planter who is sent to a target community with a three- to-five-year support plan from a denomination or church planting network is not utilizing tentmaking. Obviously, they are not supporting themselves, so they do not meet the definition of tentmaking. If a church planter works at a part-time job while planting the church so they can make community connections, they are not utilizing tentmaking as a missiological method. Even though they are providing some of their own support, they are still drawing some support from the church planting ministry and the part-time job was not selected for evangelistic or didactic reasons. If a church planter labors for two years and is not meeting predetermined benchmarks so the denomination discontinues its financial support and the church planter begins to work full-time while continuing the ministry, they are not utilizing tentmaking. It cannot be biblical tentmaking because they were forced to come up with an alternative funding strategy.

If someone takes a secular job overseas in Europe, Africa, or Asia, and while they are working overseas they intentionally present the gospel to people and live openly as a Christian, they are not using tentmaking. If someone takes a secular job that allows them to work in Turkey and, after they are in the country for a year, they hold Friday night Bible studies with some of their neighbors and co-workers, they are not utilizing tentmaking. If a civil engineer takes a secular job in Iran and while working there presents the gospel to non-Christians and twenty people come to Christ, that is not tentmaking.

In all of the examples in the preceding paragraph, those people are simply doing what they *ought* to be doing. As followers of Jesus Christ, we are commanded to intentionally present the gospel to people and live openly as Christians. We should expect all Christians to hold Bible studies in their homes as needed or as the opportunity presents itself and as prompted by God. All Christians should be thinking and praying for their unbelieving co-workers. All Christians should be presenting the gospel to unbelievers when given the opportunity, no matter where they live and work. None of the above examples qualify as tentmaking because, among other things, none of them had purposefully selected to support themselves based on the needs of their evangelistic context, and some of them were not adequately trained or called by the church. I am aware that there may be people who are in the above situations and ministry contexts who demand that they be recognized as practicing biblical tentmaking. While they may persist in calling themselves tentmakers, they are not doing what Paul did.

Now, let us say someone had at least an undergraduate degree in biblical studies or perhaps an MDiv degree. In addition, this person had an internal call to plant churches in Europe or Iran or in Wyoming or in Orlando, Florida, and that call had been recognized, validated, and affirmed by a sending church or church planting network or organization. Let us assume also that this person could receive a full salary and benefits package from their sending church or organization, but based on the evangelistic or didactic needs of their target community, they purposefully decided to fully support themselves by taking a non-ministry job while planting the church. That person would be correctly utilizing tentmaking as a missiological method.

13

Bivocational Ministry and Contemporary Need for Tentmaking

After comparing and contrasting the biblical and theological foundations of Pauline tentmaking with the historical and contemporary church's understanding and application of tentmaking, three salient distinctions were made. These distinctions shaped an objective and biblically accurate definition of tentmaking. For clarity, that definition will be restated: *Tentmaking is the biblically grounded missiological method of complete self-support, which may be used purposefully and selectively by an internally (self) and externally (church) called and adequately trained Christian leader for evangelistic or didactic reasons when establishing churches.*

It was noted that there may be several pastors, missionaries, and Christian leaders who, although they currently view themselves as tentmakers, would no longer qualify because they fail to meet this relatively narrow definition. By relatively narrow, I mean that when compared with some of the existing definitions of tentmaking and some of the examples of people who have been lifted up as tentmakers, the definition above may appear restrictive. The initial reaction may be to assume that a narrow definition of tentmaking will somehow impinge on current ministry and evangelistic efforts.

For example, the above definition would not consider a structural engineer who intentionally took a secular job within the 10/40 window to evangelize and hold home Bible studies with neighbors during free hours a valid expression of tentmaking. The objection might be made that the definition presented here is turning the clock back to a time when closed- or limited-access countries were not missionally pursued, and that tentmaking is sometimes the only way into these areas. But notice that this definition does not prohibit the structural engineer from carrying out that exact same ministry and strategy. That person would be encouraged to proceed with their plans, but they could not legitimately call themselves a tentmaker, or more accurately, claim to be using tentmaking as a missiological method. My comment to them would be, "You are not a tentmaker. You are just being a faithful follower of Jesus. Let me pray for God to use you in a mighty way."

While it is true that the above definition does restrict the total number of people who can legitimately claim to be utilizing biblical tentmaking, it does not and should not decrease the number of people engaged in Christian mission and evangelistic work.

BIVOCATIONAL MINISTRY

Before moving ahead, we first need to distinguish between tentmaking and bivocational ministry. Now that we have arrived at our tentmaking definition, it should be apparent that tentmaking and bivocational ministry are not synonymous, although they are often treated that way within contemporary literature. For example, an article by David Whitlock, Mick Arnold, and R. Barry Ellis states, "Bivocational ministers, often referred to as tentmakers, are a growing population in today's churches."[1] One of the titles by a popular tentmaking author, Dennis Bickers, equates the two terms.[2] Likewise, C. Peter Wagner writes, "Frequently the founding pastor is bivocational or a tentmaker," and then the rest of Wagner's paragraph makes it clear that he regards the two terms as synonymous.[3]

The problem is that they do not mean the same thing. Tentmaking is a missiological method with one of its defining characteristics being complete self-support. When church planters select tentmaking as a missiological method, they choose not to accept payment for ministry and support themselves completely through a non-ministry job, whereas bivocational ministers, or bivocational pastors, earn part of their income from ministry and part of their income from a non-ministry job. Hence the term bivocational, meaning "two vocations."

1. Whitlock et al., "Examination of Tentmaker," 41.
2. Bickers, *Tentmaking Pastor*.
3. Wagner, *Church Planting*, 72.

The question might be raised, *Can't tentmaking and bivocational ministry be viewed as the same thing if the bivocational minister purposely chooses bivocational ministry and meets all the other definitional criteria?* No. Remember, in all three ministry contexts that Paul selected tentmaking as a missiological method, he refused to accept support from the target ministry group. In other words, he was not bivocational. He was not receiving some support from the local church and augmenting that income through tentmaking (2 Cor 11:9; 2 Thess 3:7–8; Acts 20:34). Paul was so committed to supporting himself that he would not even accept a loaf of bread without paying for it.

What does this tell us? It tells us that Paul was not bivocational. He did not supplement traditional support from the churches he was actively ministering to with tentmaking, and he did not supplement his tentmaking by accepting partial traditional support from the churches where he was actively ministering. It also tells us that taking any percentage of support from the churches to which he was ministering would have neutralized and negated the reasons why he purposefully chose to support himself in those particular ministry contexts. If he received 10 percent of his income from the church and 90 percent from tentmaking, his opponents could still point to his willingness to receive money from the church where he was actively ministering. Therefore, the false apostles could correctly state that Paul took money for ministry services from the people he ministered to, just like they did. As a result, there would be less of a discernable difference between the false apostles and Paul. In Ephesus and Thessalonica, Paul would be unable to teach benevolence and a proper work ethic if he received any amount from those churches. Paul would no longer be able to boast about not taking anything, including something as small as a loaf of bread. He would not be able to state with integrity that it was his hands that ministered to his own necessities and those of his companions.

The conclusion then is that while the biblical definition of tentmaking must include the qualifying word *complete* when describing self-support, all other combinations of local ministry support and secular employment would fall under the category of bivocational ministry. A minister or church planter that is simply augmenting their church salary, even if it is a small percentage, could not claim to be utilizing tentmaking as a missiological method.

There is no need to generate a new definition of bivocational ministry. We do not need more definitions cluttering up an already crowded room of missionary terminology, and J.D. Payne has provided one for us: "A bivocational missionary is someone who receives a portion of his or her salary from a church and/or denomination and another portion of salary from a non-clergy type of employment."[4] The only change I might make to this definition is to substitute the word *support* for *salary* because I think the word *salary* denotes some sort of fixed level of income, whereas *support* does not. Yes, I realize I am splitting hairs with this observation. It does not appear that Paul supported himself to maintain an unchanging level of monthly income, but he did work enough hours to meet his needs and the needs of others at times. This definition could apply to both bivocational church planters and ministers working in established churches who are bivocational. Missionaries, ministers, and church planters who receive some percentage of support from their ministry work and another percentage from secular employment can and should refer to themselves as bivocational.

CONTEMPORARY NEED FOR TENTMAKING

It might be helpful at this point to display what we know about tentmaking in list format. That way, we can quickly scan the list and see if there are any contexts in which tentmaking might be selected for establishing churches today:

1. Tentmaking is a missiological method, not a type of missionary.
2. Tentmaking is purposefully selected based on the needs of the ministry context.
3. Tentmaking may be used by called and adequately trained Christian leaders.
4. Tentmaking is used to plant and establish churches.
5. Tentmaking involves securing 100-percent self-support, but not necessarily full-time employment.
6. Tentmaking may be utilized anywhere and with any people group.

Since tentmaking is a missiological method intended to be used for planting churches, it seems prudent to consider it for contemporary church planting efforts. There is nothing in the above list that suggests tentmaking is applicable only to the first century or restricted to a certain place or people group. Therefore, since tentmaking is not temporally, culturally, or geographically bound, then we need to understand that this Pauline missionary method may be used anywhere, among any people, as long as there is a legitimate need. Conversely, it should not be utilized when there is an absence

---

4. Payne, *Discovering Church Planting*, 364.

of genuine didactic or evangelistic need. Paul did not make tents to give the church a universal practice to follow at all times. In other words, Paul's tentmaking in the NT does not lay down a principle that all ministers, pastors, church planters, and gospel workers should support themselves through non-ministry jobs. Additionally, it does not mean that self-support is the preferred option, but traditional support (or a combination of self-support and traditional support) is allowed as a concession if and when 100-percent self-support is not possible.

The only time tentmaking should be used is when there is a genuine didactic or evangelistic need. If that need is not present, then traditional support may be used, or any level of bivocational support may be utilized. The last thing I would want to happen is to see a renewed interest in tentmaking that resulted in leaders championing the use of tentmaking in all church planting contexts indiscriminately. Or worse, shaming those who receive traditional support as being second-class church planters because they are unable to secure the necessary employment to support themselves. The biblical evidence suggests that when there was not a specific need for tentmaking, Paul defaulted to traditional support. We are to go and do likewise.

If there is anyone who is still having trouble picturing what a genuine didactic or evangelistic need would look like today, consider the following questions: Are there any places in the world today where people need to be taught benevolent giving through example and modeling? Do all people excel at regular, disciplined, proportionate, sacrificial giving? Are there any ministry contexts where people might need to be taught that they should work *if able* and not be dependent on someone else or on government assistance? And lastly, are there any ministry contexts in which the gospel is in danger of being confused with whatever happens to be proclaimed by popular false teachers? Might there be a situation in which it would be helpful for a lead pastor to be set apart from his contemporary peers that often proclaim a different gospel; let's say, one that is divorced from repentance? The above questions are directly related to Paul's original reasons, but there may be other valid didactic or evangelistic reasons for church planters to purposefully choose self-support. Honest answers to the above questions reveal that, yes, there remains a contemporary need for tentmaking.

14

Reviving Tentmaking

Tentmaking as a purposeful missiological method was born with the Apostle Paul in the first century. It enjoyed a healthy infancy and a vibrant early childhood in the first church where Paul supported himself in Thessalonica. As tentmaking passed through adolescence and early adulthood, first at Corinth and then at Ephesus, it grew and became strong. Paul utilized a physically fit and muscular tentmaking missiological method during his missionary journeys. It ran along the coastline of the Aegean Sea and filled its lungs with fresh salt air and the Holy Spirit.

Over time, tentmaking became less active. Its muscles atrophied from lack of use and it began to forget that it was once an evangelistic and missional champion. Once in a while, tentmaking would attempt to move with agility like it did with Paul, but for the most part it spent its days reclining in a soft chair with heavy eyelids.

More time went by, and tentmaking became advanced in years. Its beard grew out in course stubble and its hair became unkempt. A man named Roland Allen found tentmaking sleeping and almost completely covered by the bed sheets of time and neglect. Allen asked tentmaking to stand so he could perform an examination. Allen instructed tentmaking to walk and it did, slowly at first and then, after a brief rest, more quickly. J. Christy Wilson saw tentmaking and asked it to make great leaps across oceans. Others began to notice tentmaking and made their own personal requests. Over the next forty years, tentmaking attempted all sorts of physical feats of strength, but something was wrong. Tentmaking was not moving like it once did and complained of chest pains and shortness of breath. It was taken to the emergency room where an electrocardiogram revealed an erratic heartbeat that could not support the demands of its current lifestyle. As tentmaking laid on the gurney staring up at the bright lights in the ceiling, it wondered if it would ever run again and bring glory to its Heavenly Father.

It is time. It is time to revive this once-strong missiological method so that it can once again run and glorify God.

TENTMAKING RETRAINING AND EDUCATION

The only reason we find ourselves in the position of reviving tentmaking and not attempting to resurrect it is because it has not completely died. It is still being utilized, or at least some are attempting to utilize a modified form of tentmaking in selected ministry contexts. The problem is the erratic heartbeat. It was observed in chapter 11 that the church's understanding of tentmaking is moving from unclear to even less clear. There are multiple understandings and definitions of tentmaking, many of which are incongruent with apostolic practice and the biblical record. It is no wonder that tentmaking's heart is experiencing arrhythmia. As Allen stated, "From this apostolic practice we are now as far removed in action as we are in time."[1]

The first step in reviving tentmaking for contemporary church planting is retraining and education. Church planting and missionary authorities will need to retrain their students, staff, and clergy and clarify what tentmaking is and what it is not. A biblically faithful and objective definition of tentmaking will need to be decided upon and then used *consistently*. With all humility, I would offer my definition. If someone is able to definitively show from Scripture a better definition, or if someone is able to improve upon my definition, then praise God. The point is that the church will need to be held accountable and hold to an agreed-upon definition of biblical tentmaking. This means that future tentmaking literature *will have to resist* the urge to enlarge the tentmaking tent with additional definitions and increasingly complex subcategories. The importance of exercising this type of ongoing internal discipline among missiologists and church planting leaders *cannot* be overstated.

Every component of the tentmaking definition must be met in order to qualify for tentmaking. In this sense, tentmaking is similar to the office of elder or deacon. In order to be eligible to hold one of these offices, a

---

1. Allen, *Missionary Methods*, 52.

candidate must meet all of the qualifications listed in First Timothy. It is not enough to meet some of them, or even to meet all of them except one. In the same way, adequately trained and equipped Christian leaders using this method must meet all of the defining components of tentmaking before claiming to follow in the footsteps of Paul.

The church must recognize that her current practice is not helpful. When so many people advocate such significantly different understandings and definitions of tentmaking, the church is inadvertently encouraged to walk past the tentmaking buffet with her plate and pick the ones that are most appealing to her ministry palate. The more definitions the church has available to her, the less tentmaking is defined and the more shapeless it becomes. Moreover, if we are simply stating our own opinions about what we think it should be, or importing self-serving elements into tentmaking definitions, then all we have is useless prattle.

In addition, when potential church planters and missionaries are presented with such a dizzying array of understandings and definitions, they are less likely to see value in tentmaking. Who would buy something if they did not know what it was they were purchasing? How could someone purposefully and faithfully utilize tentmaking when it is so clouded in a morass of conflicting voices? Why choose self-support if the full amount of financial resources have already been raised? Without an agreed-upon definition and biblically based rationale, there is no underlying reason to select tentmaking.

In addition to rallying around an agreed-upon definition of tentmaking, the church will need to be taught. She must educate herself by direct means. For example, typical church planting or missionary courses will need to discuss how tentmaking has traditionally been practiced, both in the past and in more recent church history. The historically inconsistent and chaotic understanding of tentmaking will need to be exposed. Students, church planters, and missionaries will need to be encouraged to discard previous misconceptions of tentmaking and embrace the Pauline understanding of tentmaking as a purposeful missiological method. Paul did not utilize tentmaking in struggling churches that were at the end of their life cycle. He planted energized and spiritually charged churches that grew by conversion.

The church will need to be shown the clear distinction between tentmaking as a purposeful missiological method and bivocational ministry. There is nothing wrong with bivocational ministry, but it is not synonymous with tentmaking. Bivocational ministry is in no way devalued or cheapened by standing apart from tentmaking. I believe most people will respond positively to this type of clarification. It is helpful. Instead of someone becoming offended and exclaiming, *What do you mean I am not a tentmaker? I most* certainly am and have been for twenty-five years. I anticipate they would respond by concluding, *That makes sense. I have always wondered why no one can agree on what tentmaking means. It also explains why Paul was not consistent between churches, thanks.* Not everyone will respond positively, and that is both understandable and disappointing.

PURPOSEFULLY PREPARED FOR TENTMAKING

The second step in reviving tentmaking is to provide a strategy for intentionally preparing church planters to use tentmaking. At this point, someone might raise a hand of objection and say, *This all sounds good. I am convinced from a biblical standpoint and I see a need for change, but how does the church go about practically implementing tentmaking as a purposeful missiological method? Do we just ask pastors to find a job and support themselves?* These are valid questions. It is difficult for an adequately trained Christian leader to abruptly begin utilizing tentmaking. Usually, this is because it is not easy to secure non-ministry employment that will adequately meet the financial demands of tentmaking without specialized training. If someone has an undergraduate degree in biblical studies and an MDiv from an accredited seminary, the only type of jobs they have been professionally trained for are ministry related.

To obtain guidance on how to resolve this concern, we again turn to the Bible. Earlier in chapter 2, I noted that we cannot conclusively determine how and why Paul learned the trade of making tents. The evidence disfavors the idea that it was part of formal rabbinical training that combined Torah with trade. Most likely, Paul learned how to make tents from his father. Although we cannot pinpoint when Paul learned this skill or definitively state who taught it to him, we do know that Paul, at some point, was taught how to make tents. It would also seem reasonable to conclude that he learned how to make tents before he started to support himself with that trade. Therefore, if the church would like to follow apostolic practice as much as possible, that means that those who utilize tentmaking as a purposeful missiological method for planting churches should receive any specialized training they might need for non-ministry employment before they set out to plant churches.

In order to accomplish this, the church must be willing to acknowledge the need for increased intentionality in the areas of church planting strategy and in the preparation of her leaders. What I outline below is a suggested plan for the purposeful preparation of church planters who are equipped to utilize tentmaking. It is neither complex nor burdensome. It is not radical, in the sense that it will require unrealistic changes. In fact, in some ways this strategy could potentially improve the stewardship of God's resources that are made available to denominations and church planting networks.

The first step of an intentional strategy is to identify potential church planters who would be open to utilizing the tentmaking missiological method as part of a church planting effort. This should not be an additional burden on the church because most denominations require written assessment as well as face-to-face interviews and a thorough review by denominational officers when identifying potential church planters. This appears to be fairly standard practice. For example, in my own denomination, the PCA's Mission to North America (MNA) website includes a navigation link titled, "Church Planter Recruiting." Alan Foster, MNA Church Planter Recruiting Director, writes, "My role is to pray for, identify, and recruit laborers for the harvest to plant the scores of new churches needed to impact North America with the good news of the gospel of Jesus Christ. I will work with local churches, presbyteries, and networks in finding men to plant churches in their area."[2]

The point in sharing this example, which is representational of other denominations and church planting networks, is that a new tentmaking candidate identification infrastructure does not need to be built from the ground up in order to identify potential church planters who would be willing to implement tentmaking as a purposeful missiological method. The vast majority of all denominations and church planting networks already have these types of identification and, let us be honest, screening processes in place. I am suggesting that an additional component be added to these types of identification and assessment processes that would ask the candidate if they would be willing to utilize a tentmaking missiological method in appropriate ministry contexts. Some retraining and education will need to occur with these potential church planting candidates to ensure that they fully understand what tentmaking is and what it is not.

Step one, then, is to identify potential church planting candidates who would be willing to utilize tentmaking as a purposeful missiological method. I would suggest including pre-seminary students in this identification process. The earlier the church can identify potential candidates, the better. Furthermore, according to our biblical Pauline model, Paul received his training before he arrived at the ministry site requiring self-support, not after. Identifying potential church planting candidates early allows a greater chance for this training to take place before they are given the responsibility to plant a church. As always, we are looking for *spiritually mature* candidates.

---

2. Foster, "Church Planter Recruiting."

Step two is to obtain the necessary training for the previously identified church planting candidates so they are prepared to support themselves through non-ministry employment. Asking church planters to support themselves when the only training they have had is ministry related is unreasonable. What I am suggesting would include a purposeful break in seminary education in order to secure whatever degree or technical training is necessary to place persons in a position where they could support themselves using a tentmaking missiological method. Candidates who pass the assessment process should be brought under the care of the denomination or church planting network as soon as possible. After students have completed their first year of seminary, they would take a break from seminary. At that point, between year one and year two of seminary, the students would receive whatever technical or academic training would be required to achieve a reasonable and adequate level of self-support in a non-ministry field. This could take several months and even involve an additional master's degree. This training would be paid for by the candidate and the denomination or church planting network that has taken the candidate under its care. I would suggest an even split of the costs between the student and the denomination or church planting network.

Step three, the candidates would resume seminary education for the remaining two years. This second portion of seminary training would be paid for by the denomination or church planting network that has taken the student under care. Upon graduation, the students should not only have a seminary degree and meet the tentmaking qualification of being adequately trained Christian leaders, but they would also have the necessary training or education needed to achieve a viable and reasonable level of self-support for themselves and any dependents.

In order for this type of intentional preparation to take place, the student would enter into some sort of binding written agreement with the denomination or church planting network in which the student would promise to answer a call to plant a church using tentmaking as a purposeful missiological method. They could begin immediately after graduation from seminary, if there was a need. If the new seminary graduate was not needed immediately after completing their degree, they would be free to answer a call at an established church, another church plant, or wherever God was calling them. However, whenever the denomination or church planting network identified a particular ministry context that could benefit from a self-supporting church planter and the tentmaking missiological method, the graduate would have a predetermined amount of time to answer that call. Say, for example, three to four months. They would resign from wherever they were at the time of the tentmaking call and transition to the church plant that could benefit from having a tentmaking pastor.

There could be additional stipulations incorporated into this model to make it even more flexible and accommodating. For example, if the graduate was deeply immersed in implementing a vision for a church, or if there were extenuating circumstances such as critical health issues that the church planter or their immediate family were dealing with, or if there was a crisis in their current church, then they could be allowed one "pass" so that they could resolve whatever pressing issue(s) they were immediately confronted with. The denomination could then move on to the next best intentionally prepared graduate. In addition, the graduate themselves could be involved in actively identifying potential church plant locations that would be best suited for a lead pastor who was tentmaking.

There could be some sort of commitment cap on the agreement so that the denomination or church planting network could not wait indefinitely before calling the graduate to fulfill their church planting commitment. Say, for example, if after ten to twelve years, the denomination or church planting network has, for whatever reason, not called upon the graduate to fulfill their commitment to them, the graduate would then be released from the agreement without penalty or repayment required.

There could even be an option for the candidate to buy out their commitment if life circumstances or their sense of calling changed. If the candidate elected the buy-out option, then they would be required to make full repayment for all expenses incurred by the sending ministry while the candidate was under care. And, obviously, if the candidate refused to answer a tentmaking call from the sending agency, then they would be contractually responsible for full repayment, possibly with interest.

The above strategy is for students who are headed into seminary directly from undergraduate studies. Obviously, for second career seminary students, that is, those who have been called to ministry after already spending time employed in non-ministry occupations, the process can be streamlined significantly. The second career students would already possess the training and skills needed to secure self-support as church planters. As a result, the out-of-pocket expense for denominations and church planting networks would be much less because they would not have to pay for half of the costs of the non-ministry training.

This is not some kind of radical or untested strategy. The State of Illinois offers a full tuition waiver for college students who promise to work and teach special education in Illinois public schools. This offer is called the Illinois Special Education Teacher Tuition Waiver Program, and it has been around for decades because Illinois was (and is) experiencing a special education teacher shortage. The agreement stipulates that students may receive full tuition assistance for up to four years when they attend an Illinois-approved college or university in exchange for a five-year work commitment once they have graduated. If a student graduates and does not fulfill their commitment, they are required to repay the full amount of tuition assistance, plus interest. However, once the graduate has worked five years in Illinois public schools, they are released from any further obligations and are not required to repay any of the tuition.[3] The State of Illinois is willing to make an investment in students and intentionally prepare them for specific service. Is the church willing to make a similar investment?

From a practical standpoint, this intentional model of preparing candidates may actually cost denominations and church planting networks *less* than a traditional model for a three-to-five year church planting commitment. A lead pastor's complete salary and benefits package for a church plant can range anywhere from fifty-thousand dollars to over one-hundred-thousand dollars for one year. How much would two years of seminary tuition and half of some information-technology technical training cost? A lot less. Once again, it may be necessary to emphasize that tentmaking as a missiological method should *not* be utilized as a way to cut costs; however, long-term reduction in overall costs may be an unintentional but welcomed consequence of faithfully utilizing tentmaking in conjunction with an intentional preparation strategy.

As I review the biblical and theological foundations of this research and survey the extensive contemporary literature, I am aware of what seems to be a lack of complexity in the actual solution I am suggesting. It consists of a correct definition, direct education, intentional pathways for preparedness, and one other component. In the next chapter, I will discuss the importance of faith and the desire to cooperate with the Holy Spirit.

I do not think it is helpful to attempt to identify and discuss what types of employment would be most compatible with tentmaking. The reason for that, and the reason for not providing additional details on the exact nature of what training church planters will need to obtain before graduating seminary, is because those types of concerns should be left open. I will leave it to denominations, church planting networks, and the church planters themselves to determine what types of work would be best suited for self-support because the "best" jobs are likely to change frequently and at far greater pace than tentmaking training can keep up with.

I am convinced that at least 70 percent of reviving tentmaking is grasping a correct understanding of what tentmaking is (i.e., a method, not a

---

3. Illinois Student Assistance Commission, "Illinois Special Education."

missionary) and reaching a biblically accurate definition. Think of a correct understanding of tentmaking and a correct definition of tentmaking as the two defibrillator paddles. Once tentmaking has been shocked with these two paddles and the erratic heartbeat has been stabilized, some of the other concerns, such as training and implementation, should also return to health.

15

The Gift of Faith and the Spirit of God

In the foreword to Allen's *The Spontaneous Expansion of the Church*, Lesslie Newbigin writes, "The very heart and life of his [Allen's] message was that the mission of the Church is the work of the Spirit."[1] Allen believed that missionary zeal and work were inextricable bound to the Spirit of Christ: "If the Holy Spirit is given, a missionary Spirit is given."[2] Moreover, Allen believed the greatest missionary methods were the methods that cooperated with the Holy Spirit. He advocated for methods that most accurately reflected the Spirit of Christ in his ministry. Allen wrote, "But whilst almost any material thing, however poor in itself, can be made the instrument by which the Spirit works, the Spirit ever seeks the best possible vehicle for its manifestation."[3]

Paul acknowledged that there were some who proclaimed Christ out of what he called, "envy and rivalry," and, "others from good will" (Phil 1:15). Both were operating from vastly different motives and methods, and we can assume that God used the proclamation of the gospel in both cased to call people, because Paul said, "What then? Only in every way, whether in pretense or in truth, Christ is proclaimed, and in that I rejoice" (Phil 1:18).

---

1. Allen, *Spontaneous Expansion*, iii.
2. Allen, *Missionary Principles*, 24.
3. Allen, *Missionary Principles*, 71.

However, we do not have to ask which group of people proclaiming Christ most glorified God.

God is pleased when we not only proclaim the gospel, but when we proclaim the gospel with the right heart posture, motives, and methods. Just as "the eyes of the LORD run to and fro throughout the whole earth, to give strong support to those whose heart is blameless toward him" (2 Chr 16:9), the Spirit of God seeks those who have enough faith to trust God with their missionary methods.

Allen wrote, "The method is subject to the Spirit, not the Spirit to the method. Nevertheless, the Spirit cannot be satisfied with any but the best methods."[4] Are there any better methods than the ones used by Paul? Or are we to arrogantly conclude that Paul was naïvely misguided and could benefit from our advice on how to plant churches? I hope not.

One of the reasons the church is so resistant to following in the footsteps of arguably the greatest missionary of all time is because people do not want to. Working at another non-ministry job while attempting to plant a church is hard work, takes time, and gives the impression of illegitimacy and weakness. Working two jobs is difficult and tiring. As someone who at one time was working one full-time job and two other part-time jobs in addition to preaching weekly and leading a church, I can testify that it is not glamorous. It is tough and extremely demanding. It is all too easy to avoid a missiological method that by its nature robs a person of time that could be used elsewhere. Some people will not want to work that hard or give up that much time.

Because of the misunderstanding and misuse of tentmaking in the church, tentmaking has garnered the reputation of being something that part-time or relatively uneducated pastors do when they serve small congregations who cannot afford a "real" pastor. When I was first ordained as a minister of word and sacrament in the RCA, I experienced a rude and unsettling awakening. I had genuinely believed that all of the ordained pastors serving in my denominational region would display grace toward one another and would operate with an understanding of collegial parity. What I found was a professional pecking order. Ministers were valued, respected, and given a voice based *solely* on the size of the congregations they served. I remember getting sick to my stomach as I watched behavior that rivaled and sometimes exceeded the egotism and vanity I had witnessed in the corporate world. My point is that, for some leaders, their pride would never allow them to voluntarily step into something that had the potential to jeopardize their social and professional standing. Bickers states, "Bivocational ministry

---

4. Allen, *Missionary Principles*, 74.

is looked at by some as 'second-class' ministry performed by people who don't have the gifts to serve a larger church."[5] This image is burned into the retinas of most pastors and, for some, it is too high of a price to pay.

Yet this is exactly what Paul did when he proclaimed the gospel. He became weak. He allowed himself to be viewed by others as not worthy of full support. Allen states, "It is the Spirit that matters. God has chosen the weak things of the earth to confound the mighty."[6] The church cannot avert her eyes away from tentmaking because it is hard work and takes time, or because it carries overtones of weakness and illegitimacy. Allen writes:

> Refusal to study the best methods, refusal to regard organization as of any importance, is really not the denial of matter, but the denial of the Spirit. It is sloth, not faith. We ought not to treat the external form as something to be despised as a sort of accessory of spiritual life. It is in truth the very body of the Spirit without which the Spirit is unclothed and impotent.[7]

If Paul has shown us the best methods for planting churches, then we would do well to pay attention to them and use them no matter how they make us look or how they make us feel.

When we consider Paul and Timothy, we see men who were willing to sacrifice everything for Christ. Paul stated, "For though I am free from all, I have made myself a servant to all, that I might win more of them" (1 Cor 9:19). Paul selectively and purposefully chose to make tents in certain ministry contexts because it would mean a greater spiritual harvest. Specifically in Corinth, it was a way to set himself apart from the false teachers who were proclaiming another Jesus and different gospel. In the same way, we see that Timothy was also willing to order everything in his life around reaching people with the gospel.

In his first letter to Timothy, Paul parenthetically instructed Timothy, "No longer drink only water, by use a little wine for the sake of your stomach and your frequent ailments" (1 Tim 5:23). The reason for this statement, we deduce, was to clarify that Paul did not agree with Timothy's apparent decision to completely abstain from alcohol. Given the ministry context described in First Timothy and Second Timothy, and the false teachers at Ephesus who were most likely participating in sexual immorality and drunkenness, it seems likely that Timothy had elected to completely abstain from drink in an effort to distance himself from the false teachers. Timothy was sacrificing his own health in order to ensure that people did not confuse

---

5. Bickers, *Bivocational Pastor*, 8.
6. Allen, *Missionary Principles*, 75.
7. Allen, *Missionary Principles*, 75–76.

him with the false teachers. Timothy was willing to suffer for the sake of the gospel.

Paul wrote to Timothy, "For to this end we toil and strive, because we have our hope set on the living God who is the Savior of all people, especially of those who believe" (1 Tim 4:10). The ESV has a footnote after the word "strive" that alerts the reader to an alternate reading in some manuscripts that says, "and suffer reproach." What end is Paul talking about in that verse? The end described is Paul and Timothy's role in reaching people with the gospel, building up the church, and presenting as many people as possible mature and sanctified to the Lord. Colossians has a similar statement from Paul: "Him we proclaim, warning everyone and teaching everyone with all wisdom, that we may present everyone mature in Christ. For this I toil, struggling with all his energy that he powerfully works within me" (Col 1:28–29).

Listen to those words, *strive* and, *struggle*. Paul and Timothy were not only willing to suffer reproach and become weak in appearance, they were willing to do whatever it took and to engage in hard labor and to struggle and strive in order to faithfully carry out their calling to Jesus Christ and his church. They both had a strong gift of faith and trusted in Jesus Christ who had sacrificed everything for *them*. Allen comments:

> The most spiritual sacrifice is not a sacrifice without any visible offering, but the most spiritual offering of the material sacrifice. So it was with our Lord, so it is with us. As His spiritual offering was the offering of a Body, so our spiritual offering is the offering of ourselves, all that we are and all that we have, body and soul, affections and possessions. So clothed, the Spirit of Christ can work out through us that for which the Spirit is given to us, the Revelation of Christ to the world.[8]

Where are these leaders? Where are church planters like Paul and Timothy that have the gift of faith? Where are the followers of Christ who are willing to do whatever it takes for the sake of the gospel? The church desperately needs more leaders who have a strong gift of faith and who are willing to cooperate with the Holy Spirit. The church needs pastors who are willing to sacrifice themselves and their temporal comfort for the sake of the gospel. If the Holy Spirit is going to fill the lungs of tentmaking so that it runs again, church planters must step out in faith and trust God to work through them and through biblically sound methods.

In the last installment of the Rocky movies, *Rocky Balboa*, the movie opens with an unseen crowd chanting, "Rocky! Rocky!" over and over again. The iconic Rocky theme song begins to play and after a few seconds,

---

8. Allen, *Missionary Principles*, 76.

the picture of a boxing ring fades in with ominous bass music playing. A character named Mason Dixon, who is the currently reigning heavyweight world champion, is seen fighting another boxer. Dixon knocks out his opponent, but the crowd is not pleased. The unspoken reality is that Dixon is fighting unqualified and pushover boxers as a way of perpetuating his status as heavyweight champion. The ringside announcers provide a summary of what should be a thrilling competition between champion and challenger, but instead is faux showmanship. And then one of the announcers declares that all the fans are yearning for a warrior. Someone with fire and determination to take up the challenge and do whatever it takes to legitimately win the title. Someone like Rocky.

Are there any church planting Rockys out there? Are there any pastors left who, like Paul and Timothy, are willing to do whatever it takes for the sake of the gospel? Are there any church planters who are willing to toil and struggle so that people do not go to hell? Are they willing to appear weak and be viewed by their peers as lacking the giftedness to serve a large or established church? Is there anyone who is willing to submit to an additional year or two of training and education so that they will be able to answer a call to plant a church and utilize tentmaking like Paul? The church is looking for some warriors who are willing to put it all on the line and sacrificially die to themselves because of their passion for Jesus Christ, the gospel, and others.

If there is any hope in reviving tentmaking so that it can run again and glorify God as a powerful missiological method, the church will need to retrain and re-educate herself with a biblically sound definition and understanding of tentmaking. There will also need to be some intentional and practical pathways in place to provide training so that church planters have marketable skills in place before they are called to plant a church and utilize tentmaking. And finally, the church needs followers of Jesus who have a strong gift of faith who are convinced that methods are important when cooperating with the Holy Spirit. The church needs warriors who are driven by an insatiable desire to sacrificially serve Christ.

There is a ray of hopeful light. I have seen it. I have seen young men and women who are spiritually hungry and have the gift of faith. There are warriors for Christ who have not had their idealism and faith dulled and desensitized by years of commuting to work and sitting behind a desk. Among the next generation of Christ followers, there are some whose zeal for Jesus and proclaiming the gospel have not been tempered by denominational executive committees, spreadsheets, and realistic goals. When I look into their eyes, I genuinely believe they would be willing to toil and struggle and sacrifice everything for their Lord. May God raise them up and may they answer the call.

16

Answering the Crucial Questions

In chapter 1, I introduced this book with some crucial questions about tentmaking that demanded answers. I want to revisit and answer those questions here, because I do not want to leave any of them unanswered. Although I have addressed the issues broadly, I want to answer the questions directly.

One of those questions asked whether Paul's use of tentmaking during his missionary work was intentional or pragmatic. Was it an expedient choice? That question was summarily answered in chapter 4 and was incorporated into the final biblically accurate and objective definition of tentmaking. Paul's use of tentmaking was intentional. Paul intentionally utilized tentmaking as a purposeful missiological method in selected ministry contexts. Tentmaking was not an expedient choice or a fallback strategy that he was forced to use because traditional support was unavailable, or because he did not want to place financial strain on poor congregations. Tentmaking was not, and should not be, a financial backup plan. Paul intentionally chose to make tents and support himself for didactic and evangelistic reasons.

Another opening question raised was: Is tentmaking prescriptive and desirable for new church plants today, or is it a practice to be avoided when possible? The answer to the first part of that question is: sometimes. Tentmaking is not prescriptive in the sense that all church planting efforts should utilize tentmaking. However, if the unique ministry context and target people would benefit from the use of tentmaking for didactic or evangelistic reasons, then yes, tentmaking is prescriptive and desirable. In ministry contexts where self-support of the adequately trained Christian leader would not accomplish didactic or evangelistic goals, then no, tentmaking is not prescriptive or desirable. This inconsistent application of tentmaking as a purposeful missological method is congruent with the Pauline application and use of tentmaking. We remember from chapter 2 that Paul did not approach the issue of his missionary support consistently, unless we understand that he consistently used tentmaking in a purposeful and selective manner. However, there was no overarching rule or principle that drove him to *always* support himself with tentmaking.

I asked if tentmaking was strategically and missiologically irrelevant. This question was answered in the previous chapter, where we discussed the gift of faith and the Spirit of God. We concluded that methods are important when cooperating with the Holy Spirit. We also decided that the methods that Paul used are revealed to us by God in the Bible, and we would be wise to follow the patterns that God has given us. So, no, tentmaking is not strategically and missiologically irrelevant.

A fourth introductory question was: Is bivocational ministry only preferred within limited contexts, such as small dying churches or oversees missions? The answer to this question is resounding and emphatic. No, Paul did not use tentmaking as a means to alleviate the financial burdens on financially struggling churches. Paul was planting robust and spiritually charged churches that were growing by conversion. He did not minister to churches at the end of their life cycle that could no longer afford to pay a full-time minister. Tentmaking was not intended to be used as hospice for churches, nor was it intended to be used exclusively overseas or in closed- or limited-access countries. Despite what some of the literature states, Paul did not utilize self-support in order to give us a blueprint for creative access. Paul never gained access to his ministry locations under the guise of a legitimate businessman.

Another question: Is the recent concept of Business as Mission really the same as biblical tentmaking? The answer to this question became apparent in chapter 10. No, BAM is not the same as tentmaking. There is no need to review those findings here.

There is one last question that was raised at the very end of chapter 1: Why is the church so resistive to following in the footsteps of arguably the greatest missionary of all time? This is the one question that has not been exhaustively answered thus far. Part of the answer is that because tentmaking has been so misunderstood, even if someone wanted to faithfully follow in the footsteps of Paul and utilize biblical tentmaking, they would have a difficult time finding Paul's original footprints. With so many guides and signposts pointing in different and sometimes opposite directions, are we surprised that tentmaking has been relegated to the rural dying church that is unable to afford a pastor, or the politically hostile nation? An incorrect understanding of what tentmaking is has contributed to its neglect and misuse.

Another reason may be because there is no clear pathway to intentionally prepare church planters so they are in a position to utilize self-support. The challenges of attempting to secure 100-percent self-support for the church planter and any dependents were discussed earlier. One does not simply *get a job* that provides sufficient income to support a family in today's marketplace without some kind of training.

Yet, even if tentmaking was clearly defined and explained to the church so that the majority held a firm grasp of biblical tentmaking as a purposeful missiological method and not a type of person or missionary, I suspect there would be resistance. Even if there was a clear pathway for purposefully preparing church planters so they would graduate from seminary with additional marketplace training, I think many would hesitate to embark on that pathway and make the investment of a few additional years of training and preparedness. Why? Because even if biblical tentmaking is correctly understood and everything is in place for proper implementation, the church still needs leaders who are willing to live sacrificially. In the previous chapter, I mentioned that many people will not want to follow Paul because they will not want to put in the additional work. It takes up too much time. It gives the impression of illegitimacy and weakness. In order for tentmaking to run again, there must be a constant stream of new warriors, church planting Rockys, who refuse to view the pastorate as a profession, but instead accept the challenge of living a hard and reproach-filled life for their Lord and Savior.

Tentmaking was strong and healthy when Paul utilized self-support. How did it slip into disuse and become deconditioned so quickly? How is it possible that entire books can be written about Pauline missionary practices and completely leave out Paul's use of tentmaking? The bottom line is this: if tentmaking is going to be revived, the church must not only understand tentmaking and create purposeful and practical pathways to prepare church planters who are in a position to utilize self-support, but she must also have leaders with the gift of faith who are willing to do whatever it takes to win people for Jesus Christ. When Christ followers like Paul and Timothy step up, tentmaking will run again.

The church will need strong, prepared, and called leaders who gaze out onto their particular church planting target community and discern if self-support is needed for teaching or evangelistic purposes. If self-support would be beneficial, if there is a chance that it would increase the spiritual harvest, or if self-support would show and teach people an important principle by example and modeling, then the church planter will need to secure enough non-ministry employment to provide self-support. It will be tough and demanding. It will mean they have to work twice as hard. It will be costly. It will mean they are following in the footsteps of Paul. It will be tentmaking.

Bibliography

Allen, Hubert J.B. *Roland Allen: Pioneer, Priest, and Prophet*. Cincinnati, OH: Forward Movement and Grand Rapids: Eerdmans, 1995.
Allen, Roland. *Missionary Methods: St. Paul's or Ours?* Grand Rapids, MI: Eerdmans, 1972.
———. *Missionary Principles—and Practice*. Cambridge: Lutterworth, 2006.
———. *The Siege of the Peking Legations*. London: Smith, Elder & Co., 1901.
———. *The Spontaneous Expansion of the Church*. Eugene, OR: Wipf and Stock, 1997.
Baer, Michael R. *Business as Mission: The Power of Business in the Kingdom of God*. Seattle: YWAM, 2006.
Barnett, Paul. *The Second Epistle to the Corinthians*. The New International Commentary on the New Testament. Grand Rapids: Eerdmans, 1997.
———. *A Short Book About Paul: The Servant of Jesus*. Eugene, OR: Cascade, 2019.
Beale, G.K. *1-2 Thessalonians*. The InterVarsity Press New Testament Commentary Series. Downers Grove, IL: InterVarsity Academic, 2003.
Bickers, Dennis. *The Bivocational Pastor: Two Jobs, One Ministry*. Kansas City: Beacon Hill, 2004.
Blomberg, Craig L. *1 Corinthians*. The NIV Application Commentary. Grand Rapids, MI: Zondervan, 1994.
Bock, Darrell L. *Acts*. Baker Exegetical Commentary on the New Testament. Grand Rapids, MI: Baker Academic, 2007.
Bosch, David J. *Transforming Mission: Paradigm Shifts in Theology of Mission*. Maryknoll, NY: Orbis, 1991.
Bruce, F.F. *The Book of the Acts*. The New International Commentary on the New Testament. Grand Rapids, MI: Eerdmans, 1988.
———. *The Epistles to the Colossians, to Philemon, and to the Ephesians*. The New International Commentary on the New Testament. Grand Rapids, MI: Eerdmans, 1984.
———. *New Testament History*. Doubleday-Galilee ed. New York: Doubleday, 1980.
———. *Paul: Apostle of the Heart Set Free*. Grand Rapids, MI: Eerdmans, 2000.
Carey, William. *An Enquiry into the Obligations of Christians to Use Means for the Conversion of the Heathens*. USA: Book Jungle, 2007.

Carini, Edward. *Take Another Look*. Englewood Cliffs, NJ: Prentice-Hall, 1970.
Ciampa, Roy E., and Brian S. Rosner. *The First Letter to the Corinthians*. The Pillar New Testament Commentary. Grand Rapids, MI: Eerdmans, 2010.
Cox, John. "The Tentmaking Movement in Historical Perspective." *International Journal of Frontier Missions* 14, no. 3 (July–Sept 1997) 111–17.
Danby, Herbert. *The Mishnah: Translated from the Hebrew with Introduction and Brief Explanatory Notes*. Peabody, MA: Hendrickson, 2012.
Daniel-Rops, Henri. *Daily Life in the Time of Jesus*. Ann Arbor, MI: Servant, 1980.
Danker, William J. *Profit for the Lord*. Grand Rapids, MI: Eerdmans, 1971.
Dorsett, Terry W. *Developing Leadership Teams in the Bivocational Church*. Bloomington, IN: Crossbooks, 2010.
Evans, Craig A., ed. *The Bible Knowledge Background Commentary: Acts-Philemon*. Colorado Springs: Cook Communications Ministries, 2004.
Fee, Gordon D. *The First and Second Letters to the Thessalonians*. The New International Commentary on the New Testament. Grand Rapids, MI: Eerdmans, 2009.
———. *The First Epistle to the Corinthians*. The New International Commentary on the New Testament. Grand Rapids, MI: Eerdmans, 1987.
———. *Paul's Letter to the Philippians*. The New International Commentary on the New Testament. Grand Rapids, MI: Eerdmans, 1995.
Fernando, Ajith. *Acts*. The NIV Application Commentary. Grand Rapids, MI: Zondervan, 1998.
Finn, Bruce R. "Small Churches Can Plant Churches." DMin diss., Reformed Theological Seminary, 2000.
Foster, Alan. "Church Planter Recruiting." PCA MNA. https://pcamna.org/church-planting/church-planting-ministries/church-planter-recruiting/.
Garland, David E. *1 Corinthians*. Baker Exegetical Commentary on the New Testament. Grand Rapids: Baker, 2003.
Gentry, Kenneth L., Jr. *The Greatness of the Great Commission*. Tyler, TX: Institute for Christian Economics, 1990.
Green, Gene L. *The Letters to the Thessalonians*. The Pillar New Testament Commentary. Grand Rapids, MI: Eerdmans, 2002.
Greenway, Roger S. *Go and Make Disciples!: An Introduction to Christian Missions*. Phillipsburg, NJ: P&R, 1999.
Guder, Darrell L., ed. *Missional Church: A Vision for the Sending of the Church in North America*. Grand Rapids, MI: Eerdmans, 1998.
Hafemann, Scott J. *2 Corinthians*. The NIV Application Commentary. Grand Rapids, MI: Zondervan, 2000.
Hansen, G. Walter. *The Letter to the Philippians*. The Pillar New Testament Commentary. Grand Rapids, MI: Eerdmans, 2009.
Harris, Murray J. *The Second Epistle to the Corinthians: A Commentary on the Greek Text*. The New International Greek Testament Commentary. Grand Rapids, MI: Eerdmans, 2005.
Hesselgrave, David J. *Planting Churches Cross-Culturally: North America and Beyond*. Grand Rapids, MI: Baker, 2000.
Hock, Ronald F. *The Social Context of Paul's Ministry: Tentmaking and Apostleship*. Minneapolis, MN: Fortress, 1995.
Hunter, George G., III. *The Celtic Way of Evangelism: How Christianity Can Reach the West . . . AGAIN*. Nashville: Abingdon, 2000.

Hutchison, William R. *Errand to the World: American Protestant Thought and Foreign Missions*. Chicago: University of Chicago Press, 1993.
Illinois Student Assistance Commission. "Illinois Special Education." https://www.isac.org/students/during-college/types-of-financial-aid/scholarships/illinois-special-education-teacher-tuition-waiver-settw-program.html/.
Johnson, C. Neal. *Business as Mission: A Comprehensive Guide to Theory and Practice*. Downers Grove, IL: InterVarsity Academic, 2009.
Keller, Timothy J., and J. Allen Thompson. *Church Planter Manual*. New York: Redeemer Church Planting Center, 2002.
Klauber, Martin I., and Scott M. Manetsch, eds. *The Great Commission: Evangelicals and the History of World Missions*. Nashville: B&H Academic, 2008.
Lai, Patrick. *Tentmaking: The Life and Work of Business as Missions*. Downers Grove, IL: InterVarsity, 2005.
Latourette, Kenneth Scott. *A History of Christianity*. Peabody, MA: Prince, 1997.
Lewis, Jonathan, ed. *Working Your Way to the Nations: A Guide to Effective Tentmaking*. 2nd ed. Downers Grove, IL: InterVarsity, 1996.
Malphurs, Aubrey. *The Nuts and Bolts of Church Planting: A Guide for Starting Any Kind of Church*. Grand Rapids: Baker, 2011.
———. *Planting Growing Churches for the 21st Century: A Comprehensive Guide for New Churches and Those Desiring Renewal*. Grand Rapids: Baker, 2004.
Martin, D. Michael. *1, 2 Thessalonians*. The New American Commentary. Nashville: B&H, 1995.
McCarty, Doran C., ed. *Meeting the Challenge of Bivocational Ministry: A Bivocational Reader*. Nashville: Seminary Extension of the Southern Baptist Seminaries, 1996.
Moreau, A. Scott., ed. *Evangelical Dictionary of World Missions*. Grand Rapids, MI: Baker Academic, 2000.
Murray, Stuart. *Church Planting: Laying Foundations*. Scottdale, PA: Herald, 2001.
———. *Planting Churches in the 21st Century: A Guide for Those Who Want Fresh Perspectives and New Ideas for Creating Congregations*. Scottdale, PA: Herald, 2010.
Newbigin, Lesslie. *A Word in Season: Perspectives on Christian World Missions*. Grand Rapids, MI: Eerdmans, 1994.
O'Brien, Peter T. *The Epistle to the Philippians*. The New International Greek Testament Commentary. Grand Rapids, MI: Eerdmans, 1991.
———. *The Letter to the Ephesians*. The Pillar New Testament Commentary. Grand Rapids, MI: Eerdmans, 1999.
Packer, J.I., and M.C. Tenney, eds. *Illustrated Manners and Customs of the Bible*. Nashville: Thomas Nelson, 1997.
Paton, David, and Charles H. Long, eds. *The Compulsion of the Spirit: A Roland Allen Reader*. Cincinnati, OH: Grand Rapids, MI: Eerdmans, 1983.
Paton, David M., ed. *Roland Allen: The Ministry of the Spirit*. Cambridge: Lutterworth, 2006.
Patrick, Darrin. *Church Planter: The Man, the Message, the Mission*. Wheaton, IL: Crossway, 2010.
Payne, J.D. *Apostolic Church Planting: Birthing New Churches from New Believers*. Downers Grove, IL: InterVarsity, 2015.
———. "A Brief Biography and Missiology of Robert E. Logan." *The Journal of the American Society for Church Growth* 13 (Fall 2002) 29–65.

———. *Discovering Church Planting: An Introduction to the Whats, Whys, and Hows of Global Church Planting*. Colorado Springs: Paternoster, 2009.

———. "An Evaluation of the Systems Approach to North American Church Multiplication Movements of Robert E. Logan in Light of the Missiology of Roland Allen." PhD diss., Southern Baptist Theological Seminary, 2001.

———. *Roland Allen: Pioneer of Spontaneous Expansion*. CreateSpace Independent Publishing Platform, 2012.

———. "Tentmaking and North American Church Planting." Paper presented to the Southeastern Regional Evangelical Missiological Society, Louisville, KY, Mar. 18–19, 2005.

Peterson, David G. *The Acts of the Apostles*. The Pillar New Testament Commentary. Grand Rapids, MI: Eerdmans, 2009.

Plummer, Robert L., and John Mark Terry, eds. *Paul's Missionary Methods: In His Time and Ours*. Downers Grove, IL: InterVarsity Academic, 2012.

Rundle, Steve, and Tom Steffen. *Great Commission Companies: The Emerging Role of Business in Missions*. Downers Grove, IL: InterVarsity, 2001.

Russell, Mark L. *The Missional Entrepreneur: Principles and Practices for Business as Mission*. Birmingham, AL: New Hope, 2010.

Rutt, Steven Richard. *Roland Allen: A Missionary Life*. Cambridge: Lutterworth, 2018.

———. *Roland Allen: A Theology of Mission Towards a Missiology of Spirit and Order*. Cambridge: Lutterworth, 2018.

Seebeck, Doug, and Timothy Stoner. *My Business, My Mission: Fighting Poverty through Partnerships*. Grand Rapids, MI: Partners Worldwide, 2009.

Siemens, Ruth E. "The Vital Role of Tentmaking in Paul's Mission Strategy." *International Journal of Frontier Missions* 14, no. 3 (July–Sept 1997) 121–29.

Silva, Moisés. *Philippians*. Baker Exegetical Commentary on the New Testament. Grand Rapids, MI: Baker Academic, 2005.

Simson, Wolfgang. *The House Church Book: Rediscover the Dynamic, Organic, Relational, Viral Community Jesus Started*. Wheaton, IL: Tyndale, 2009.

Sjogren, Steve, and Rob Lewin. *Community of Kindness: A Refreshing New Approach to Planting and Growing a Church*. Ventura, CA: Regal, 2003.

Smith, E. Elbert. *Church Planting by the Book*. Fort Washington, PA: CLC, 2015.

Spencer, F. Scott. *Journeying Through Acts: A Literary-Cultural Reading*. Peabody, MA: Hendrickson, 2004.

Stetzer, Ed. *Planting Missional Churches: Planting a Church That's Biblically Sound and Reaching People in Culture*. Nashville: B&H Academic, 2006.

Stetzer, Ed, and Daniel Im. *Planting Missional Churches: Your Guide to Starting Churches that Multiply*. Nashville: B&H Academic, 2016.

Stetzer, Ed, and Thom S. Rainer. *Transformational Church: Creating a New Scorecard for Congregations*. Nashville: B&H, 2010.

Stetzer, Ed, and Warren Bird. *Viral Churches: Helping Church Planters Become Movement Makers*. San Francisco: Jossey-Bass, 2010.

Stott, John. *Acts: Seeing the Spirit at Work*. Downers Grove, IL: InterVarsity Connect, 1998.

———. *The Message of 1 & 2 Thessalonians*. The Bible Speaks Today. Downers Grove, IL: InterVarsity, 1994.

Sweet, William Warren. *Religion on the American Frontier*. New York: Cooper Square, 1964.

———. *The Story of Religion in America*. New York: Harper & Brothers, 1939.
Thielman, Frank. *Philippians*. The NIV Application Commentary. Grand Rapids, MI: Zondervan, 1995.
Thiselton, Anthony C. *The First Epistle to the Corinthians: A Commentary on the Greek Text*. The New International Greek Testament Commentary. Grand Rapids, MI: Eerdmans, 2000.
Thrall, M.E. *2 Corinthians 8–13: A Critical and Exegetical Commentary*. International Critical Commentary. London: T&T Clark, 2004.
Wagner, C. Peter. *Church Planting for a Greater Harvest: A Comprehensive Guide*. Ventura, CA: Regal, 1990.
Whitlock, David, Mick Arnold, and R. Barry Ellis. "An Examination of Tentmaker Ministers in Missouri: Challenges and Opportunities." *JBTM* 5, no. 1 (2008) 41–52.
Wilson, Cory. "An Evaluation of the Missiology Count Nicholas von Zinzendorf in Light of Roland Allen's *Missionary Methods*." Paper presented to the *Southeast Regional Meeting of the Evangelical Theological Society*, Southern Baptist Seminary, Wake Forest, NC, Mar. 23–24, 2012.
Wilson, J. Christy, Jr. *Today's Tentmakers: Self-Support: An Alternative Model for Worldwide Witness*. Overseas Counseling Service Ed. Wheaton, IL: Tyndale, 1979.
Yamamori, Tetsunao. *God's New Envoys: A Bold Strategy for Penetrating "Closed Countries."* Portland, OR: Multnomah, 1987.

Author Index

Abel, 74
Abraham, 74
Allen, Hubert J.B., 84, 86, 87nn16–17, 88nn18–21, 89n23, 89nn25–26
Allen, Roland, 7, 83–102, 103, 110, 124, 126, 143, 144, 153–54, 155, 156, 158, 173, 174, 182, 183, 184
Ananias, 150
Antiphon, 11
Aquila, 21, 22
Arnold, Mick, 169
Asbury, Francis, 80

Bacon, David, 80
Baer, Michael R., 135–37, 140, 141
Balboa, Rocky, 185, 186
Barnabas, 25, 75
Barnett, Paul, 12, 13, 14, 46–50, 51, 58, 64n21, 97, 99
Beale, G.K., 29, 30
Bickers, Dennis, 6, 169, 183–84
Bird, Warren, 111
Bishop Westcott of Durham, 84n2
Bloecher, Detlef, 108, 148
Boaz, 75
Bock, Darrell L., 22, 24, 33, 40
Bosch, David J., 51–52, 56
Bruce, F.F., 10, 18–19, 20, 22, 23, 30, 31n5, 32, 40, 42
Burrows, Winfred, 84

Carey, William, 72–74, 79, 143, 148
Carini, Edward, 1n1
King Christian VI, 71
Ciampa, Roy E., 37–38, 40
Cleanthes, 10
Clitophon, 61
Columbus, Christopher, 69, 74, 148
Constantine, 66
Cotto, Cisco, 112
Cox, John, 72

Danker, William J., 70
David, 117, 118
Dio Chrysostom, 10
Dixon, Mason, 186
Dober, Leonhard, 71, 153

Ellis, R. Barry, 169
Euthydemus, 11
Evenus, 11

Fee, Gordon D., 30n3, 57, 58, 64–65
King Ferdinand II, 69
Finn, Bruce R., 144–45
Foster, Alan, 177

Gamaliel, 8
Garland, David E., 38n12
Gore, Bishop, 84
Gorgias, 11

AUTHOR INDEX

Green, Gene L., 36, 40

Hafemann, Scott J., 13–14, 14n26, 48n20
Hagar, 74
Hamilton, Don, 107
Harris, Murray J., 12, 41–46, 46n16, 50, 51, 57n5, 97
Hesselgrave, David J., 124–25, 126, 144, 145, 161
Hillel, 9
Hippias, 11
Hock, Ronald F., 9, 10, 11, 18, 53, 58, 59–60, 61, 62, 63
Holmberg, Bengt, 16
Hus, John, 70

Im, Daniel, 4n10, 111n32, 112n33, 112n35, 113n36
Isaac, 75
Queen Isabella I, 69
Isocrates, 11

Jesse, 117
Jesus Christ, 21, 24, 25, 27, 29, 30, 32, 33, 34, 35, 36, 41, 45, 46, 47, 50, 55, 56, 57, 58, 59, 60, 63, 64, 68n7, 71, 75, 76, 92, 101n55, 105, 106, 107, 107n7, 120, 122, 131, 137, 140, 147, 150, 153, 160, 164, 165, 166, 169, 177, 182, 184, 185, 186, 189
Johnson, C. Neal, 131, 133–34, 135, 137, 138, 139–40, 156
Joseph (husband of Mary), 75
Joseph (son of Jacob), 75
Joseph of Arimathea, 75

Keller, Timothy J., 126, 146
Kling, August J., 69–70
Kruger, Kurt T., 112n34

Lai, Patrick, 131–33, 135, 137, 139
Latourette, Kenneth Scott, 24, 81–82
Lewin, Rob, 4, 110, 113–14, 128, 149
Lewis, Jonathan, 106–7, 116n53, 160n1, 164n5
Luke, 8, 32

Lydia, 15, 30, 31, 44n13, 99

Malphurs, Aubrey, 3, 119–21, 126, 146, 147
Marshall, I. Howard, 29
Martha, 75
McCarty, Doran C., 12, 13nn21–22
Miriam, 75
Moreau, A. Scott, 21n9
Murray, Stuart, 4, 109–10, 148

Neusner, J., 9n6
Newbigin, Leslie, 89, 182
Nicodemus, 75
Nitschmaun, David, 71, 153

O'Brien, Peter T., 15

Packer, J.I., 9–10
Paton, David, 84n4, 88–89, 90nn28–29, 91nn30–31, 93nn33–36, 94n37, 100nn50–51
Patrick, Darrin, 125–26, 144
Payne, J.D., 67, 84n3, 126–29, 144, 155, 162, 170–71
Peter, 33, 67, 68, 154
Peterson, David G., 22–23, 24, 32–33, 40, 104
Plummer, Robert L., 24n16
Polo, Marco, 69, 74, 148
Porter, H. Boone, 88
Porter, Mr., 144n1
Priscilla, 21, 22
Prodicus, 11
Protagoras of Abdera, 11

Rebekah, 75
Rose, Brother, 144n1
Rosner, Brian S., 37–38, 40
Rowe, Thomas, 70
Rundle, Steve, 6–7, 138–39, 140
Ruth, 75
Rutt, Steven Richard, 83–84, 84n1, 84n2, 85n5, 96–97

Samson, 75
Samuel, 117, 118
Sanneh, Lamin, 89

Saul, 117
Shelton, Seth, 112–13
Siemens, Ruth E., 6n13, 11n13, 26, 116n53, 121–23, 144, 149, 156, 164
Silas, 20–21, 22–23, 25, 26, 27, 40, 54, 115, 121n67
Sjogren, Steve, 4, 110, 113–14, 128, 149
Smith, E. Elbert, 115–18
Socrates, 62
Steffen, Tom, 6–7, 138–39, 140
Stetzer, Ed, 4, 110–13, 148–49
Stott, John, 24, 30n4
Sweet, William Warren, 77–81, 82

Tenney, M.C., 9–10
Terry, John Mark, 24
Thiselton, Anthony C., 13
Thomas Aquinas, 66
Thompson, J. Allen, 126
Thrall, M.E., 16, 45–46, 50–51, 64, 97
Timothy, 20–21, 22–23, 25, 26, 27, 40, 54, 115, 121n67, 184, 185

Urbach, E.E., 9n6

Waggett, Father, 84
Wagner, C. Peter, 3, 114–15, 149, 169
Watteville, Frederick de, 71
Wesley, John, 77
Whitlock, David, 169
Wilson, Cory, 71–72, 148, 153
Wilson, J. Christy, Jr., 67–70, 72, 74–76, 104–6, 108, 154–55, 156, 164, 165, 173
Winter, Ralph, 131
Worcester, John, 110
Wundt, Wilhelm, 1

Yamamori, Tetsunao, 22, 106, 107, 108, 160, 164
Yamasaki, April Nora Chiu, 13

Zaccaeus, 75
Zinzendorf, Nicholas Ludwig von, 70–71, 153

Scripture Index

OLD TESTAMENT

1 Samuel
16	118
16:2	117

2 Chronicles
16:9	183

Proverbs
16:16	33

RABBINIC WORKS

Mishnah

Abot ("The Ethics of the Fathers")
1:13	9n3
2:2	8n2

NEW TESTAMENT

Luke
9:22	59
10:7	29

Acts
3:6	33, 66
9:1–19	161
9:15	150
13:1–4	145, 161
13:44–47	25, 151
13:46–47	25, 26
15:39–40	145, 161
16:5	44
16:15	15, 98, 145n8
18:1–5	21, 22
18:2–3	132
18:3	2, 2n2, 8n1, 145n8
18:3–6	23
18:3–6 NIV	24
18:4	24, 25n18
18:4–6	25
18:4–6 RSV	26
18:4–7	151
18:5	20, 21, 22, 23, 26n19, 27, 40, 54, 115, 116, 121n67
18:6	25
19:11–12	62
20:18–35	32
20:32	33, 34
20:32, 33	34
20:33	34
20:33–34	99
20:33–35	145n8

Acts (continued)

20:34	34, 163, 170
22:3	162
22:28	10
33–35	32

Romans

1:1	150
1:16	24
5:15–16	57
15:24	43

1 Corinthians

1:1	150
1:23	58
1:26	13
2:12	57
4:1, 19a	38
4:10	58
4:11–12	58
4:14, 16, 18, 23	38
4:15	38, 64
4:19b-22	38
5:18–20	107n7
9	143, 150
9:1	150
9:1–2	56
9:1–12	36, 116
9:1–18	36, 151
9:2	64
9:3–14	29
9:3–18	112
9:6–14	9n4
9:6–18	145n8
9:11–12a	64
9:12	36, 37, 38n12, 42, 64, 99, 101, 120, 132
9:14	64n21
9:15	121
9:15–18	55, 56n3, 57
9:16	55
9:16–18	48
9:17	56
9:17–18	56
9:18	57
9:19	184
9:19–22	151
9:19–23	101, 125, 150
9:22	37, 151
11:9	119
12:27–30	105n4
12:28	139
16:6	43

2 Corinthians

1:1	150
1:5	58
1:16	43
2:1	64
2:17	36
3:1–3	64
5:20	106, 107, 107n7
8:1–2	115
8:1–5	16
8:2	13
10–13	51
11	143
11:1–15	116
11:4	36, 47
11:7	41
11:7–12	41, 44–45, 145n8
11:8	12, 48, 48n22, 98, 100, 163
11:8–9	43
11:9	12, 16, 37, 41, 46, 48n22, 163, 170
11:9–10, 12	41
11:10	43
11:12	37, 47, 49
11:12–13	37
11:12–15	43
11:13	47
11:23–27	48
11:27	60
12:10	60
12:13	12
12:13–16	145n8
12:14	37

Galatians

1:15–16	150
2:7	150

Ephesians

2:8–9	57
4:28	34, 35
4:29	35

Philippians

1:3–5	15
1:5	15, 44
1:15	182
1:18	182
2:6–8	58
4:14	12
4:14–16	43
4:14–20	48
4:15	15, 44, 52, 98
4:16	12, 16, 43, 163
4:16–17	98
4:17	163
4:17–18	100

Colossians

1:28–29	185
2:16–23	9

1 Thessalonians

1:9	145n8
2:9	30, 59, 99, 102, 132
4:11	29
4:11–12	28, 30, 145n8
4:13—5:11	29
5:14	29, 145n8

2 Thessalonians

3	143
3:6–12	30
3:7–8	163, 170
3:7–12	145n8
3:9	29, 31, 32

1 Timothy

2:7	150
4:10	185
5:17–18	9n4, 29
5:23	184

James

5:2–3	34

1 Peter

1:18–19	33

Revelation

22:17	57

www.ingramcontent.com/pod-product-compliance
Lightning Source LLC
Chambersburg PA
CBHW070321230426
43663CB00011B/2188